Purgatory

Purgatory
and the means to avoid it

Martin Jugie

Roman Catholic Books
Post Office Box 2286, Fort Collins, CO 80522

NIHIL OBSTAT
>JACOBUS P. BASTIBLE,
>*CENSOR DEPUTATUS*

IMPRIMATUR
>DANIEL,
>*EPISCOPUS CORCAGIENSIS*

15 FEBRUARII, 1949

ISBN 1-929291-17-5

AUX CROISÉS DU PURGATOIRE

Under the Patronage
of
St. Gertrude

CONTENTS

PREFACE

PART ONE

PURGATORY

CHAPTER   PAGE

I—THE CATHOLIC DOCTRINE OF PURGATORY   1
    1.—General Notion.
    2.—Why Purgatory?
    3.—Purgatory: an Expiation.
    4.—Prayer for the Dead.
    5.—State of Souls in Purgatory.

II—THE SWEET REASONABLENESS OF PURGATORY . . . . ,   18
    1.—Purgatory, Masterpiece of Divine Wisdom.
    2.—Purgatory, Masterpiece of Divine Goodness.
    3.—Purgatory, a Dogma of Consolation.
    4.—Purgatory, a very Sanctifying Dogma.

III—PLACE, POPULATION AND SOCIETY OF PURGATORY   30
    1.—The Place of Purgatory.
    2.—The Population of Purgatory.
    3.—The Society of Purgatory.

IV THE PAINS OF PURGATORY   44
    1.—Nature of Pains.
    2.—Intensity of Pains.
    3.—Duration of Purgatory.
    4.—Purgatorial Pain and Private Revelations

V—LIFE IN PURGATORY   61
    1.—Erroneous Conceptions.
    2.—Relations with God.
    3.—Relations with Church Triumphant.
    4.—Relations with Church Militant
    5.—Joys of Purgatory.

CHAPTER	PAGE
VI—THE CHURCH TRIUMPHANT AND PURGATORY	79

    1.—The Fact of Intercession.
    2.—Mode of Intercession.

VII—THE CHURCH MILITANT AND PURGATORY	88

    1.—Foundation and Mode of Our Power.
    2.—Means of Helping the Holy Souls.
    3.—Reasons for Helping the Holy Souls.
    4.—Prayer to the Holy Souls.

PART TWO

MEANS OF AVOIDING PURGATORY

I—GENERAL CONSIDERATIONS	108

    1.—Is avoidance possible?
    2.—True for some Souls.
    3.—The Best Means of Avoiding Hell.
    4.—Why Avoid Purgatory?
    5.—Various Means.

II—THE SACRAMENTAL MEANS	116

    1.—Baptism.
    2.—Martyrdom.
    3.—Frequent Confession.
    4.—Indulgences.
    5.—Frequent Communion.
    6.—Extreme Unction.
    7.—Mass of the Living.
    8.—The Religious Life.

III—HOLY DISPOSITIONS AND SALUTARY PRACTICES	141

    1.—Spirit of Penance.
    2.—Acceptance of Trials and Death.
    3.—To do All for Love.
    4.—Remission of Debts.
    5.—To Avoid Judging Others.
    6.—Spiritual Infancy.
    7.—Detachment.
    8.—Constant Remembrance of the Last Things.
    9.—To ask for One's Purgatory on Earth.

PAGE

IV—OF CERTAIN EXCELLENT ACTS OF CHARITY   174
    1.—Apostolate of Purgatory.
    2.—Prayer for Deserted Souls.
    3.—The Heroic Act.
    4.—To Offer Oneself as a Victim.
    5.—Apostolate of Prayer.
    6.—Prayer for those in their Agony.
    7.—Catholic Action.
    8.—The Apostolate after Death.
        (i) Work of Priestly Vocations
        (ii) Foundation Masses for the Dead.
        (iii) Foundation of Parochial Missions.
        (iv) The Good Book.
    9.—Material Alms.

PREFACE

*F*OR man here on earth, there can be no greater problem, no more pressing subject for reflection, than the hereafter. The future life, indeed, is very near to him. He brushes shoulders with it, so to speak, for a mere nothing separates him from it. No one has any security against death, since youth and age, riches and poverty are all powerless against it. We listen to the last swing of the church bell, tolling someone's death. It dies in the silence of the meadows. Its next toll may be for any one of us.

This is true of all times, but more especially so of ours, when the scourge of war is laid on us, and the daily death-roll grows ever greater. Every book, therefore, that treats of the future life, ought to receive a welcome.

Such books are not wanting in French. Some treat the subject fully, dealing with the four last ends: death, judgment, Hell, Heaven. Others treat of one of these truths, and a great number of these deal with Purgatory. Purgatory does not figure in the list of the four last ends, for it is essentially a passing state, wholly orientated towards Heaven, of which it is the ante-room. Moreover, for the greater part of those who are saved, it is the state which they first experience on leaving this world. It is not to be wondered at, then, if a dozen or more books have appeared in France on the subject, in the present century. We have no wish merely to add another to the list, covering the same ground. Our reasons for writing this is that we have remarked how other writers have treated of Purgatory in itself and for itself —that is to say, with a view to making known the state of these suffering souls and inspiring the living to aid them. Now, Purgatory can be looked at from a different point of view, which without excluding the first, tends directly, however, to another end. The others have written with their eyes primarily on the dead. We write with our eyes on the living—the faithful on earth—and we strive to foster in them a salutary fear of the pains of Purgatory, and point out to them the means of avoiding them. This is a resumé of our point of view in the following pages.

The first point is, above all, an exposé of the doctrine of Purgatory, according to definitions of the Church and the con-

clusions of sound theology. Theology pursues its investigations beyond dogma, having dogma always for its guide. It attempts to throw light on what is obscure in the definitions ; to make precise what they leave vague ; sometimes, to guess at the implications of their silence. It is evident that much of what we say must needs be a repetition of what others have said before us, for it is difficult to add much at this time of day. We believe, however, unless we are greatly mistaken, that we have exposed certain truths on the state of souls in Purgatory, here and there in our work, which if not altogether new have rarely received sufficient attention. We have drawn the logical conclusions of the truth of faith, which defines that these suffering souls are established in a state of grace and holiness, and that this state is definitive, secure, incapable of substantial progress—since there can be no question of merit after death.

As to the second part : " The Means of Avoiding Purgatory," it has appeared as articles in that excellent revue " Les Croises du Purgatoire," and is assembled here, at the request of of many of those to whom the book is now dedicated.

The dedication, and the choice of the patronage of her who first began the glorious " Heroic Offering," are sufficient indication that, while " Purgatory and the Means of Avoiding It " envisages primarily the living, the dead are not forgotten. It seeks, indeed, to convince the first that one of the securest means of avoiding Purgatory is to aid the souls suffering therein. Let us remark, in passing that the sufferings of war and the hardships of its aftermath, provide a splendid occasion of salutary penance and of aid for the Holy Souls. Generous acceptance of all hardships in a spirit of penance, with the intention of aiding the souls in Purgatory is all that is needed. Thus we will realise the words of St. Paul : " All things work together unto good for those that love God " (Rom., vii, 28). If we know how to make wise use of the treasures that are in our daily sufferings, we shall enrich ourselves with merits for eternity, we shall be the benefactors of Purgatory, and we shall prepare ourselves for immediate entry into Heaven.

Lyon, 9th January, 1940.

Translator's Note :
   My thanks are due to Miss Cecilia Patterson of Notre Dame, Glasgow, for the proof-reading of Part Two.   M.G.C.

Chapter I

THE CATHOLIC DOCTRINE OF PURGATORY

1.—General Notion of Purgatory

THE CATHOLIC DOGMA OF PURGATORY supposes the immortality of the human soul, and the existence, for that soul, of another life, after death has separated it from its vesture of clay. We are not concerned here with demonstrating the immortality of the soul. That is a truth of the rational order, confirmed by Christian Revelation—a truth which is fundamental, which is basic to the whole moral order, and which, despite all the efforts of materialism, shines with undimmed splendour.

Death is, therefore, for the human soul, the beginning of a new life, about which, though the Catholic Religion furnishes us with certain precise ideas, our curiosity is far from being satisfied. Yet what we do know is no mere guess work. It comes to us, stamped with the infallible teaching authority of the Church.

According to this teaching, the soul immediately after death, goes to Heaven, or to Hell, or to Purgatory, according to the nature of its relations with God at the precise moment of death.

If it is in a state of perfect friendship with God, being entirely free from both mortal and venial sin and having done sufficient penance for sins committed after Baptism, it is immediately admitted to the Beatific Vision—the Vision of the Three Divine Persons in One Only God, which renders the soul ecstatically happy. This state of beatitude, given to man in proportion to the love of God he attained to while on earth, is known as Heaven. Heaven, for the soul separated from the body, is above all a *state*, the state of perfect felicity. It is also, according to our manner of conceiving it, a *place*, but a place in the wide sense, in the improper, analogical use of the word, since the soul being a spirit, cannot be properly speaking localized. Heaven is where Jesus Christ, true God and true Man, with His glorified Body, lives with His Virgin Mother and the glorified of the first Paschal day. However, one can say that Heaven, considered as a state, is everywhere in which God is. But God is everywhere.

If the soul, at death, is constituted in a state of enmity with God, through having one or more mortal sins unrepented of to the very last breath, it is driven away from Him and plunged into a state of damnation. This state will be eternal, for, after death, the soul does not change. It remains immutably fixed in the dispositions in which it was at the moment of death. After death, there is no repentance, there is no conversion, according to a dogma of Catholic Faith. The damned soul no longer desires God. It detests Him and will detest Him eternally. God can no longer pardon that soul, for it no longer wishes to ask for pardon, and there is thus fixed between them, a great chasm. This state of damnation is called Hell. Notice that it is primarily a *state*. It is also a place, but in the analogical sense pointed out above in reference to Heaven. Just as the blessed soul, wheresoever it be, carries its heaven with it, because it is united to God by vision and love ; so the damned soul cannot escape from its Hell, because it is deprived of the beatific vision of God, Whom it detests, eternally resenting the weight of His justice.

Finally, if at death the soul is in the state of grace and amity with God, but is as yet unworthy to be admitted to the Beatific Vision—either because of venial sin unrepented, or the lack of sufficient penance for both mortal and venial sins, or both—it must pass some time, long or short according to the amount of its debt, in an intermediate state between the state of beatitude and that of damnation. This state is designated, in the Latin Church since the 11th century, by the word *Purgatory*, that is, a state or place of *purification*, of *expiation*. This state is characterised : 1° by eternally assured amity with God, arising immediately from the changelessness of the soul, fixed in the certain hope of sooner or later coming to the Beatific Vision ; 2° by the temporary privation of that vision ; 3° by mysterious sufferings arising from that privation and proportionate to the number and gravity of sins not sufficiently expiated here below. Like Heaven and Hell, Purgatory too is a state; but they are eternal states and it will pass. Purgatory is also a place, in the sense in which separated souls can be said to be in a place. It is a station of penance, where the soul must endure the rigours of chastisements : a kind of Marshalsea, where the soul is detained for spiritual debts it has failed to meet on earth : an exile, full of sorrow, far from the fatherland, far from the father's house—an exile which of its nature will end happily, and which the Church Militant and the Church Triumphant, each in its own fashion, can alleviate and shorten. But the imprisoned and exiled souls can do nothing for themselves to sweeten or take away the pains to which they were condemned at the particular judgment. Such is the general idea of the state called Purgatory. It remains to sift and analyse it.

II.—Why Purgatory at All?

Purgatory is a fruit of sin : not of that habitual sin, which we ourselves have not committed, but which has come to us as an hereditary stain from Adam, and which we name *original ;* but of personal sin, committed through the perverse will in each one of us, and known to Theology as *actual sin.* Take away actual sin, and Purgatory ceases to exist.

What, therefore, is the raison d'être of Purgatory? What is the obstacle which impedes a soul in the state of Grace from entering into Heaven? It is sin, and that which is called the relics of sin. Sin, in this context, can mean only venial sin not pardoned on earth. There must surely be a small margin of difference between the number of those who died in venial sin, and the number of the full toll of death. It is very seldom that one whom death surprises, and who has not been given the time in which to make his soul, to breathe an act of contrition, or to receive the Last Sacraments, does not bring with him one or more venial sins. These unremitted venial sins must be cleansed in Purgatory.

What, now, do we understand by the relics of sin? There is question, firstly, of vicious inclinations, resulting from bad habits, which inclinations affect especially the sensibility, as witness, for example, gluttony or anger ; or they affect especially the higher faculties, as pride or vanity. There is question, above all, of the temporal pain due to every sin committed after Baptism, even when that sin has been wiped out, as to its guilt, by contrition and Sacramental Absolution.

A soul may go to Purgatory, then, for three reasons: 1° on account of venial sins not remitted here on earth; 2° on account of vicious inclinations left in the soul through habits of sin; 3° on account of the temporal punishment due to every sin, mortal or venial, committed after Baptism and not sufficiently atoned for during life. Certain souls go to Purgatory for the third reason only, for they have brought to the Judgment Seat neither venial sins nor ingrained inclinations to vice. If a person dies with one single venial sin on his soul, he is condemned to Purgatory for the first *and* the third reasons, since venial sin, too, must be atoned for. Then, again, it can be safely said that no one goes to Purgatory solely for the second reason, since vicious inclinations do not in themselves constitute sins, and the majority of theologians hold with St. Thomas that these inclinations do not survive the first instant that follows separation of soul and body. They disappear in that instant; for the soul in a state of grace, once it finds itself in the presence of God, strains towards Him with ardour and hates intensely all that displeases Him. This violent turning-away from sin suffices to detach the soul from every inclination to commit sin, and gives to it a perfect moral rectitude. The position becomes perfectly clear, when it is remembered that the greater number —if not all—of vicious inclinations are linked in some fashion to sensibility and the organs of sense, whose exercise is suspended by the separation of body and soul effected by death.

What is said of vicious inclinations is true also of venial sins not remitted here below. The act of perfect Contrition breathed by the soul at the moment of death suffices to wipe out the *guilt* of venial sin, but there remain the expiatory chastisement fixed by Divine Justice. Here again is the doctrine of St. Thomas, and held by the best theologians. It would appear to be the only true one. The idea of progressive purification from venial sin *as such* and from vicious inclinations, ought to be discarded as not in harmony with the state of souls separated from their bodies. We will demonstrate this presently.

It follows from all this, that the principal—one might even say the unique—reason for the existence of Purgatory, is the temporal punishment due to sins committed after Baptism, since neither venial sin nor vicious inclination survives the first instant that follows death. Immediately on its entering Purgatory, the soul is perfectly holy, perfectly turned towards God, filled with the purest love. It has no means of bettering itself nor of progressing in virtue. That would be an impossibility after death, and it must suffer for love the just punishment which its sins have merited. It is not suprising, therefore, that the official definitions of the Church regarding Purgatory mention only the temporal punishment due to sin. Let us examine some of these. The Council of Florence, in the " Decree of Union with the Greeks," says :

> " As regards the faithful who die in true repentance, before having satisfied for their sins of action and omission, their souls are purified after death by expiatory pains ; and for their deliverance from pain, the suffrages of the living faithful—the Sacrifice of the Mass, the prayers, the alms and the other works of piety which the faithful are accustomed to offer for the dead—are very efficacious."

The Council of Trent, also, when it had affirmed the existence of Purgatory and the fact that souls therin detained are helped by the suffrages of the faithful, especially by Holy Mass, goes on to define, against the Protestants, the existence of a temporal pain due for all sins committed after Baptism even when those sins have been effaced by Absolution or by Contrition with the desire of Confession : " If anyone says that to every penitent sinner who has received the grace of justification, the sin is to such an extent remitted, and the sentence of eternal punishment to such an extent effaced, that there remains no obligation of temporal punishment to be paid either in this world, or in the next, that is to say, in Purgatory, before Heaven is opened for that soul, let him be anathema." (*Session* vi, *Canon* 30). The Council does not deny, that in certain rare cases, all the punishment due to sin is lifted from the soul in the instant when the Priest pronounces the words of Absolution, on account of a vehement contrition inspired by perfect charity ; but it affirms that, in most cases, there remains a punishment to be undergone for sin, even when it has been effaced by Absolution. Hence the reason why *satisfaction*, meaning the penance imposed by the confessor, is an integral part of the Sacrament of Penance. That penance ought theoretically to suffice for the payment of our debt to Divine Justice. One could well believe that this was the case formerly, when the Church was in the habit of imposing, for certain sins, a very long and very severe satisfaction. But, in our days, the penances imposed in Confession are generally too light to allow us to hope for a complete remission of the temporal punishment due for our sins. To supply the deficit, the Church offers us the treasury of its Indulgences, and exhorts us to inflict voluntary penances on ourselves, or at least to accept, in a spirit of penance, the trials of life, the crosses which Providence sends us. For the rest, the value of our satisfaction depends ever so much more on our interior dispositions than on the rigour of the penance imposed.

In this connection, it is well to notice the difference that exists between the Sacrament of Baptism and the Sacrament of Penance, as regards the remission of sins. At Baptism, God shows Himself royal and magnificent in His pardon, in forgiving, with a total and plenary forgiveness, all the recipient's sins. On leaving the Baptismal Font, the neophyte is white as snow ; were he to die, he would immediately enter heaven, for he is clothed with the innocence and the merits of Jesus. Looking on that soul, God sees in it His well-beloved Son : " All you who have been baptized in Christ," says St. Paul, " you have put on Christ " (*Gal.*, iii, 27).

That grace of Baptism is so grand and so splendid that, in the designs of God, it should be the first dawn-flush of eternal life, a dawn ever growing in the depths of the soul to the effulgent splendour of an eternal noon, according to that saying of Holy Writ : " The path of the just is as the brilliant light of morning, whose light will grow in splendour unto noon " (*Prov.* iv, 18). One can, therefore, conceive the indignation of our Heavenly Father, when He sees us extinguishing in ourselves this aurora of eternal life by mortal sin, or dimming its light by deliberate venial sin. Doubtless, His merciful Heart is touched by our cries of repentance. Foreseeing our weakness, he has established a second stream to wash us from our iniquities and restore to us the whiteness of the robe we have tarnished. That second stream is the Sacrament of Penance. But this time, the pardon will not be so generous as at Baptism. Outraged love will raise the arm of avenging justice. The soul is released from the sin and from the eternal punishment which was its due; but it must submit to a temporal chastisement proportionate to the gravity of its offence. There is no absconding from this chastisement. If the debt is not paid here below, it is carried forward to the next life. All this is clearly taught by the Council of Trent: " The fruit of Baptism differs from the fruit of Penance. By Baptism, we are clothed with Christ, we become in Him truly a new creature, for we receive the full and entire remission of our sins. By the Sacrament of Penance, it is impossible for us to come to that new and perfect life without great efforts and abundance of tears, according to the exigencies of Divine Justice. That is why the holy Fathers have called Penance a toilsome Baptism" (*Session* xiv, *Ch.* II).

III.—PURGATORY IS BOTH A PURIFICATION AND AN EXPIATION—BUT PRINCIPALLY, AN EXPIATION

There is a marked difference between the words *purification* and *expiation*, and they cannot be interchanged without regrettable confusion. As applied to the moral sphere, the word *purification* is primarily a metaphor. To purify, properly signifies the removal of a blotch, a physical stain, the making clean. By extension, we speak of moral purification, because there is question of removing a stain of the spiritual order. The word *expiation*, on the contrary, belongs in its own right to the vocabulary of morality and spirituality. It can be used only of free persons. To expiate is to repair a fault by a pain, by a chastisement which the guilty one imposes on himself, or to which he submits as imposed by the person he has offended. Of itself, expiation does not tend towards the good or the amelioration of him who does it, but it aims at making an honourable amend to the person injured at the cost of the offender. Doubtless, such expiation, accepted in a spirit of justice and reparation, registers moral growth; but that is not its direct end. Before all else, it envisages the good of the person offended. The difference is clear.

According to what we have just said about the 'raison d'être' of Purgatory, it emerges that Purgatory is both a purification and an expiation. For certain souls, indeed, it may be an expiation only.

Purgatory is a purification, in as much as it delivers souls from venial sins not remitted here below, and from disordered inclinations of the sensible and spiritual powers of the soul. But we have seen that, according to the best Theologians, following St. Thomas, venial sins and vicious inclinations disappear on the threshold of Purgatory, with the engulfing of the whole soul in the virtue of charity—queen, mother, and nurse of all the virtues. For charity is the nuptial robe which instantly imparts its many-coloured glory to the spouse of Christ. No longer is there spot or wrinkle in her: all is perfectly ordered, pure, holy, immaculate. From the moment it gets free play in the soul, Charity destroys the least disorder, the least imperfection. Such is the doctrine of St. Paul in the 13th chapter of his First Epistle to the Corinthians. The Apostle shows that charity is the synthesis of all the virtues. Besides, it is of Catholic faith, that after death one cannot merit, one cannot make progress, one can no longer better oneself. The degree of charity to which the soul has reached at its last breath, is the eternal degree of its charity. It marks, as it were, the eternal temperature of our soul, its place in the hierarchy of supernatural values, its diapason in the chant which the elect sing around the throne of the Most Holy Trinity.

If the purification, properly so called, which one attributes to Purgatory, is realised from the first instant of its entry into that state, it follows that the rest of the time the soul spends there is consecrated to one single object—to *expiation*. Expiation is a debt for sins committed, which is paid by suffering; it is a reparation offered to the holiness and the justice of God, offended by sin. The payment of a debt does not merit a reward. The repairing of an injustice cannot bring with

THE CATHOLIC DOCTRINE ON PURGATORY

it any personal profit, for one merely rights a disturbed order of justice, at one's own expense. This is exactly the situation of the souls in Purgatory. They are debtors, bound to reparation for sins they have themselves committed. The pains and sufferings which they endure do not procure for them any merit, any progress in charity or in virtue. All the profit they draw from them is the removal of the obstacle to their entry into Heaven.

What underlines the unmixed expiatory and objective character of their sufferings, without any spiritual profit in the order of merit and of subjective perfection ; what gives to these sufferings the name of a *debt to pay*, is simply the fact that the Church Militant can pay these debts for the Church Suffering by offering suffrages to God for that intention, and by offering, through the Sacrifice of the Mass and through Indulgences, the satisfactions and the merits of the Redeemer. The saints in Heaven, too, can exercise on behalf of the souls in Purgatory, by their intercession and in a manner not easy to explain, that measure of suppliance which is fixed by God and of which we are entirely ignorant. If Purgatory had for its end to better these souls, to make them progress in perfection, to educate them little by little for their entry into Heaven, it would be incomprehensible that we could take their place, alleviate their pains, shorten and even end them by their intervention. But as there is question above all of an objective debt to be paid, it is quite natural to expect that the members of the same family, of the same Mystical Body, should be allowed to take in common the debts of its erring members. In a word, Purgatory must be looked on as a liquidation of the past, not as a march with face lifted towards a future, towards an ideal not yet attained.

These considerations are important, for they help to remove an eroneous conception which one can form of Purgatory, and to which the word itself easily gives rise.[1] From the manner

---

[1] Note that the word *Purgatory* (Latin : *Purgatorium*) is a substantive which, towards the XI century, began to replace *ignis purgatorius, the purifying fire*, of which the Greek and Latin Fathers since Origen had spoken. The ancient tradition, basing itself on certain Scriptural passages, speaks of a purification and an expiation of souls by this fire, without clearly determining, however, whether the word ' fire ' is to be taken in a real or in a metaphorical sense. The Origenists have even confused this fire with that

in which they express themselves, certain theologians and spiritual writers appear to describe Purgatory as a sort of purification, of progressive, *unmerited* amelioration, by which the souls lay aside the dross which renders them ugly to the eyes of their Lord. That would make it an ascending by steps to the Beatific Vision, a kind of heavenly noviciate, a course of supernatural education to refine the souls and to prepare them for the Divine Union. Such a comparison, employed by St. Catherine of Genoa in her celebrated " Treatise on Purgatory," can give that impression. A frequently quoted passage from one of Mgr. d'Hulst's letters of direction, contains the same idea of progressive purification :

" On leaving this world, many souls, saved by mercy after a life estranged from Heaven, *are not clothed as befits their entry into the Kingdom. Then the Divine Mercy sends them to purify themselves*, and that purification has three phases.

The first is humiliation : God gives His light, and they see themselves as they really are. Inexpressible for them is the confusion born of this knowledge. On earth these poor souls drank sin like water : now they have a loathing for the sins they see scored up against them. *This torment endures for a long time*, unless it is shortened by the prayers and the sacrifices which rise from the earth.

When these souls have acquired, by their suffering a true knowledge and a real hatred of sin, God, by a second illumination, shows Himself to them from afar in His beauty, and inflames their desires to the point of utter ravishment. Then they recall the time when God was very near to them, when He knocked unheeded at their door, because they preferred a pleasure, a bauble, a mere nothing. Now they burn with

---

of Hell, for, in denying the eternity of the pains of Hell, they have made it in very truth Purgatory. The Latin words ' purgare,' ' purificare,' ' purificatio,' signify ' to purify,' ' to make clean,' in their primary sense ; but they have equally the sense, ' to expiate,' ' to repair,' ' to pay,' ' to liquidate.' With Pliny the Younger, ' purificatio ' signifies ' expiation,' ' an expiatory ceremony.' Ovid has ' purgare nefas ' (=' to expiate a crime '). The word ' Purgatory,' then, contains the two ideas of ' purification ' and ' expiation.' The term ' poenis purgatoriis ' of the Council of Florence can be equally translated ' expiatory pains ' and ' purifying flames.' What has been said of the Latin words ' purgare,' ' purificare,' ' purificatio,' is equally true of the corresponding Greek words : cathairein, catharismus, cathartérion (=purgatorium). These words contain the two senses, purification and expiation, which, though cognate ideas, are not to be confused with each other.

desire to go to Him, but it is His turn to remove Himself from them. These desires are a suffering, but a suffering which purifies and leads on to love.

When this second stage has been completed, the scene is prepared for love : it penetrates these souls and makes them rush into the flames. Then they remember their negligences, *and Perfect Contrition, the Contrition of the great penitents, the Contrition of love, overwhelms them, purifies them interiorly* and brings them to the Kingdom of Heaven.

See, then, Purgatory with its three hours agony ! What prevents us from anticipating it all ? From beginning through humiliation, continuing through desire, ending through love ? "[1]

The author of these lines certainly appears to regard Purgatory as a purification only. It would seem that the very word "Purgatory" misleads him. Were one to follow him in this, it would be necessary to accept Purgatory at one time as an act of mercy, and again as before all else an act of justice. It would have for its end to purify the soul little by little by moral amelioration, rendering it worthy of the Beatific Vision, even though such amelioration is impossible after death, and even though Purgatory is above all a penal expiation of sin, a debt to be paid to the justice and the holiness of God. According to the author, the soul condemned to Purgatory would not be clothed *comme il faut* for entering the nuptial guest-feast. Perfect Contrition would come only in the last place, when a long time had been spent in passing through three stages, very suggestive of the Purgative, Illuminative and Unitive Ways of Ascetic and Mystical Theology. This is to forget that the soul in Purgatory is clothed, from the moment of its entry into the beyond, with the nuptial robe of charity ; of that charity which is inseparable from the perfect detestation of sin, and which we name Perfect Contrition. It is impossible to conceive how the soul, clothed with charity, should not from the moment of its separation from the body, utterly detest sin in all its forms. Divine love, in the soul separated from its body, takes on immediately all its efficacy and the fulness of its extension. It kills all that could turn the soul

---

[1] Mgr. d'Hulst, "Lettres de Direction," N., cvii. We have italicized the passages most flagrantly in contradiction with sane theology.

from God, and renders it perfectly pure. When Jesus could say of His Apostles in the Cenacle: " You are clean " (*John* xiii, 10), with how much stronger reason can the words be applied to the soul in Purgatory, utterly possessed by divine charity.

The conception of Purgatory as having for its sole end the amelioration, the progressive purification of the subject, must therefore be regarded as false. Rather is it, before all else, a reparation for sin by a chastisement proportioned to its gravity. Mgr. d'Hulst's view is in danger of linking itself with the Protestant theory of the amendment of sinners after death. This is to forget the wonderful transforming, even divinizing power of charity in the separated soul—a power that takes immediate possession, like the power in the vision that struck down Paul on the road to Damascus.

IV.—Prayer for the Dead

The dogma of Purgatory is intimately bound up with another truth of Catholic Faith. That truth affirms the efficacy which the prayers of the living faithful possess to alleviate the souls in Purgatory. That alleviation should be understood of the mitigation in the intensity, the shortening of the duration and even the total deliverance from the pains which the souls endure, according to the state of each, the nature of the suffrage offered by the living, and the decrees of divine justice concerning them.

Prayer for the souls of the faithful departed is as old as the Church. It was already a practice of the Jews, as is witnessed by the second book of the Macchabees (xii, 39-46). In the text of all the ancient Masses of both East and West, there are many passages where the celebrant recommends to God the souls of those who rest *in the faith, in penitence, in the sleep of peace, in the hope of resurrection to life eternal,* and asks for them *the place of refreshment, light and peace, the remission of their sins, especially those of fragility, deliverance from chains, darkness and prison, entry into beatitude, the luminous abode where shines the face of God,* etc. These expressions, in the normal course, can designate only those souls in the intermediate state between Heaven and Hell, for the Church does not pray for the damned, who are forever cut off from her communion, nor for the Blessed in Heaven who have no need of prayer.[1] Prayer for the dead is equally attested to by inscriptions in the Roman catacombs—the most ancient of Christian cemeteries.

By the generic expression, *prayer for the dead*, is to be understood all the means by which the faithful of the Church Militant come to the aid of the souls in Purgatory, whether it be prayer properly so called, or good works offered to God for this intention. The ensemble of these means gets the name *suffrages*, that is, assistance in the form of requests and supplication to God. For the Church on earth no longer possesses jurisdiction over the dead. It can no longer accord to them the remission of their sins or of the punishment due to sins by means of sacramental absolution. The Church can but intercede for those near to God, but knows that its prayer is effective for them. When, how and in what manner, these suffrages bring solace, consolation or deliverance, is something unknown to the Church. It is a secret hidden in God.

V.—State of the Souls in Purgatory

We have already indicated above what essentially characterizes the state of the souls in Purgatory. It is de fide that they are in the friendship of God, and since there can be no change in soul after death, they will remain eternally so. They are therefore sure of their salvation, with a certitude given to them from the moment of the particular judgment. But they are temporarily deprived of the Beatific Vision and are *delivered from all stain by expiatory and purifying sufferings*, according to the expression of the Council of Florence.

The principal of these pains—if not the only one—is certainly the delay of the Beatific Vision, from which must proceed, by consequence, all their other pains. This retarding of perfect beatitude is called, by the greater part of theologians, *the pain of the damned*. The phrase is not of the happiest,

---

[1] One finds, however, prayers in favour of saints, in certain eastern liturgies. These can be explained as requests for the augmentation of their beatitude in that which is accessory and accidental to it. It is in this sense that Our Saviour says that the angels in Heaven rejoice more over the conversion of one sinner, than over the ninety-nine just who need not penance.

for it can give the impression that these pains produce the same effects in these souls as in the souls of the damned. Between the soul in Purgatory and the damned soul there is a vast difference as regards moral dispositions. The first is in the embrace of God's love, wholly submissive to His Will, accepting with joy and even with gratitude the chastisement which it has merited by its sins. The other, on the contrary, is devoured by hatred of God : it is in perpetual rebellion against Him, and it kicks against the goad of divine justice punishing it. The first has the joyful hope of being soon admitted to the banquet of the elect. The other lives in eternal despair. Could there possibly be a more violent contrast between the two states ? So it is, that certain recent theologians have rejected the phrase *pain of the damned*, and substituted happier terms, as : *delay of the Beatific Vision, the pain of the expectation of God, the pain of exile.* Quite recently, a theologian has written in the " Dictionnaire de theologie catholique " (*tome* xiii, *Col.* 1291) :

"We, for our part, consider that the term ' pain of the damned ' should be altogether eliminated from the terminology of Purgatory. All agree in recognising that the analogy between the so-called ' damnation ' of Purgatory and the damnation of Hell, is a very tenuous one. Why retain an expression which is apt to mislead the unwary as to the true state of the souls in Purgatory ? The one fact of the certain hope of salvation takes from this temporary deprivation of the Vision of God, the character of real damnation."

We are fully in accord here with M. l'Abbé A. Michel. When there is question of expressing the doctrine, the most exact terms must be used, and all vigilance exercised lest expressions capable of ambiguity creep in.

Apart from the delay of the Beatific Vision, the Church has given no definition bearing on the nature of those other pains, known to theologians as ' the pain of sense.' It contents itself with affirming that souls are *purified by expiatory pains*, without telling us if these pains differ from the great torment of love which the temporary privation of total union with God in the Beatific Vision causes in these souls. We will later attempt to explain this torment of love and to show that it is the source of all the other pains, which are linked to it as effect to cause.

The phrase ' fire of Purgatory ' comes readily to everyone. At the Council of Florence (1438-1439), the Greeks and the Latins discussed at great length the existence of this fire. Its existence could not be proved from Scripture and Tradition, much less its nature be determined : so that agreement was reached with the vague expression *purifying or expiatory pains*. Anterior to this discussion between the Greeks and the Latins, that is to say up to the beginning of the thirteenth century, the current opinion in both East and West was that the souls in the intermediate state suffered a pain of fire.[1] But there is nothing known of the nature of that fire. It could be looked on as a metaphorical expression designating a very real torment, which would have a certain analogy with the sensation of burning provoked by our earthly fire. It must not be forgotten that separated souls are deprived of their bodies and normally exercise only their spiritual activities.

Be all this as it may, it is important to remember that, on the nature of the pains of Purgatory, we have no official, obligatory teaching from the Church's magisterium. All concerning it, lies in the domain of opinion. We will see later what certain private revelations, in no way ' of faith,' can tell us.

We have no certain knowledge of the duration of these pains, save this : that the state of Purgatory will cease at the last judgment, at the general resurrection. The sentence which the Sovereign Judge will pronounce over the whole human race on the last day, will envisage but two definite

---

[1] It is from a spirit of controversy that the Greeks attack the fire of Purgatory. They pretend to see in it the purifying fire of which the Origenist heretics speak and which includes in its rôle the purifying of even the damned. The liturgical books of the Greco-Russian Church speak in many places of the fire wherein are plunged those souls for which the Church prays. Even in our own days, there is read, on the Saturday preceding Sexagesima Sunday in Churches of the Byzantine Rite, a little treatise, erroneously attributed to St. John Damascene, on " Those who sleep in the Faith." It speaks of a negligent monk who was delivered from the lake of fire into which he was plunged, by a gradual alleviation due to the sacrifices and prayers of his spiritual father. The " Dialogues " of St. Gregory the Great, translated into Greek at the beginning of the seventh century, are known to have had great vogue in the East. In them there is frequent mention of a fire of Purgatory.

and immutable situations : the state of eternal felicity and the state of eternal damnation.

As regards the duration of Purgatory for each particular soul, it is clear that this will be more or less long according to the degree of gravity and the number of the sins which have not been atoned for on earth by penance and good works. The duration can be shortened, and in the normal course should be, both by the suffrages of the living and the intercession of the elect. By common suffrages : that is, those which are offered in general for all the souls in Purgatory ; by particular suffrages : those offered for some particular soul. God certainly ought to respect the intention of those who, in offering good works for the dead, name a soul or souls which they wish to aid. But there is no infallible certainty that this will be so in every case. For example : a rich man who has led a lukewarm and negligent life, who has been wanting in charity towards the poor, leaves on his deathbed a huge sum to obtain Masses for the repose of his soul. It could very well happen, that, by a just judgment of God, a good part of these Masses should go to the neglected and forgotten souls of the poor. If we can credit certain private revelations, God does sometimes act thus. And who, indeed, could question the wisdom of this ? Divine justice will not be circumvented. When necessary, God knows how to establish a just equilibrium between the rich and the poor. Those who calculate that their money will serve to run a fine establishment even in the next life, sadly deceive themselves. Those only who consecrate their riches to good works, to the helping of the poor, and this *during* their lives, will find that their money passes currency in Heaven. They are truly happy, for Jesus Christ has said : " Blessed are the merciful for they shall obtain mercy " (*Matt.* v, 7) ; and again : " Make for yourselves friends of the mammon of iniquity, that when you shall fail, they may receive you into everlasting dwellings " (*Luk.* xvi, 9).

It only remains to add, that as far as we can conjecture, the soul will be notified at the moment of the particular judgment of the time which it must normally spend in Purgatory, unless its sentence is shortened through the prayers of the Church Militant or the intercession of the Church Triumphant. It follows from this that the souls in Purgatory may be ignorant of the precise time when their exile will finish.

Chapter II

THE SWEET REASONABLENESS OF PURGATORY

Among the doctrines of our faith, there are some which are simply transcendent, mysterious, inaccessible to human investigation, such that they are difficult to positively reconcile with reason. We accept them on the sole authority of God, Who has revealed them to us, and Who cannot Himself be deceived nor can He deceive us. We must await the supreme revelation of Heaven in order to know them. All that our earth-bound reason can do, does not reach to the explaining of these dogmas : it can only defend them against the attacks of the incredulous, by showing that they involve no contradiction, and that the objections raised against them are useless, since they do not even touch them. Such, for example, are the Mysteries of the Holy Trinity, of the Real Presence of Jesus Christ, God and man, in the Sacrament of the Eucharist.

Other revealed truths, on the contrary, are also truths of reason. We find in Holy Scripture, inspired by God, a whole assembly of rational truths, which constitute a veritable revealed philosophy : the immortality of the soul, for instance, or the existence of human liberty. The witness of Divine Revelation has contributed in no small way towards setting the seal of truth on these doctrines, which the sophisms of so many philosophies have striven to cloud.

There is, in fine, a third category of doctrines, placed between the mysteries, properly so called, and the truths of the rational order. In certain respects, they lie outside the limits of our intelligence ; in other respects, their truth is seen clearly by the light of reason. Considering them attentively, we find them eminently and sweetly reasonable. The doctrine of Purgatory, which we have outlined in the foregoing chapter, belongs to this category. Doubtless it draws its sap from many other revealed truths, which reason alone can never discover or demonstrate : but its general trend agrees, in a wonderful manner, with the exigencies of right reason in the domain of morality.

First among the buttressing proofs, is that those heretics who have striven to cast out the doctrine of Purgatory—certain dissident Orientals of mediaeval and modern times, with the Protestants of the XVIth century—have lost no time in re-accepting it, at the peril of a flagrant contradiction. Denying the existence of Purgatory, they have illogically drifted into accepting it under another name—Hell: for they denied the eternity of Hell, thus making it Purgatory. They who rejected Purgatory, have come to the stage of accepting Hell only as a Purgatory, for, in denying the eternity of the pains of Hell, so clearly proclaimed by Jesus Christ in the Gospels, they have subscribed to the age-old error of Origin. But, in effect, Purgatory can be called a postulate of right reason. Its harmony with reason may be indicated in a multitude of ways.

I.—Purgatory, the Masterpiece of Divine Wisdom

Purgatory first presents itself to us as an admirable compromise between the sanctity of God and His justice, as a masterpiece of Divine Wisdom. What is, at the moment of death, the state of those who go to Purgatory? They are the friends of God. Their soul is lovely with sanctifying grace, and afire with Divine Charity. They have not merited, therefore, to be removed from the Face of God for all eternity. On the other hand, however, they have not sufficiently satisfied the Divine Justice by fruits worthy of penance, for sins committed after their baptism. Or again, at the moment of death, they find their conscience stained with one or many venial sins, and in this state, they appear before the tribunal of Jesus Christ: and it is written that nothing defiled, nothing that is not completely purified, shall enter into the Kingdom. The gate of Paradise is closed against them: they stand midway, unworthy both of Hell and of Heaven. The existence of a state, intermediate between that of damnation and that of perfect and eternal beatitude, thus emerges as one in which the dead of whom we speak make to the justice of God an expiation for the sins they have committed. Such is the 'raison d'être' of Purgatory. The sanctity of God is respected: the soul, not yet completely cleansed, will not be admitted to the vision of the Saint of saints, to unite itself with Him Who is Purity itself. Again, the Divine Justice does not conflict with itself, in sending to Hell a soul which does not merit such a sentence. The Catholic Dogma of Purgatory is thus seen to be redolant of sweet reasonableness.

Certain adversaries, however, here make an objection, which, at first sight, is devastating enough. It is seemly, they say, that God, Who is a good Father, should not watch with steel-pointed eye the peccadilloes of his children. Why should He not gratuitously remit these venial faults ? Why should He not give to them, at the hour of death, a complete amnesty in respect of the pain the sinner ought still to suffer ? Certainly, God could do that. But would it be wise ? Would it be just ? If Purgatory did not exist, God would treat in precisely the same manner, the fervent and the lukewarm, the hero and the slacker, the perfect and the imperfect. Doubtless, he could accord to the saint a more exalted place in Heaven. Yet, see the immediate consequence of that theory. If the menace of Purgatorial pains hardly suffices to inspire in us a horror of sin in general, and of venial sin in particular, what would be the case if the gates of Heaven were, so to speak, half-opened immediately after death to those who lead a a lazy and lukewarm life, to those who loiter about the thin line that marks the frontiers of mortal and of venial, to those who shrug their shoulders over expiatory penance, once they have received absolution for mortal sin ? Such a doctrine would favour laxity : it would be the ruin of the life of perfection : still more, it would conduct the souls quickly to mortal sin, towards death, for the dividing line of mortal and venial sin can often be difficult to determine. A fully deliberate venial sin is a horrible thing : God must indeed be exceedingly good and exceedingly merciful not to withdraw His friendship from him who dares thus to insult His love, with such words and provocations as no human friendship would survive. In a word—take away the doctrine of Purgatory : immediately you open to human souls that great way and that wide path leading to eternal perdition of which the Saviour speaks in the Gospels. You will suppress effectively the works of penance. Luther was not deceived when he wrote: "When you reject Purgatory, you suppress with it the vigils and the fasts: you seal up the doors of convents."

It must be remembered that *venial* sin is called such, only by comparison with *mortal* sin. Considered in itself, it is a great disorder. Every sin, because it is an offense offered to God, is an evil as great as God is great. It merits punishment, and God would not be a wise legislator, had he not established a sanction for this disorder—a sanction which the sinner ought to undergo either in this life or in the next. For the moral order must be repaired in the measure it has been disturbed.

That first ground of reason for the existence of the intermediate state between Heaven and Hell, was appreciated by the pagans themselves. The philosopher Plato speaks of it in truly remarkable words, in which the Catholic theologians need hardly make a change. "Immediately on separation from the body," he says, "the souls come before their judge to be attentively examined. Does he see a soul disfigured by sin? Heaped with ignominy he will send it to the dungeon where it will suffer the just chastisement of its crimes. But there are some who profit by the pains which they endure: these are they whose faults are of such a nature that they can be expiated. Sometimes that amendment is effective only by the way of sorrow and sufferings, for it is impossible to be delivered otherwise from injustice. As for those who have committed heinous crimes, and who, by reason of their perversity, have become incurable, they serve as an example. Their suffering is of no value to themselves, because they are incapable of being healed." (See the "Gorgias" and the "Phaedo").

The doctrine of Purgatory is so reasonable, that the disciples of Luther and Calvin have not hesitated to criticize on this point the teaching of their masters. For the Protestant, Lessing, it is evident that Luther has changed the very idea of justice, much as he has changed the texts of the Bible. The theologian, K. Hase, wrote in the last century, in his "Manuel de polemique protestante" (*Berlin*, 1864, p. 422):

"The greater part of those who die are, it must be admitted, too good for Hell: but it is none the less sure that they are too bad for Heaven. It must be frankly admitted that there existed at this point, a certain obscurity in the doctrine of Protestants. The new science has, for a long time now, testified to this."

Other Protestants have gone still further. As we have just noticed, in denying Purgatory they have been driven to transform Hell into Purgatory. Joseph de Maistre makes the point in his " Soirées de Saint-Pétersbourg," viii :

" One of the grand motifs in the 16th century confusion was the doctrine of Purgatory. The insurgents held doggedly to a single and a pure Hell. However, when they developed the implications of their thought, they were driven to deny an eternity of pain. They invented a Hell of time, solely for good policy and with a panic lest their doctrine should place Nero beside St. Louis, and Messoline shining in glory with St. Thèrése, in the Kingdom of God. But a temporary Hell is nothing else but Purgatory. After having embroiled themselves with us in their denial of Purgatory, the Protestants have embroiled themselves with us anew because they will now admit Purgatory only. What an extravagance!

II.—PURGATORY—MASTERPIECE OF DIVINE GOODNESS

Required alike by the sanctity, the justice and the wisdom of God, Purgatory is also a creation of His goodness. Purgatory is no exception to the general law that God made all things for love. A father shows his goodness towards his children when he threatens them with punishment, if they expose themselves to danger of body or of soul: he will, for example, forbid them to bathe in a dangerous river or to read an immoral book. In establishing Purgatory to punish sin, to turn us away very specially from those faults which are called venial and are in reality so dangerous, God has not only safeguarded the rights of His holiness, justice and wisdom, but he has also consulted our own best interests. He foresaw that venial sin of its nature would lead straight to mortal sin—a fact, indeed, of everyday experience—and He underlined it when He said that " he who is unfaithful in that which is least is unfaithful also in that which is greater " (*Lk.* xvi, 10.). Startling words, from the Divine Mouth of Him Who is Truth itself, worthy of our deepest reflection. It is that we may be faithful in the small and avoid the great, thus escaping damnation, that Our Saviour has established Purgatory. It would be therefore unjust to accuse God of severity, when He hangs over our heads the threat of Purgatory. Rather is this a proof of His infinite goodness.

III.—Purgatory—a Dogma of Consolation

Besides setting in relief the wisdom and the goodness of God, the doctrine of Purgatory is also a consolation for our weakness. When we reflect that at any moment death can surprise us, setting before our startled soul the dread tribunal of God ; and when we remember our lack of preparation, our miseries, our faults, our unworthiness to look on the face of Purity and Sanctity, despair of our salvation would catch us by the throat, were we not consoled by the doctrine of Purgatory. We find ourselves so ugly, so deformed, spiritually so ill-adjusted, that we would not dare to enter the nuptial banquet hall, even were the door flung open to us and we were invited to enter. Our weakness demands a kind of antichamber, where, after death and above all after a sudden and unforseen death, we may be able to repair our past negligences. No doubt we find here below in the Holy Church all the means to prepare ourselves for immediate entry to the Vision of God. But that demands a white purity of life, much vigilance, and a constant fidelity to Divine Grace : in a word—the fervent and heroic life. Alas ! heroes are rare : sinners and the imperfect are as the sands of the seashore. For the greater part of men, Purgatory is certainly a doctrine that drips with consolation.

St. Gertrude had a revelation which accords very well with what we have just said. She saw in spirit the soul of a religious who had passed her life in the exercise of the most exalted virtues. This soul stood in the presence of Our Saviour, adorned with the ornaments of her great charity : yet she would not dare to raise her eyes to Him. She kept them cast down as if she were ashamed at finding herself in His presence, and she pressed backwards from Him in her desire to remove her unworthiness from the face of Purity itself. Gertrude, amazed at such conduct, addressed herself to Christ, that she might learn the cause. " God of goodness," she said, " why will you not receive this soul into the bosom of your infinite charity ? What mean those strange movements of defiance which I watch in her ? " Then Our Saviour stretched out His right arm towards the soul of the religious to draw her to Him ; but she, overwhelmed with humility and modesty, turned from Him. The saint, now a prey to an ever growing amazement, asked the religious why she fled the caresses of a spouse so worthy of being loved. The religious replied : " Because I am not entirely purified from the stains which my sins have left behind them. Even if the good God were to permit me to enter freely into glory, bearing the scars of my sins, I would not accept even such a gracious invitation. For, how brilliant soever I may appear to your eyes, I am not yet a worthy spouse of my Saviour."[1] The attitude of that religious is perfectly comprehensible. Would it not be boorish in the extreme to attend a royal festival or a marriage feast in soiled and torn clothes ? Now, holy souls are souls truly refined, having in the highest degree the sense of the divine fastidiousness. It would be impossible to lack that sense, were one able to see oneself in the light of God's glory, and it is precisely thus that the soul sees itself at the moment of the particular judgment. The divine light reveals to the soul that which she owes to the justice and sanctity of God, so that of herself, with great eagerness, she flies towards the place of expiation, where she can be cleansed, and appear without a blush of sensitive shame before God and His saints.

From another point of view, Purgatory is a consoling doctrine. It consoles the living as they watch their dear ones part from them in death. If Purgatory did not exist, if there were only Heaven and Hell, relations and friends could have no illusions about the eternal lot of those whom they have loved on earth. It would be impossible for them to know that hope where there is no hope : they must remain in tears for the eternal loss of those whom they know to be manifestly

---

[1] See *Faber*, " All for Jesus," Ch. ix.

unworthy of Heaven, both by reason of the tenor of their lives and of the sentiments of their last moments. But let Purgatory exist. Immediately, hope springs eternal, for there is an intermediate state between the two where poor spotted humanity can sink down that it may rise in purity. They who mournfully follow the coffin, are consoled with thoughts of the mercy of God ; of the expiation of venial sin and the cleansing of the wounds, left by mortal sin, after death ; of extenuating circumstances which may have rendered certain sins venial for the dear deceased one. The anguished heart, torn with dread about the fate of the loved one, clings to this last hope, and there finds solace and some peace.

Private Revelations worthy of belief assure us that this hope is no deceptive will-o'-the-wisp—the revelation, for instance, of Soeur Marie-Denise of the Order of the Visitation, who died at Annecy in 1653. It is recorded at full length in that well-known work of Fr. Faber : " All for Jesus." To that saintly religious, wholly devoted to expiation for the release of the souls in Purgatory, Our Lord deigned to show the soul of a very powerful prince, recently killed in a duel, but to whom the Divine Mercy had come with an act of Contrition breathed in his dying breath. Marie-Denise received an order to pray fervently for him. For nine years and three months, she laid siege to Heaven for this soul, even to the length of offering her own life in ransom. But it all seemed in vain. Words are powerless to describe the mental and physical sufferings endured by this holy nun to assuage the torments of this hapless prince. After a long martyrdom, it pleased God to show her, in vision, the soul of the prince released from the lowest depths of the fire. At the same time, she received the assurance that he would be delivered a short time before the day of General Judgment, and also that a remission of *some hours* of Purgatory had been granted to him. The sister asked Mother du Châtel to pray for her intention. This good religious consented gladly, but she could not hide her surprise at such a meagre remission in return for such sacrifices. " Ah ! my Mother," the holy sister answered, " it is already a great mercy that God should let the cooling balm of my prayers reach him. Time in the next life is not measured as it is in this. Whole years of sorrow, of weariness, of poverty, of sickness are nothing in comparison with one hour of the Purgatorial fires."

That story is at the same time terrifying and consoling, but the consolation outweighs the terror. The unhappy prince had died in the very act of mortal sin. He ought, in the ordinary course, to have gone to Hell, if the mercy of God had not accorded a moment of recollection to him, in which he breathed his dying act of contrition. According to Marie-Denise, this grace had been accorded in answer to the prayers of saintly souls.

The biographer of the Curé d'Ars recounts a similar experience. A woman had lost her husband, an irreligious man, who had committed suicide. Inconsolable at what she believed to be his eternal damnation, she chanced one day to visit Ars, and desired to speak with the Curé about her husband. She pushed her way through the crowd to where the holy man stood. Then, before she could say a word, he bent down and murmured in her ear: "He is saved. Yes, he is saved." The poor woman shook her head in a gesture that said—impossible, impossible. Then, in a still surer voice, he went on:

"I tell you he is saved; that he is in Purgatory and that you must pray for him. Between the parapet of the bridge and the water, he had time to make an act of Contrition. He owes the grace to the Blessed Virgin Mary. You remember how your irreligious husband allowed you to keep the month of May in your room . . . how he sometimes joined with you in the prayers. That has merited for him the supreme pardon."[1]

If the first account is both terrifying and consoling, the second is entirely consoling. It shows that, thanks to the existence of Purgatory, we can still hope for the salvation of those, who, to all appearances, ought to go to Hell.

IV.—Purgatory—a Very Sanctifying Dogma

The Christian dogmas are not simply speculative truths which claim the assent of our reason, on the authority of God revealing them. They are also instructions of a practical import which point the way to the realization of our divine

---

[1] F. Trochu. "L'admirable Vie du Curé d'Ars." Lyon, 1932.

destiny. But the doctrinal element and the moral element are unequally mixed in different dogmas. In some the doctrinal predominates: in others, the moral. It is difficult to say which of the two predominates in the dogma of Purgatory, for it is intimately bound up with many other revealed truths, while at the same time, its moral import is immense. It is therefore, a most sanctifying doctrine.

Examined from the doctrinal aspect, this dogma, both by reason of its own formulation and of the devotion to which it is fundamental, is inseparable from many other revealed truths which continually exercise our Faith. Passing over the immortality of the soul and the existence of a future life, both necessarily presupposed, Purgatory implies the infallibility of the Church, on the authority of which we accept that truth, which is indicated in Holy Scripture in but an obscure manner—a fact which explains its rejection or its modification by the dissident Churches.

" Moreover, devotion to the souls in Purgatory exercises our faith in the effects of the Sacrifice of the Mass and of the Sacraments ... in that we take for granted their efficacy in aiding the dead. It increases our faith in the Communion of Saints ... so that the idea of Indulgences becomes quite easy and familiar to us. Around the doctrine of Purgatory, many other doctrines necessarily gather. By exercising our faith in this doctrine, we do so in all the others, too " (*Faber*). St. Paul says that " the just man liveth by faith "—and the thought of Purgatory, with prayer for the souls therein, causes us to live that life of faith, which is a primordial condition of holiness, and familiarises us with the supernatural world.

But who will measure the moral content of this dogma ? It touches all Christian morality, at its principles equally with its practical applications. It proclaims the infinite sanctity of God, Who cannot suffer in His elect the least blemish: it preaches His infinite justice which leaves no disorder unvisited with punishment. It thus inspires in us a profound horror of sin, even of sin labelled venial. It is principally, though not uniquely, for the expiation of venial faults that Purgatory has been instituted. It therefore inculcates the grave necessity for our doing penance to pay off the debt left by our sins, for we know the alternative—that of doing so in the next life under conditions incomparably harder and entirely without merit for the increasing of our eternal glory. One of the best ways of doing penance is simply to multiply good works, especially works of charity and of mercy towards the dead. To pray for the souls in Purgatory, to offer for them works of reparation, what a splendid way to wipe out one's own debts to the justice of God! For this act of charity is particularly agreeable to the Saviour, Who has said that mercy shall be to the merciful. "Blessed are the merciful," He said, "for they shall obtain mercy."

Often, moreover, in praying for the dead, in offering good works for them, we not only make simple acts of mercy, but we also discharge personal debts of justice and of gratitude. How very many souls in Purgatory have a claim on our suffrage, by the double title of justice and gratitude! While they were here below, they have heaped our lives with their kindnesses. Because of us and through our fault, they have committed certain sins, for which they are undergoing a rigorous chastisement—sins due either to the scandal they have received from us, or to our actions having been the occasion to them of acts of impatience, of murmuring, of anger, of slander. Is it not indeed just that we should come to their aid, and thus look to our own best interest, in wiping out the scores marked up against us for our injury of these souls?

Add to this, the fact that the thought of Purgatory is in itself a sanctifying one, inasmuch as it brings before us vividly the great last things: death, judgment, the sanctions of the next life. Devotion to the souls in Purgatory detaches us from the vain and passing things of the earth. It establishes a contact between us and our dear ones, which does not allow their memory to sleep with their dust. Not knowing whether they may not yet need our prayers to release them from their prison of sorrow, we multiply for them our prayers, our sacrifices, our good works. And of all that, nothing is lost, for if they for whom we supplicate are happily in no need of such attention, God will mercifully apply to other souls the satisfactions we offer. There are multitudes of forgotten souls, whose names are never uttered in prayer to God. To these must be given the overflow from the prayers offered for others. Mary distributes to them these merciful alms. They are strange alms, these alms given by the living to the dead, for they are alms given and kept. In the hands of God, they become for their givers a treasure, a capital, the interest of which will be paid at their death in merit rich for Heaven, in a shortening —even an annulment—of the Purgatorial pains. Thanks to the dogma of Purgatory, how many souls follow the recommendation of Our Saviour, and lay up to themselves treasures in Heaven, thus becoming rich before God (*Mat.*, vi, 20 ; *Lk.*, xii, 21).

Chapter the Third

PLACE, POPULATION AND SOCIETY OF PURGATORY

WITH THIS CHAPTER, we leave the firm ground of dogma and theological certitudes to pass to that of opinion and pious conjecture. These are not all of equal value. Some would appear to belong to the domain of pure imagination. Others, on the contrary, have some foundation in the principles of a sane theology. We will confine ourselves to these.

I.—THE PLACE OF PURGATORY

We have already pointed out in the first chapter, that Purgatory, according to the definitions of the Church, ought above all to be regarded as a state, even though the definitions are sometimes couched in terms belonging to the category of place, in order that things spiritual may be presented in a manner nearer to our way of thinking. Separated souls, being spiritual substances, cannot be localized in the proper sense of the word. But they must exist in some place, according to the mode proper to them. To determine where this *somewhere* is in space, is the question raised when one speaks of the *place* of Purgatory.

Let it be understood from the outset that the magisterium of the Church has defined nothing as to the *localisation* of Purgatory. The question is freely open to hypotheses. These have not been wanting throughout the centuries, and they are most divergent. Although certain Greek Fathers, as St. Gregory of Nyssa and St. John Chrysostom, seem to have placed Purgatory in a superterrestrial region near to the terrestrial paradise—the latter being supposed a garden planted by God between Heaven and earth; although certain Byzantine and Greco-Russian theologians have also placed their Purgatory in the air, making it consist of a voyage more or less long, very painful and laborious, across the customs-regions of the beyond called 'telonies,'[1] where the souls must suffer the vexations of demons on account of their sins ; the western tradition has habitually placed Purgatory in an inferior place, and more precisely, at the centre of the earth, in the neighbourhood of Hell. In the "Divine Comedy," Dante imagines Purgatory as a conical mountain, which has strange resemblances to the little volcanic island of Stromboli, to the northeast of Sicily. Loaded with the debt of their sins, the souls climb painfully the ascending circles which will conduct them to the summit, from which, their expiation ended, they will fly to the celestial Jerusalem. On the other hand, certain Latin Doctors, as St. Gregory the Great (+604) and St. Peter Damien (+1172), imply that the souls endure their Purgatory in the very places in which they have sinned. Private revelations and visions accord with this opinion. St. Thomas Aquinas attempts to reconcile these divergent hypotheses. He writes :

"Holy Scripture gives nothing precise on the location of Purgatory, and there is no reason to place it here rather than there. However, regard having been had to the words of the saints and to private revelations, it is probable that there are two places for Purgatory. The first is fixed by the common law : it is an inferior place, situated in such contiguity to Hell that the same fire serves both the tormenting of the damned in Hell and the purifying of the just in Purgatory. But as the damned are lower than the just, Hell must be placed below Purgatory. The second place of Purgatory is an exceptional one. It explains those narratives of certain souls being chastised in different places, whether for the instruction of the living or for the comfort of the dead—for by their suffering being revealed, they procure the prayers of the faithful. How-

---

[1] The oriental 'telonies' are a kind of aerial customs-stations, presided over by demons. After death, the soul, accompanied by its guardian angel, must present itself at each of these stations to be examined under a special category of sins. According to the nature and the number of the sins which it has committed and for which it has not sufficiently atoned, the soul is held for a time more or less long at such-and-such a station. If it is completely pleasing to Divine Justice, the soul passes on unhindered to the region of the Blessed. The number of 'telonies' varies with the author's imagination, from six to twenty two. This naive and rather crude fiction has been invented to give in one image the idea of the particular judgment and of Purgatory. Certain oriental theologians of to-day attach an importance to it which is certainly excessive.

ever, certain authors teach, that, according to the common law, the place of the soul's Purgatory is that in which the person has sinned: an opinion hardly tenable, seeing that the same person is being punished at the same time for sins committed in different places. According to others, the place of their punishment must be above us, because, they argue, their state places them between God and us. This reasoning is valueless, since sin, the cause of their chastisement, makes them our inferiors rather than our superiors."[1]

The liturgy of the dead, which is very ancient, does not enter into all the distinctions worked out by a later theology. It keeps to the biblical manner of expression. In the Old Testament, the Jews, to whom the precise states of the next life had not been clearly revealed, envisaged all the souls of the dead as inhabiting the same place, called shéol, in which they did not distinguish different pasts. Shéol was an *inferior* subterranean place, a dark prison. The Psalmist speaks often of "an inferior and black lake, placed in the shadow of death, the shadow of the land of forgetting." This inferior place has been translated by *inferus, inferi, infernus, inferni,* in the Latin version of the Bible. This *inferus* or *inferni* in the Latin text of the Bible, and very often in the liturgical texts, means at one time Hell in the strict sense of our usage; at another, Purgatory; again, the sojourn of the just before the coming of the Saviour, called " Abraham's bosom " in the Gospels and " The Limbo of the Fathers " by theologians; yet again, the vague complexus of all these without distinction. The invocation which occurs so often in the Office for the Dead: " A porta inferi erue, Domine, animas eorum," ought not to be translated: " Lord, deliver the souls of the dead from the gate of Hell," but rather : " Lord, deliver their souls from the gate of the inferior region," or, in our term, from Purgatory. This inferior region is opposed to the *superior region* or Heaven. When we say in the " Apostles' Creed " that Christ descended into Hell " after His death on the cross, this " hell " designated above all—and *perhaps exclusively according to the safer doctrine*—the region of the just souls in Shéol, whom Our Saviour in His human soul, ever hypostatically united to His

---

[1] **Summa Theologica, Supp.,** *q.,* lxix, *a.* 8.

Divine Person, went to visit, console and bless. For before His coming, these just souls—that is, those in a state of perfect charity and complete deliverance from the temporal punishment due to sin—did not yet enjoy the Beatific Vision of God, but only a foretaste analogous to that given in the peace and joy of the saints here below.

The Church has also adapted Psalm 129 to the Holy Souls: "Out of the depths have I cried to thee, O Lord." In the literal sense, this psalm is a prayer of the exiles of Babylon making their supplication to God from the depths of their misery and anguish. In the figurative sense in which the Liturgy uses it, the ' depths ' signify Purgatory.

One hesitates, however, to apply to Purgatory the words used in the Offertory of the Requiem Mass: "*Lord Jesus Christ, King of Glory, deliver the souls of the Faithful Departed from the pains of Hell and from the deep pit; deliver them from the mouth of the lion; let them not become the prey of Tartarus, that they may not fall into darkness: but may the holy standard-bearer, St. Michael, present them into the holy light, which Thou didst promise to Abraham and to his seed.*" Certain theologians, among them Pope Benedict XIV, does not hesitate to say that, in this prayer, the Church prays for the souls in Purgatory. The ' Hell ' of which it speaks ought to be translated ' inferior place,' that is, Purgatory. Similarly, *the deep pit, Tartarus, the dark prison* are all synonyms for the word, Purgatory. As regards the *deliverance from the lion's mouth*—the lion is evidently the demon, according to St. Peter's (1st *Epist.*, v, 8-9) comparison—that also can be interpreted as deliverance from Purgatory. Purgatory, indeed, which mediaeval theologians place near to Hell, makes a part in some fashion of the domain of the devil, in as much as it is an effect of sin. God has, so to speak, given jurisdiction to the devil over all that, immediately or remotely, concerns sin. Some authors have even had the bad taste to suggest that the devils are allowed to torture the souls in Purgatory.

The majority of theologians, however, following St. Bellarmine, hold that the Church, by that prayer, has indeed the intention of praying for the deliverance of the souls in Purgatory ; but, in a vivid image, the Church takes its place at the bedside of the departing soul, at the precise moment of death when it is in danger of eternal damnation. It prays the Lord Jesus to assure the salvation of the departing souls by delivering them from both Hell and Purgatory, and to introduce it, under the conduct of St. Michael, into the abode of eternal light. It is by a similar fiction, that the Church celebrates the great mysteries of the life of Christ as if they were taking place there and then before its eyes.

Sufficient has been said concerning the place of Purgatory. Since Purgatory is first and foremost a state of the separated soul, it can be said that Purgatory is where the soul in Purgatory is. The suffering soul brings with it its Purgatory, just as the blessed soul takes with it the heaven from which it can never be separated. All the other localizations are in grave danger of being pure products of the imagination.,

II.—The Population of Purgatory

When we undertake to discuss the population of Purgatory, we make no pretence, be it clearly understood, to give even remotely approximate statistics. To make a census of Purgatory is something entirely beyond our means. Only God and His saints—for to them He has surely revealed it—know what, at any given moment, is the exact population of the Church suffering. But we may speak of that population without hazarding any figures.

The first most striking trait is that it is a continually floating population. Purgatory is like a huge harbour or an important railway station or airport where crowds are continually arriving and crowds departing : arrivals from the earth, departures for Heaven. In our day, when the population of the world is about two thousand million, the mean death-roll is 6,000 per hour, giving 140,000 per day, How many of that number go to Purgatory ? This is a completely insoluble question for us, especially when we remember that in this matter, we are concerned only with the minority in that 6,000 who are baptized ; and of that minority, again, scarcely half belong to the Catholic Church. As far as we can conjecture from our own experience of this Catholic minority in a minority, very few Catholics merit on their death to pass straight to Heaven. And who will count the number lost in Hell ?

As regards the joyous phalange on phalange of delivered souls who see heaven opened to them at each successive moment, we cannot calculate their number, for we are in complete ignorance of all that would be necessary to attempt the remotest of approximations.

The question now arises, whether there are souls in Purgatory whose sojourn on earth preceded the Incarnation and the Sacrifice of the Cross. To that curious but far from idle question, the Greek Church would seem to give an affirmative answer. Since the XI century at least, it has established a general commemoration of the dead for the eve of Pentecost, when it prays *for all men who have died in holiness since Adam*. It may be, then, that Purgatory still contains souls who came to it before the birth of Our Saviour. This ought not to surprise us, when we remember that before God and His justice " one day is as a thousand years, and a thousand years as one day " (ii *Pet.* iii, 8), and if we can give credence to certain revelations made to saintly souls, which go to show that certain souls are condemned to Purgatory till the day of Final Judgment. St. Thomas also gives an affirmative. In the " Summa " (iii, *qr.* lii, *a*, 8), he will not admit that Christ, when he descended into Hell, emptied Purgatory by granting *motu proprio* a plenary indulgence to all the souls He found there. He maintains, on the contrary, that this visit of Our Saviour did not change in any way the normal course of divine justice as regards Purgatory. Only those souls were delivered whose term of expiation was completed, or whose life had merited that their deliverance should coincide with the coming of the Redeemer. Dante is equally of that opinion, since he chose for his illustrious Purgatorial guide the poet Virgil, who died in 19 B.C. And there are a whole body of theologians, who will not deviate a hair's breath from the opinion of St. Thomas in this matter.

Certainly, the answer given by St. Thomas is the safest one, from the point of view of God's strict justice; but there were special circumstances which would seem to justify an exception to the general rule, for this was the moment when Christ, having finished the work of our salvation, come to announce the joyful tidings to that part of humanity that had been faithful before His Incarnation and Death. It is the consideration of these special circumstances that has drawn other theologians, saints and even some brethren of St. Thomas among them, to favour a contrary opinion, by affirming that Our Saviour then really delivered all the souls in Purgatory and allowed them thus to keep the first Jubilee of the Redemption.

Among the theologians, we find a Dominican in the first rank—the celebrated St. Vincent Ferrer—who makes a distinction, in one of his sermons for Holy Saturday, between the rights of strict justice and the sweetness of mercy. St. Thomas has spoken according to the rights of strict justice. St. Vincent opts for the sweetness of mercy: Purgatory was emptied on the evening of Good Friday, and the souls detained there were allowed to join the company of the Just to whom Our Saviour opened the splendours of the vision of God.[1]

Here is a Jesuit, the Ven. Louis Du Pont, in one of his meditations: " It is probable that the Son of God drew from the flames of Purgatory all the suffering souls, either by shortening the term of their suffering, or by remitting their debts through the merits of His Blood newly shed for them. Perhaps he sent his angels to them, to deliver them one by one." (*Méditations sur les mystères de la foi*, pp. 14-15).

Suarez does not doubt the intrinsic probability of this pious conjecture, and St. Robert Bellarmin declares that there can be no error in maintaining it, since the mercy of Our Saviour is not necessarily linked with the sacraments or with our satisfactions, in such a manner that it cannot operate outside them.[2]

What reasons can be brought forward in favour of this thesis of mercy? One reason arises from a comparison with that which takes place among men. On the day of triumph and victory, the victor grants an amnesty to the guilty who have not merited capital punishment, especially to those guilty of light offences. When a king comes to the throne, he acts in like manner. On his patron's day, the father of a family pardons the little shortcomings of his children. This last is the most pleasing comparison. Jesus is the new Adam,

---

[1] See " Commentaire sur la Somme " of de la Ponetta O.P., iv, p. 395.
[2] Opera Omnia, Paris 1870, t., i, p. 433 ; De Christo, i, iv, c., xvi.

the Father of regenerated humanity. All those who have been saved owe their salvation to the merits of Christ, applied by anticipation before the great drama of Calvary. What more natural than that, on the evening of this day of triumph the Saviour should accord to the souls in Purgatory that plenary indulgence of which we speak.

Perhaps we may see a small indication that this is the true view, in the perfect absolution which Jesus gave to the thief who proclaimed his innocence and asked for a remembrance in His Kingdom. According to all appearances, this thief, in spite of his repentance—which was indeed serious but not very likely different from that of an ordinarily well-disposed penitent—ought to have gone to purgatory for a long time. Yet see how the Saviour canonizes him immediately, and unites him that very evening to the assembly of the saints who see God and rejoice in eternal happiness. Is it not an indication that, on this evening, Christ opted for that judgment of sweet mercy of which St. Vincent Verrier has spoken?

Another reason would appear to be even stronger. The people who lived before Christ had been, as regards eternal salvation, in a much less favourable situation than that in which we live our lives—we, the happy privileged ones, who have seen arise the star of Bethlehem, and to whom the treasures of superabundant redemption lie open. They were in darkness, scarcely seeing even the dawn : we live in the full noontide. They had not before their eyes, for safe guidance, the example of a God made man : no cross, no tabernacle, no confessional. Dead, they were not followed by Masses to assuage and shorten their Purgatory. Since the coming of Christ, even those souls who come to Purgatory in schism, in heresy, in infidelity, have a share in the fruit of the Masses celebrated in the whole universe, in the numerous suffrages offered by the Church militant. Would it not indeed have been in accordance with His Wisdom, if Christ, in the overflowing mercy of that first Good Friday, had balanced the scale of mercy between the two humanities—those before and those after His coming—by granting a plenary indulgence to those under the Old Law, who knew not the riches given to us with regal largesse ?

In spite of these considerations, certain theologians hesitate to accept this idea of a general Purgatorial amnesty affecting those souls of what we have called ' the first humanity.' They opt for a compromise: a great number were delivered, and many others were not. Here is an expression of this " mean of justice ":

"We maintain that Christ, descending into hell, probably delivered a certain number of souls from Purgatory. This assertion is perfectly consonant with what we have in the first place affirmed. It is one thing, indeed, to say that Christ's descent into hell was not a means of applying the merits of Christ, and therefore could not *per se* have delivered the souls from Purgatory; it is quite another to say that Christ, descending into Hell, did not obtain for any soul—by His own will, or by His Prayer—the application of the merits of His Passion and Death. We cannot deny that second assertion, without equivalently denying the first, or seriously questioning it. Therefore, we can affirm that Christ, in descending into Hell, on the one hand, delivered certain souls from Purgatory; and, on the other, did not exempt other souls from its pains. The reason for this opinion must now be outlined. During His life on earth, Christ, by a particular grace and a special mercy, gave remission of sins to certain people. On the cross, He pardoned the good thief. Rising, he opened the graves of many dead. Is it not indicated, therefore, that in descending into Hell, He should have delivered certain souls, eminent for their faith or their devotion? Who will tax with error the opinion, that, at present, certain souls are delivered from Purgatory, in virtue of the Passion of Christ, not by a law of justice, but by mercy gained by their faith or by their merits. And therefore, in a parallel way, may we not say that certain souls, by a similar faith and similar merits, have been delivered on Christ's descent into Hell, in virtue of that same mercy. We know that the suffrages of the saints aid mightily the souls in Purgatory. A fortiori, the prayer of Christ must have a power to aid them. If to-day, there are souls who, on some title or other, merit favours obtained through the prayer of Christ, why should there not have been similar cases, when Christ descended into Hell?"[1]

---

[1] P. Stentrup: "De Verbo Incarnato."

For our own part, we incline to the thesis which favours the greatest mercy, for the reasons we have already set forth. The very doctrine of St. Thomas, indicated earlier on, of the instantaneous disappearance of the moral stains of venial sin and the similar disappearance of disordered inclinations, with the souls in Purgatory, favours this opinion. For in what, in effect, consists this favour accorded by Jesus to these souls? In a simple remission of the temporal punishment due to sin, in a shortening of the expiation, properly so called, by that granting of an Indulgence we call Plenary. This is not to overthrow the requirements of divine justice. When one considers the reasons that weighed in favour of such an indulgence, on the evening of Good Friday, the possibility of an exception in favour of these souls certainly looms large.

III.—The Society of Purgatory

Taken in its totality, the Church consists of three parts: the Church Militant on earth; the Church Suffering in Purgatory; the Church Triumphant in Heaven. These three divisions of the Universal Church constitute one only Mystical Body, the Head of which is Jesus Christ, Who gives to it its supernatural life of grace—a veritable created participation in the very life of God. Each division is distinguished from the others by the state of development of this supernatural life, found in each. In the Church Militant, this life is seen at its beginning and in a state of progress; in the Church Triumphant, it has reached its full plenitude; in the Church Suffering, it no longer grows, but it is liberated from the fetters that shackled it on earth in its efforts to reach perfect charity. The soul in Purgatory no longer opposes the action of God within it; it is totally possessed by divine love. But it pays its debt of just punishment for its sins. That is the obstacle which for a time hides from it the Face of its Beloved.

Each of these three Churches forms a society apart, with its own organization, but in constant communication with the other two.

This is true of the Church Militant, constituted in a visible hierarchical society, in which—always mindful, of course, of the invisible primacy of Jesus—we find Christ's first and universal vicar, the Pope ; his subordinate and local vicars, the bishops and the other members of the Clergy, according to their function ; and the body of the faithful obedient to their superiors.

One also speaks of the society of the elect and of a celestial hierarchy, of which angels and human souls, arrived at the perfection of supernatural life, form part. This celestial hierarchy, of which Jesus, in the spledour of His glorified Humanity, is the summit, is not based on titles and exterior dignities, but on the personal merits of each of the elect, on the soul's degree of charity which measures for it the field of the Infinite Vision. The celestial hierarchy is, therefore, very different from the hierarchy of the Church Militant. It is in Heaven that one finds the most surprising and the most unexpected applications of that saying of the Saviour : " The last shall be first, and the first last "

Is there also a hierarchy in Purgatory ? We answer : the souls in Purgatory live in a society, but there are not, properly speaking, any grades in that society, since the " grouping," so to speak, is provisional, not permanent. Purgatory is a kind of station on the line leading to Heaven ; a delay more or less long on the way to the lasting city ; it is the vestibule to the Father's home. For a hierarchy supposes stability. Moreover—and here we have the most solid argument of all —the same reason for being in Purgatory is shared by all the souls therein, for they are united in the expiation of sin. This places the souls on the same level, and cannot serve as a basis for the establishing of a hierarchy among them. They are all in prison, and there cannot be any reason for declaring one superior to another. They all have the same motive for humility : all have been sinners, through their own fault.

Purgatory must therefore be conceived as a republic of souls in distress, rivalling each other only in humility, and no one striving with another. All are animated with the most tender, the most compassionate mutual charity, practising to perfection the counsels of the Apostle in the Epistle to the Romans (xii, 10-11, 16) and in that to Philemon (ii, 3-4).

The souls in Purgatory, then, do not live in isolation from each other. They have also relations with the other two divisions of the Church—but of that later. Among themselves, they form a society, knowing each other, loving each other, aiding each other.

The souls in Purgatory know each other. This does not necessarily suppose their being gathered together in one place, for separated souls, spiritual substances, are not subject to the laws of material space. Spirits must have a means of communication, absolutely unknown to us. When one considers the possibilities of long-distance communication, latent in television, surely it is not too much to suppose that spirits can know each other, even though separated the one from the other.

In Purgatory, one is known and one makes new friends. How many contemporaries, citizens, neighbours, friends, relations, the newly arrived must find in Purgatory! A son finds himself again with his parents, a brother with his sister, a religious with his superior. At death, all social distinctions disappear, for the Sovereign Judge regards only merits and demerits. There one meets the great ones of the past, whose exploits one has admired or censured. They will be able to reveal to their fellows why they are still in Purgatory, and by what mercy they have escaped Hell. All those who are reunited there are holy and confirmed in grace, destined to life eternal together. After a time, more or less short and certainly finishing with the General Judgment, they will be forever assembled together in the celestial Fatherland. What more natural, then, than that the souls in Purgatory should know each other?

The souls in Purgatory love each other with a supernatural charity which has its source in God. Purgatory is a region of that perfect fraternal charity, so easily missed on earth where the commandment of Jesus: " Love ye one another as I have loved you," is so often disobeyed. There is scarcely a soul in Purgatory that is not expiating some faults against charity. How all resentment, all rancour, all bitterness must disappear, when hardened hearts are softened in the furnace of charity. Those who have least to suffer condole with those who have more; and these in turn rejoice that their consolers will soon be in Heaven, to aid them with their supplication, for envy and jealousy are unknown in Purgatory. Each rejoices with each in its happiness, and sorrows with it in its sorrows. Hence the incessant departures for Heaven are one of the joys of Purgatory, and the incessant arrivals from earth are one of its sorrows.

This mutual love of the souls in Purgatory is not a mere love of compassion or kindness. We may suppose, with certain theologians, that there is also, perhaps, a love of benevolence. Doubtless, each soul is impotent to help itself; but is it impotent as regards its companions in exile? It can hardly be so, since the general belief in our own days that they can intercede for *us*, leads on naturally to the conclusion that they can pray for one another. Prayer is the common manifestation of that fraternal charity which unites among themselves all the members of the Mystical Body of Jesus. This common means of communication must be available to all the faithful of all three divisions of the Church, that they may communicate with each and all of their brethren. The prayer of a soul in Purgatory for a fellow soul has not, of course, satisfactory value: it has impetratory force, the proper efficacy of prayer considered in itself. It could be compared to the gesture of a poor man who holds out his hand to a rich.

Other considerations make this thesis even more plausible. We have just remarked on the surprise that must be experienced by a soul on finding its contemporaries in Purgatory— a parent his children, friends their old friends, creditors their debtors, enemies their enemies. Parents are eager to aid their children, friends to deliver their friends, debtors to pay their debts, enemies to show the sincerity of their reconciliation. How can family love, friendship, gratitude and above all justice be allowed to satisfy themselves, if the souls in Purgatory are not permitted to aid each other, at least by prayer.[1] What

---

[1] Is it possible that there may be another way in which the souls in Purgatory can aid one another? Could a soul, on the instant of departing from Purgatory, offer itself as a voluntary victim, to take on itself a part of another's Purgatory? No theologian, to our knowledge, has posed the question. In itself, there can be no objection to such substitution, since it is possible between the living and the dead. One cannot doubt that there are souls in Purgatory generous enough for this. The whole question is whether such *vicarious satispassion*, to use the theological term, is reconcilable with the demands of divine justice. It must be carefully noted that, in this hypothesis, the soul that thus offers itself cannot gain by its act any merit, properly so called, any new degree of charity. The same must be said of the prayer of one soul in Purgatory for another. That prayer is an act of charity, but that act does not augment the personal merit of him who makes it.

these virtues demand among relations and contemporaries, compassion, the daughter of charity, claims for all souls in general, because all are worthy of pity and commiseration; they suffer unspeakable pains.

What these pains are must now claim our attention.

Chapter IV

THE PAINS OF PURGATORY

IN THEIR ESSENCE, we have already dealt with the pains of Purgatory in our first chapter. The Church, in her official teaching, speaks only of the purifying or expiatory pains, without determining their nature save on one point: one of the pains, doubtless the principal, is the temporary privation of the Vision of God. Catholic theologians have endeavoured to make this more precise. They point out that, by these expiatory pains, the suffering souls offer reparation and satisfaction for their sins to God, but that this differs in certain respects from the satisfaction offered while on earth. The difference concerns two points, mainly. Firstly, our satisfactions while on earth, not only appease the justice of God, but win for us grace and merit, for they are good works at once satisfactory and meritorious. The pains of Purgatory, on the contrary, are purely satisfactory, for there is no meriting after death. Secondly, other things being equal, the justice of God is probably less exacting on earth than in the beyond, for the present life sees the reign of mercy, the next the reign of justice—even though it is true to say that God always shows Himself mercifully in the sense that He always punishes the sinner less than he deserves, even in the next life. Besides, here below, the sinner in accepting fully the chastisement for sin, merits, with a merit of congruity, a diminution of his punishment. This congruous merit exists no longer for the soul in Purgatory, even though it accepts the punishment with a mightier élan of love than earth could ever know.[1] To distinguish the two types of satisfaction outlined above, theologians have coined the term *satispassion* for the satisfaction of Purgatory.

I.—NATURE OF THE PAINS

Purgatorial pains, as we have seen, are both *expiatory* and *reparatory* of sins committed. They are also *purifying* in the

[1] Cf. Suarez, 'De Purgatorio,' disp., xlvii, S.2j, N.7.

broad sense of the word. The temporal pain due to sin can be looked on as a kind of blemish, which remains on the soul cleansed from sin by repentant love ; but, as we have seen at some length, that pain is before all else an expiation, a reparation for an offence offered to God : which fact explains how the faithful of the Church Militant can assume the rôle of suppliants towards the members of the Church Suffering.

A.—Variety of the Pains

What are these expiatory pains ? We can say immediately that these pains are proportioned to the number and to the *subjective gravity* of the sins to be expiated. The subjective gravity depends on the state of soul of the sinner, at the moment he commits the sin. The same fault can be more or less grave in the eyes of God, according as it is committed with more or less knowledge, advertance and consent by one who has received more or less of the divine favours and graces, and who is held, by his social position and the duties of his state, to more or less of vigilance over himself, to more or less responsibility in influencing others. God alone can measure this subjective gravity. The just judgment of God on each soul is the measure of its Purgatory, as regards the nature of its pains, its intensity, its duration. Unlike an earthly tribunal, then, there can be no uniform sentence, decreeing the same punishment for the same offence. Purgatory offers a variety of punishments, for each soul has its own measure.

" Just as, among the Elect in Heaven, it would be impossible to find two saints with exactly the same earthly history, so no two souls in Purgatory suffer the same pains. Souls, even more than faces, keep their own physiognomy. Each has also its own personal responsibility, so that the same fault committed by one is not equally culpable before God as when committed by another. The degree of guilt has been determined to a nicety by the justice of God, and now the punishment is similarly measured. Those souls are more culpable who have received greater graces and have sinned with greater light, for " to whom much is given, of him much will be expected " (*Luke*, xii, 16). Purgatory, therefore, must be rigorous for those privileged ones of God, who have responded but half-heartedly to the divine advances. Great, too, is the responsibility of those who have negligently fulfilled the duties of authority, especially when they have sought after that authority: the good which they have failed to do to their inferiors, the evils which they allowed when they should and could have prevented them—all this swells the debt to be paid in Purgatory. It must be added, however, that these same privileged persons, because they have had more occasions of virtue and acquired great merit thereby, will, when their expiation is complete, enjoy a greater glory than those less-privileged ones who, through a milder Purgatory, will rise to a less glorious Heaven."[1]

B.—GENERAL CLASSIFICATION OF THE PAINS

Theologians have reduced this great variety of pains to two heads. There is the *common pain*, the deprivation of the Beatific Vision—a pain vouched for by the definitions of the Church, and essential to the very idea of Purgatory considered as a state. They call this the *pain of the damned*—a not very happy term, for which we have suggested some alternatives. *Pain of sense* is the generic name given to the other pains, and by that is generally understood, the pain of fire, of a material fire afflicting the souls.

Perhaps *pain of sense* is equally unhappy as a term, with *pain of the damned*. It suggests, in effect, the idea of a sensible, material torture, the sensation of burning, even though the soul, separated from its body, from the bodily organs of sense, is a spiritual substance which cannot *normally* experience sensible pains, like those experienced through the organs of sense. God could, of course, *by a miracle*, cause this to happen, since the separated soul preserves radically and in potency its sensitive faculties, its power to experience sensible pain. But must one push the matter so far? Many theologians do not think so, even those who admit a material fire which torments the souls. Among these is St. Thomas Aquinas, who conceives the action of the fire of Purgatory on the soul as an imprisonment, a chaining which thwarts its normal

---

[1] L. Paré. " Les Mystères de l'au-delà." pp. 100-101.

spiritual activity in its new state of separated spirit, and causes it profound humiliation by such a chaining to a material thing. It is in the same way that St. Thomas explains the action of the fire of Hell. This is evidently possible and extremely ingenious. But we may be allowed to differ from it, as regards Purgatory, since the Church leaves us free in the matter, even to the extent of denying a material fire more or less like the fire we know on earth.

We have seen that the Council of Florence, in view of the repugnance of the Greeks to the idea of a material fire, was not precise as to the nature of the Purgatorial pains, and simply used the words *expiatory* or *purifying*. Of these pains, that which results from the delay of the Beatific Vision is the principal—and it is possible to maintain that it is, *in some way the only pain*. By this, we mean that the privation of the Beatific Vision is *directly and per se* the great torment of these souls, in such a way that those other pains, called by theologians *the pain of sense*, flow from it as consequences. Let us explain this.

C.—The Pain of the Hunger for God

The deprivation of the Beatific Vision is incontestably the principal torment of these souls. For them, this is not a purely negative pain, as we might be tempted to regard it from our experience of those who live their lives far from God, without experiencing the least inconvenience therefrom. At the moment of death, the scales fall from the eyes of the soul, and it sees God as its sovereign good and only felicity; that it is made for Him, and that He is its all. It is given a mighty revelation of the immense, gratuitous love with which it has always been enveloped, and its love for Him knows no limits. An irresistible attraction draws it to Him, but its élan is hindered by the debt of its sins, which with great willingness it must pay to divine justice—or rather, to outraged love. The great desire to offer to that love a just reparation, devours them. At the same time, their hunger and thirst for the Beloved pierces them with the agony of longing. That is their great torment—a torment of which our earthly loves can give but a pale idea; a torment far exceeding all the torments of this world, because it is of another order and surpasses all our experiences. Only the awful trials through which certain contemplative souls, whom God allows to anticipate their Purgatory, pass, can give a suspicion of what it is like. St. Catherine of Genoa, who was such a soul, attempts by a familiar comparison to give us some idea of this pain (" A Treatise on Purgatory ") :

" To understand, in some fashion, the ardour with which the souls in Purgatory desire God, let us imagine in the world one only bread, with the power to satisfy the hunger of all creatures. If a man in good health, devoured by hunger and knowing that only this bread can satisfy him, sees himself deprived of it, will not his hunger grow and become ever more intolerable the nearer he approaches that bread without being able to grasp it ? . . . The souls in Purgatory have that same ardent hunger to refresh themselves with the celestial bread —God Himself."

Inspired by this passage of the celebrated Genoese mystic, Mgr. Gay thus describes the sufferings of these souls :

" Fundamentally, it is God Himself Who is the sorrow of these souls—from which it follows that, in one respect at least, it is by reference to Him that the measure of their suffering must be gauged. In effect, the essence of their pain is the love which they bear to them : a love which is now all free and all pure, which quickens wonderfully the perfect knowledge that they have of Him. This love inevitably radiates in infinite desires to see Him and to possess Him. But how are we to name these desires ? A hunger, a thirst, a fever : hunger for God, thirst for God, fever for God. This need for God borrows something of the grandeur and the necessity of its object, so that its intensity and its urgency are altogether incalculable. With all its being, the soul reaches towards God. All the state, the life, the occupation of these souls is the hunger for God . . . They become, as it were, living hungers. That bread for which they starve, that water which they burn to drink, that indispensable good for which they long, that Being Who is all their life, their repose, their happiness, and towards which they earnestly strive—is absent and far from them. In a sense, this is but a prolonging of their exile on earth, when they felt the heavy weight of absence from God ; but this chagrin did not prevent them from enjoying a thousand pleasures. Apart from the fact that their personal state was altogether different, the absence of God during our earthly life is in the order of things. After death, that absence is a disorder, for God does not now hold His creature at a distance from Him, because it is the hour when that creature should come to Him. He claims it, He draws it . . . The soul knows Him, though it cannot see Him ; it feels Him ; all within it flings itself towards Him, but it is compelled by necessity to remain away. That necessity comes from within, and holds the soul by an inner power. The impotence of the soul causes its immobility. Like the paralytic on the pool's edge, it is completely unable to aid itself . . .

In a sense, the soul desires and loves these chains which hold it captive ; but this implies great wisdom and holiness, and this in turn implies the most ardent love—precisely the love which causes its torment."[1]

Certain saintly souls have experienced in this life the thirst for God which tortures the souls in Purgatory, but certainly in a lesser degree and in other circumstances. Many passages witnessing their experiences could be cited. These saints speak of a mysterious fire which consumes them, and this is in accord with many private revelations concerning Purgatory, as well as with the commonly accredited opinion in the Latin tradition.

D.—What, then, is this Fire ?

What is this mysterious fire ? Is it not the very fire of love, burning in the depths of the soul, while the soul, drawn irresistibly towards its Well-Beloved, can neither reach nor see Him ? Stopped in its progress by an insurmountable obstacle, that love becomes a fire, a burning sorrow, a kind of spiritual fever, which cannot be adequately expressed by the human word *fire* ; a real fire, a physical fire in some sense, but having only a faint analogy with the material fire of earth. Love can sometimes produce effects in the human breast which recall those of material fire. We read in the life of certain

---

[1] C. Gay. ' De la vie et des vertus crétiennes." Chap. xvii.

saints that they could not support the ardour of the fire which the love of God kindled within them, and to ease the burning they would uncover their breast to the cold. " Love is strong as death ; its heat as the heat of fire, the flames of Jahveh " (*Cant.* vii, 6). It is not to be wondered at, that the soul, separated from its body, should still feel in its inmost recesses those strange, sorrowful longings. Such, then, is the secret of the fire of Purgatory, lighted by love, and very different from the infernal flames, born of despair and hate : a fire producing in some fashion a suffering analogous to that of earthly fire.

Certain expressions of the mystics suggest this interpretation. " The suffering of sufferings for these souls," say St. Catherine of Genoa, " is the opposition which they find in themselves to the Will of God, which they know to burn with the most tender and most perfect love for them . . .This it is which enkindles in them a reciprocal fire of love for God—a love so living and insistent that it causes them to precipitate themselves with joy into Purgatory, that through these terrible flames they may the more quickly come to God."

Similar declarations are not far to seek in the life of contemplative saints. This interpretation of the fire of Purgatory has the advantage of resting on sure dogma—that, namely, which teaches that the souls in Purgatory are in a state of grace, of charity, and of perfect holiness. Every attempt at describing what might be called their psychology, must begin from this dogmatic fact, and must never lose sight of it.

E.—The Other Pains

In the light of this principle, the other pains of the moral order, which theologians and spiritual writers have reasonably enough supposed to be the lot of these souls, must be envisaged : regrets at having squandered the grace of God, and thus lost a higher degree of glory than that which they have merited ; pain at their neglect by the living, especially by those whom they have heaped with benefits ; sorrow at their uncertainty as to the time of their deliverance ; anxious longing for the blessed suffrages which will shorten their exile.

These pains can exist, but their bitterness cannot proceed

for these souls from any consideration of their own personal good. That bitterness has its source above all in their love for God. They regret that they have culpably missed a heaven more glorious, a field of vision more vast and more profound in the Infinite, because by raising themselves higher they could have glorified God more and responded better to the desires of the Heart of Jesus. They can suffer from the neglect of the living, but they accept that pain as just punishment for their own so frequent forgetfulness of God and His benefits. God leaves them in uncertainty as to the moment of their deliverance, but they accept this in the same spirit in which they endure their torment.

Thus does their love for God explain and penetrate all their pains. It is this love which shows the radical difference which exists between Hell and Purgatory. The one, a torment of hate and despair; the other, a torment of love, sweetened by a certain hope. In both, it is the justice of God which claims satisfaction, the difference being that, in Purgatory, the face of justice is softened by an expression of the most tender love. The punishment of the damned is that of the perverse slave, who hates the hand that strikes him. The punishment of the soul in Purgatory is the expiation of the Prodigal, casting himself at His Master's feet and asking for punishment that he may repair his offence. Were it able, the damned soul would quit its Hell and continue to sin without wishing to return to God—which would be, of course, to continue its Hell. Were it free to enter Heaven before it had paid its debt to divine justice, the soul in Purgatory would refuse, for it would find it intolerable to enter the wedding feast with the slightest stain on its wedding garment. So St. Francis de Sales : " The souls in Purgatory are there for their sins, which they sovereignly detest ; but as regards the pain they suffer from being detained from Paradise, they lovingly suffer it, ever devoutly pronouncing the canticle of divine justice : ' Thou art just, Lord, and Thy judgments are right ' (*Ps.* cxviii, 137)."

F.—CONCLUSION

In spite of the distinction between the pain of the damned

and the pain of sense, elaborated by theologians, certain private revelations exempt a great number of souls from the pain of sense considered as distinct from the privation of the Beatific Vision. St. Catherine of Genoa had such revelations. Other revelations divide Purgatory into three zones : the first, bordering on Heaven, where only the pain of the damned is felt ; an intermediate zone, where the pain of sense is mixed with that of the damned, without the torment being very rigorous ; finally, the lower Purgatory, where souls laden heavily with debts, the souls of death-bed conversions, suffer the full measure of torment. All this is plausible without being certain, since a close comparison of these revelations shows considerable discrepancies between them.

We may conclude, therefore, that the great pain of Purgatory is a torment of love, provoked by the vehement desire to see God, and that this is the source of those other pains known as the pain of sense. This explanation accords perfectly with the real state of the souls in Purgatory as taught us in Catholic dogma—a state characterized by the perfect love of God, full submission to His Will, and the ardent desire to satisfy His justice and His sanctity for their sins.

II.—INTENSITY OF THE PAINS

After our treatment of their nature, we have little to add on their intensity. That intensity is unknown to us. We can but say that they ought to vary according to the number and the gravity of the sins to be expiated, and we can suspect that, in some cases, God may shorten the duration of the exile by intensifying the suffering. We are lead to suppose this latter especially of the souls in Purgatory on the eve of the General Judgment.

The question of the intensity of the pains is for us one of comparison with the suffering of this life. Theologians have debated whether the sufferings of Purgatory are keener than all the sufferings which a man can endure in body and in soul while he lives on earth. Does the least pain of Purgatory surpass the greatest of earth ? Many, following St. Thomas, answer in the affirmative ; others, with St. Bonventure, in the negative. Judging by the trials of the contemplatives, something of which we have seen, the evidence seems to favour St. Thomas. The sufferings of Purgatory, he says, are not to be compared with those of this life, since they belong to a different order. The mystics have told us that their suffering exceeded all the torments inflicted on the martyrs. We must conclude, then, that the sufferings of Purgatory—the thirst for God—far surpass anything in our earthly experience. This should be a salutary lesson for us. We will certainly be right in persuading ourselves that the sufferings of Purgatory are extremely severe, and that the souls therein deserve our most tender compassion. At the same time, the knowledge that the pains of this life cannot compare with those of Purgatory, should stir us up to anticipate the payment of our debts and thus avoid a more rigorous exactment.

III.—THE DURATION OF PURGATORY

We are in total ignorance as to the duration of Purgatory for any particular soul. One is naturally inclined to measure the Purgatory by the number of sins to be expiated . . . But, if we may credit certain private revelations, this reasoning is not always exact, since God may diminish the time by augmenting the intensity. When St. Margaret of Cortona had prayed much for her deceased father, Our Saviour gave her this revelation: " Be not disquieted because of his past life, because the pains of Purgatory are of different kinds. He has suffered the most intense of these pains, because I will, by purifying him in the most terrible fashion, to deliver him very soon" (*Vie Intine, Ch.* viii).

The question now arises: what is the measure of time for the separated soul? Time, the measure of movement and of change, represents something objective for the souls in Purgatory. They are not fixed in a changeless present. They put forth diverse and successive acts which, by the very fact of their diversity and their succession, are measurable by duration. They have the notion of our time and of our way of measuring it. However, for them there is no day, or night, or month, or year, or season. Nothing breaks the uniformity and the monotony of their time. They do not measure the parts of time with hour-glass, or clock, or watch. Moreover, the subjective appreciation of duration in time is something very relative, even with us. How swiftly the happy moments pass, when we are absorbed in a work of love or enthralled by an eloquent voice—when hours seem minutes. How, on the contrary, sleepless nights, the time in the ante-room of an operating theatre, or the endless war-time queuing drag their slow minutes out till each seems an hour. From our own experience, we can get a vague idea of what an hour in Purgatory must mean to a soul athirst for God.

Whatever about subjective impressions as to the duration of time, it is certain that the measure is more or less that of earth—the measure these souls know well. For precision on this point, we have only private revelations, which cannot, however, furnish any general rule, since they are concerned only with particular cases. These revelations are both terrifying and consoling. They upset our calculations and our conjectures, because we can judge our neighbours only according to that which appears without, not knowing the heart that God sees. So our admiration has placed such-and-such a soul in the glory of Heaven, and we discover that it must suffer a long Purgatory. Another, like the good thief, goes straight to Heaven, yet in our estimation he must languish for a long time in Purgatory. The saints feared greatly the tendency of their friends to anticipate their canonization, for they knew it would deprive them of the prayers and suffrages which would shorten their Purgatory.

" These good souls," says St. Francis de Sales of those who sang his praises, " with all their glorifying me, will make me languish in Purgatory, for they will imagine that I have no need of prayer. Behold what such reputation will profit me." The Abbé Balley, who gave his instruments of penance to the Curé d'Ars with instructions to hide them, was inspired with the same thought.

Yes, even canonized saints have had to spend a time, more or less long, in Purgatory. St. Severinus, according to St. Peter Damian, remained there for some time. The Blessed de la Colombière, according to his penitent St. Margaret Mary, was deprived of the Beatific Vision from the moment of his death to the moment of his burial. How many other saints, especially those who exercised high authority on earth, must have known the sufferings of Purgatory.

We have said that private revelations on Purgatory are both consoling and terrifying : terrifying, when they reveal sentences of long duration, stretching out to the final judgment ; consoling, when they speak of a Purgatory of months of days, of hours. Here are some revelations of lengthy Purgatory :

" St. Veronica Juliani speaks of a sister who fought strenuously against her reforms in the matter of primitive poverty, but who had died in true repentence. Without the prayers of the saint, she would have remained as many years in Purgatory as she had lived on earth . . .

The Curé d'Ars was once asked whether a certain non-practising Catholic, M. d'Escrivieux, who had died without Confession, had been saved. He answered : " Yes, but he will be in Purgatory for a long, long time." Of another, this time a good Catholic, he said : " In three years he will go to Heaven, and you will know that through one of your children." The child had later a revelation of the fact in sleep . . .

St. Ludgarde prayed and fasted for Simon, a Cistercian Abbot who had lead an austere life but had been unbending towards his brethren. She obtained his deliverance, but she knew that, without her prayers, he would have been forty years in Purgatory."[1]

The apparition of the illustrious Pope Innocent III to St. Ludgarde, in which he revealed to her that he must suffer in Purgatory till the Day of Judgment, is arresting indeed, and so impressed the saintly Cardinal Bellermine that he carefully examined the evidence for this revelation. The Visitandine, Soeur Marie-Denise de Martignat, also speaks of a prince, killed in a duel, who was condemned to remain in Purgatory until the Day of Judgment. He had escaped Hell by last-minute Contrition. By hard penance, the saint succeeded in shortening his sentence by a few hours.

Happily, the examples of short-term Purgatory are not rare among the private revelations. What St. Thérèse tells

---

[1] Saudreau : "Pensées sur le Purgatoire.

us of her Purgatorial visions is very consoling. She speaks of a certain Father Provincial for whom she foresaw a long Purgatory, because of his heavy responsibilities. " Though he was a man of great virtue," she says, " I feared for his soul, because I always fear much for those who have charge of souls, and he had been a superior for twenty years." She goes on to speak of her prayers for him, until the happy moment when she saw him delivered. " Although he was an old man, he appeared as a man less than thirty, and his face was dazzling with light . . . That was fifteen days after his death."

The same saint speaks of a Carmelite who spent but two days in Purgatory ; of another, who had borne a heavy cross of illness, whose stay was but four hours ; of a Jesuit whose delivery occurred during the Mass following the day of his death.

" On 8th May, 1714, Soeur Maria-Imperia, a Benedictine nun of Città di Castello, who had bonds of friendship with St. Veronica, died a holy death. Veronica saw her in Purgatory, but her place there was lighted up by a ray from the Immaculate Heart of Mary. She had but to pass a few days there, but her saintly friend Veronica, obtained her deliverance on the first day.

On being asked whether a certain lady who was ill would recover, the Curé d'Ars, knowing supernaturally that she was dead, answered : " She has already received her reward . . .

Mère Moes, who saw priests in Purgatory condemned to long sentences, saw other priests whose stay in Purgatory was for a month, a week, two days."[1]

It is clear, therefore, that there are sentences of long duration and of very short duration in Purgatory. The conclusion must surely be, that in our uncertainty as to the fate of our brethren, the wisest and most charitable thing to do is to pray unceasingly for them. Let us apply to prayer for the dead, those words : " We ought always to pray and not to grow slack." In approving of Masses in Perpetuity for the dead, the Church approves of such constant remembrance. In this, she shows herself in disagreement with that strange opinion of P. Dominic Soto, who played an important part in

---

[1] Saudreau : " La Vie Spirituelle."

the Council of Trent. This theologian affirms that the sufferings of Purgatory are so terrible and the suffrages of the Church so efficacious, that a soul, no matter what its debt, cannot remain there more than ten years.[1] That would be to give the lie to many private revelations. They are not, it is true, imposed de fide on us, but they certainly merit our attention. Before concluding this chapter, it is as well to attempt a collective appreciation of these revelations.

IV.—Purgatorial Pains and Private Revelations

The detail of private revelations contrasts sharply with the laconic definitions of the Church on the subject of Purgatory. From the time of Gregory the Great and his " Dialogues " right up to our own day, this multiplication of visions and revelations concerning Purgatory in hagiographical writing, presents a curious phenomenon. The revelations on Hell and Heaven have nothing of this luxuriance of detail. Why this difference ? Without wishing to make the acceptance of all these revelations a matter of conscience, it is surely high temerity to reject them en bloc, for many of them come to us with sufficient proof of credibility and are in no way contrary to any doctrine of the Church. Of the conduct of Providence in this matter, Mgr. Henri Bolo has some good things to say :

" The revelation of Heaven and Hell in the Scriptures, fulfils the end which God proposed, in letting us know the certain, definite end of human life. Once revealed, the simple notion of Hell and Heaven ought sufficiently to influence us ... This is not the case with Purgatory, and this for two reasons. In the first place, whatever the dogmatic utterances of the Church on Purgatory, we know that the expiatory sufferings do not constitute a definitive state. We know, on the contrary, that Heaven alone is highly desirable, while Purgatory is a place into which one does not enter without a certainty of eternal salvation. From this, a very natural consequence results. All things considered, the notion of Purgatory reassures more than it frightens us. Let us be

[1] This opinion has not been condemned, but it is not the common one held.

careful not to offend God mortally, and let the rest look after itself ! The repentance which saves from Hell will suffice : let us not anticipate those troublesome expiations ! We are not playing a dangerous game, in thus letting our debt mount up, for Purgatory is the ante-room to Heaven.

Thus, instead of vividly striking our imaginations, this dogma, so full of menace, serves as a pretext for lukewarmness rather than a warning to be perfect.

Hence the reason why God gives such a vivid content to the revelations coming to us from beyond the grave, and the motive of the frequent apparitions and interventions of souls condemned to that terrible expiation.

Nothing is proved in these visions, nor is there anything certain in these phantoms, or indisputable in these accounts : what matter, if the general effect is disquieting ? Souls in pain, spectres in fire, phantoms in chains, sorrowful faces, foreheads veiled in mourning, are not meant to bring faith to the living. No one ever had the idea of basing his faith in the Purgatorial expiations on such accounts. They are given that they may disquiet us. The more indeterminate the details, the more troubling are these accounts. The most intrepid feel the sweat pearling on their brow. The most coldly rational are constrained to say : If that were true . . . The habitués of the spiritual listen with rapt attention. Everywhere, there is fear . . . And these communications are made in circumstances which impose, if not absolute belief, certainly unmixed respect. The witnesses to them are transparently sincere, of known virtue, saints even. We are still free to reject them, but we can hardly escape the impression they make on us. If the Hand of God is in this, its end is, by that very fact, secured, As the fear of Hell is the beginning of conversion, so the fear of Purgatory is the beginning of a life of mortification and perfection. It is quite understandable, then, why the souls in Purgatory have often the occasion and the permission to reveal themselves to the living.

Another and more obvious reason is sufficient of itself to explain the intervention in our life and affairs, of the souls in Purgatory.

It is ' de fide ' that we can help the souls in Purgatory by our prayers and our works, by the Mass and by Indulgences.

It is all too evident, however, that our compassion is aroused only in proportion as we are sensibly moved. A far-off disaster is a mere headline of our newspapers. A suffering, the notion of which is purely intellectual, leaves as nearly indifferent ... The most awful disasters are a three days wonder with us ... And what, indeed, is more remote from us in every way, than the sufferings of the dead?

And what shall we say, when we remember that the lukewarmness of ' little faith ' is still to be added to this natural indifference? Thus, faith tells us that every mortal sin crucifies the Saviour. How many Christians commit mortal sin, entirely without remorse?

How could such a weak faith have sufficient energy to wake us to the reality of the fearful thought that a tenderly loved being could endure such sufferings? The result is that the dead, after a long or short time, are also the forgotten. That forgetfulness would be of little moment, if it were a question only of our own fidelity. But it is the dead who must bear the brunt of this.

The Church does what she can to appeal to our sensibility and to awaken our faith, in the interest of the dead. Her funeral rites have an incomparable beauty and dramatic power. The " lessons " of the Office describe with touching eloquence, the complaints, the appeals, the heart-cries of those whom our carnal ears cannot hear calling on us. Every year, we are solemnly reminded of the dead. Does this suffice? Evidently not. And even when whole Christian families remain in communication, through suffrages, with their dead, there is still the great army of the forgotten dead. When all is said and done, it is surely just such forgotten souls who make up the greater part of Purgatory.

But to be amazed that Providence gives a remedy for this abandonment, in permitting souls to come miraculously and solicit the pity of the living, is to be amazed that charity is charitable."[1]

The author we have just cited, goes on to justify these miraculous interventions, by declaring that the principal ' raison d'être ' of miracles is to establish and to strengthen

---

[1] Bolo, ' Nos Communications avec les morts.'

faith, but that it is none the less true that the Gospel miracles had for their determining motive, the tender compassion of the Saviour for the miseries of humanity. Bossuet had already written: "I maintain that all His miracles came from a sentiment of compassion. Looking often on the miseries of our life, He did not refuse us His tears ... In all the mighty healings which He did, He never failed to give expression to His sympathy with human calamity. From this I conclude that His compassion has wrought nearly all His miracles."

Now, what misfortune is more worthy of compassion than that of the souls in Purgatory? Like the paralytic on the pool's edge, these souls can do nothing for themselves but must depend entirely on the help of others. Jesus, to Whom they bear a relation as friends and spouses, has undoubtedly exercised His mercy to them in inflicting on them a pain much less than they deserve. But His justice forbids Him to deliver them gratuitously. What He can still do, however, is to permit some of these souls to ask miraculously the assistance of the living, who, as we have seen, can assist by their prayers. This is the second reason for those relatively frequent revelations and manifestations having a bearing on Purgatory. It serves but to make the first reason all the more forceful in convincing us of the gravity of the Purgatorial pains—a gravity so overwhelming, that it disarms, so to speak the justice of the Saviour, and wrests from His compassionate goodness a new largesse of miracles.

CHAPTER V

LIFE IN PURGATORY

As REGARDS WHAT essentially constitutes the state, the life, of Purgatory, we have already said sufficient. We know that in Purgatory there are saintly souls, confirmed in grace, sure of their salvation, perfectly possessed of the love of God, perfectly submissive to His Will and accepting lovingly the just pains merited by their sins. They are saintly penitents who suffer in loving and love in suffering. This is what constitutes the foundation of their life. We have already spoken of the sweet mutual fraternal feeling of soul with soul in Purgatory. Can we push our description further, so as to speak of what one might call the occupations of the souls in Purgatory? Can we penetrate further into their psychology? Remembering our ignorance of the conditions of living of the separated soul, this is surely a hazardous and bold undertaking. We know nothing of the manner in which God treats these souls, nor of the proportion of natural and supernatural in souls that are holy but not yet beatified. We have, however, a rich help to direct us in our attempt. This help is our knowledge of the state of charity and holiness in which they live. A healthy theology can draw many and important conclusions from this—conclusions to which those writing on the subject have often failed to give sufficient attention.

I.—ERRONEOUS CONCEPTIONS

And firstly, in the interests both of theology and philosophy, certain erroneous conceptions concerning the inner activities of these souls must be removed. Since their sufferings are so extreme, it would be natural to expect that they are so absorbed by them that they could not possibly attend to anything else. It is true that when physical suffering reaches a certain intensity, this is certainly the case with us., But this arises from the fact that in our life, the exercise of the superior and spiritual faculties of our soul is bound up in some way with the bodily organism. Violent physical pain shackles thought and will and concentrates on itself all the mental activity. " Walk through a hospital ward, go to the bedside of that dying workman. Drawn into the merciless grip of a machine, he has seen in the twinkling of an eye some one of his members caught, crushed and pounded : the blood poured out, he screamed horribly, his nerves were torn, his muscles contracted, and, in the grip of excruciating torture, he awaited the coming of the doctor who could free him only by amputation. He had no power to think or to reason, but shrieked like an animal in pain. Do not ask him what went on around him, nor speak to him of anything except his suffering. Suffering kills heart and head : when one suffers, one does not think, one does not love."[1]

It would be impossible to question the truth of that description, but to apply it to Purgatory is misleading. There, suffering does not numb thought and will. " In this place, the spirit keeps all its lucidity : the thought is daughter to the sorrow ; the sorrow is daughter to the thought. When one remembers that the soul is there separated from the body, it becomes evident that the sufferings cannot injure the power of thinking. The bodily faculties have disappeared ; the organs of sense are no longer there ; there can be no wound to shackle intellectual activity. The spirit is freed from its dependence on the senses."[2]

In Purgatory, intellectual activity, so far from being suppressed or fettered, undergoes a development, the extent of which it would be difficult for us to measure. The separated soul is endowed with a new mode of knowledge much more rapid and much more powerful than the painful process that we call thinking. It no longer proceeds by way of reasoning and deduction, but it knows by intuition in the manner of the angels. That it why its knowledge is so vastly superior to ours both in extent and in profundity. To knowledge acquired here below—for one does not lose one's memory in

---

[1] Chollet : ' La Psychologie du Purgatoire.' p. 36.
[2] *Op. cit.*, p. 39.

Purgatory—new knowledge is added. Freed from the shackles of the body, the spirit sees new horizons opening before it. " The world of ideas is accessible to the soul in Purgatory. Knowledge, a high philosophy, an all consoling theology developes in the soul, giving it ideas more certain and more elevated than all the sciences of earth, revealing to it the reason of being and, as it were, the shape of the new world around it, showing it the Providence of God behind the tangled unrolling of human history, endowing it with supreme reason that it may now explain all those things of which, formerly, it could be only a witness."[1]

We say that the souls in Purgatory know what passes on earth. How, indeed, can this not be so, since they are part of the Mystical Body of Jesus, and are united by bonds of great intimacy with the Church Militant and the Church Triumphant ? Everything that concerns the Church here below ought to be known to them, either through a knowledge natural to their condition, or by a revelation of God. " Those we have lost, and for whom we weep, have not indeed left us : now immaterial beings, the question of place and distance has no meaning for them. They are very near to us. Clear-visioned beings, they are no longer impeded by a veil or by ignorance. They know us, they follow us, and in a beautiful delicacy of love, they watch with solicitude our every hour."

The souls in Purgatory, though deprived of the Beatific Vision, know, however, Heaven with its angels and saints, for they can communicate with them in a mysterious way unknown to us. They know who they are who are saved and come to be their companions, and those who are forever separated from God.

Thus, in Purgatory, the activity of the intellect, so far from being injured or shackled by suffering, enjoys a freer mode of action and a wider field of knowledge. That activity conditions and illuminates an intense moral and supernatural life, which we now pass on to consider in its triple relation to God, to the Church Triumphant and to the Church Militant.

[1] *Op. cit.*, p. 49.

II.—Relations of the Souls in Purgatory with God

As we have seen, following St. Thomas, the souls in Purgatory are instantly fully purified from venial sins not cleansed on earth, as well as from their evil inclinations and their disordered habits. They attain, from the first instant of their entry, that degree of perfection and sanctity which will be theirs for eternity and which will measure in heaven, the degree of their glory. No longer for them will there be any imperfection, any resistance to their being engulfed by the love of God, no longer any disorder. As the sacred Liturgy says, they " sleep the sleep of peace "—of that peace which is the tranquillity of order. Henceforth, perfect order reigns in them, for in nothing do they resist the divine wishes. All that now remains is for them to expiate their past sins, and doubtless one is at liberty to call this expiation a purification, in the broad sense of the word. But, in fact, they have no moral stain. All impurity has been removed by the consuming fire of divine love. What will they occupy themselves with, during the time of their exile? They will strive for the perfection of a repentant and reparatory life of holiness. They will suffer for love, and will accept the penance imposed by the justice of God, and every moment they will produce most perfect acts of all the virtues compatible with their state.

Almost all the virtues we practise on earth are accessible to them. If one excepts the virtues which have the curbing of sense appetites for their object; if one remembers that, in Purgatory, there could be no transgression of prudence or the virtues habitually connected with it, there is no virtue in the domain of morality and the highest spirituality which one may not expect to find in an eminent, purified degree among the souls in Purgatory.

Before all else, the " theological life," which consists of the virtues of Faith, Hope and Charity—called " theological," because they have God for their object —is found in Purgatory.

Faith is not yet swallowed up in Vision, but its object is increased. " The spirit no longer doubts; the will, which has its place in Faith, has no longer any hesitation ... It is with perfect assurance that it says: ' I believe.' The veils have fallen from certain mysteries, and the assent which it gave to them here below is changed into a mere statement of experience: it believed in a future life, then—it has it now; it has now proved the immortality of the soul by personal experience; it speaks with the Angels, in whom it once merely believed ... But all is not revealed to them: the Divine Substance, the Most Blessed Trinity ... must yet remain hidden from them, so that they may continue to exercise their faith, by accepting the witness of revelation."[1] It is, therefore, the continuation of the reign of Faith, in what concerns Faith's most essential object. Hope also remains, but without admixture of fear or uncertainty. The soul in Purgatory has no longer " to work out its salvation in fear and trembling," for it enjoys a complete assurance. It knows itself as one of the predestined, and this is, for it, an unalterable source of joy. However, this is not yet the actual possession of the supreme Good; the hour of full rejoicing, of unmixed happiness, has not yet sounded. The soul hopes with the hope of one who is assured of obtaining what he desires. Moreover, certain theologians accord to the souls in Purgatory that experience of God's presence which is the characteristic of the Beatific Vision. The souls know God as present, but as hidden from them, as it were behind a veil. This is quite probable, and so far from diminishing their torment of love, it rather augments it in sharpening the souls' desire to see God face to face.

Charity, which lives on earth, in Heaven and in Purgatory, holds the first place in the life of the suffering souls. Charity animates all, and is the cause of their joys and their sorrows. To manifest itself, it borrows the form of different virtues which make of Purgatory, a kingdom of suffering and reparatory holiness. Reparation through suffering accepted in a spirit of penitent love, is the dominant note of the Purgatorial life. We must suppose these souls as a society, where each offers its mead of sorrow as a just compensation to offended Love. Of the four ends of sacrifice—adoration and praise, grace, reparation, petition—it is reparation which holds the first place in what might be called the liturgy of Purgatory. The

---

[1] Chollet, *op. cit.*, p. 52.

other three ends are not excluded, but their adoration and praise is coloured by reparation, because they adore and praise before all else the justice and the holiness of God. They thank, they sing the mercies of the Saviour, but always with a backward-looking towards past sins. They petition, but for others, and for themselves only that others may be inspired by God to pray for them, that they may the sooner come to that perfect praise which knows " nor groans, nor tears, nor sorrow " (*Apoc.* xxi, 4).

The liturgy of Purgatory ! The expression is a suggestive one, lifting for us, as it were, a corner of the veil. St. Paul in the Epistle to the Hebrews, and St. John in the Apocalypse, give us a glimpse of the splendours of the liturgy of Heaven. Purgatory should have its liturgy too. Is it the same as ours ? Certainly, these souls benefit in a great measure from our liturgy. Our Masses are their most potent alms, and we may surely suppose that they associate themselves with our Masses, in a fervent spirit of grateful love. They are remembered in every Mass, and the Holy Sacrifice is often celebrated for one or some or all of them. At every moment of the day and night, the Holy Sacrifice is offered for their help and their deliverance. Those souls for whom a Mass is specially offered must surely know it, and assist thereat in an invisible manner, with tremendous sentiments of adoration, of contrition, of reparation. It is our Masses which at every moment sound the trumpet for the departure of the holy souls to Heaven. From the sorrow-draped exile of expiation, the newly-elect rise like brilliant stars to the splendour of the heavenly Jerusalem, where the welcoming applause of Heaven awaits them. These continual departures cast a ray of joy on those who remain, for Purgatory is the realm of the most delicate fraternal charity, where the ecstasy of one is the joy of all.

These departures for Heaven do not all take place in precisely the same way, according to certain private revelations. Usually, the soul's Guardian Angel descends to call on the soul ; but sometimes the angel has a cortege of saints : relations, friends, benefactors, specially honoured patrons, sometimes Our Lady in person, and—incredible almost—Our Saviour Himself. In this connection, St. Thérèse writes :

" A Brother of the Company of Jesus had died that very

night, and I recommended him to God. While I assisted at a Mass which was being celebrated for him by a Father of the Company, I fell into a profound recollection in which I saw this religious rise all glorious to Heaven, accompanied by Our Saviour. The Divine Master told me that this was a special favour accorded to this soul." What had the good Brother done to merit such an honour? This little detail can give us a beautiful glimpse of the manner in which God treats His Elect. Jesus tells us He will gird Himself that He may serve, at the celestial banquet, those of His servants who shall have been found vigilant and faithful to the end : " Amen I say to you that he will gird himself and he will make them to sit down, and passing he will minister to them " (*Luk.* xii, 37). St. Thérèse's account shows that He keeps His word.

We can conjecture, then, that the Mass is the great feast of the souls in Purgatory, the centre of the whole cult which they render to the Holy Trinity. They participate in all the ceremonies. For them, as for us, there is a distinction of feasts. All days are feasts which see the immolation of the Divine Victim on thousands of altars. In liturgical language, there is no distinction between working days and days of rest. Every day of the week, from Monday to Saturday are called Ferials i.e., holidays ; Saturday, the Sabbath, is the day of repose in the Old Law ; and Sunday is the Sabbath of the New. In so far as she is able, the Church on earth strives to imitate the Church in Heaven, by consecrating all her time to the Divine praise—the great occupation for which God created us, before that dire but just sentence was passed : " In the sweat of thy brow shalt thou eat thy bread " (*Gen.* iii, 19). To praise God in the midst of their suffering ; to honour by their expiation His Holiness and Justice ; to thank Him for His mercies —such is the sole occupation of the souls in Purgatory. There is no interruption in their liturgy. For them, our Sunday is more than the second or the third feria, because Purgatory reaps on earth a greater harvest of suffrages. The Faithful come in greater numbers to Church : the Masses and Communions, in which they are never forgotten, are more numerous : indulgences offered for them increase and multiply : before or after Mass, parents and friends gather to pray round the graves of their dear departed. A Sunday cloud, heavy with refreshing roses, shadows Purgatory, so that the Sunday is more radiant for these souls than any other day of the week. To the spiritual wealth of Sunday, must be added that of the great festivals—the spiritual alms we call Indulgences, the flowers of Communions, of prayers, of good works—and above all, the rich harvest of All Souls' Day. This is a feast which comes to us, trailing a certain sweet melancholy and a heavenly nostalgia : while to the holy souls, it brings an abundance of blessings, because of the unnumbered trinity of Masses, and the merciful rain of plenary indulgences.

Thanks to this liturgy, thanks to the ceaseless coming and going of souls from earth and of souls to heaven, thanks to the continual distribution of alms from earth and heaven, life in Purgatory is not monotonous. And when this is said, all has not been said, for the holy souls preserve their relations with their brothers and sisters of heaven and of earth. We will add a few words on this.

III.—Relations with the Church Triumphant

Purgatory being the antechamber of heaven, it would be inconceivable that there should be no communication between the two regions. We have already said that the souls in Purgatory know those in Heaven, and in a special way those who have been their relations, their friends, their contemporaries here on earth. By God's permission, Purgatory must surely speak to Heaven, that the souls in exile may speak, may plead for powerful intercession. What is the nature of this intercession of the saints for the souls in Purgatory ? What is its efficacy ? The existence of such intercession cannot be doubted, for why allow it in favour of earth, and deny it to Purgatory ? Private revelations lead us to believe that the Elect can pay visits of consolation to the suffering souls, can sweeten their pains, just as the sight of a friend can sweeten a hospital hour. The most frequent visitor must surely be Our Lady, Queen of Purgatory no less than Queen of Heaven and earth : and after her, the Guardian Angel, patron saints, relations, friends.

Many private revelations attest the visits of the Guardian Angels to Purgatory. " In the long visit which St. Magdalene

LIFE IN PURGATORY

de Pazzi made to Purgatory, she saw the Angel Guardians assisting to bring consolation to those who had sinned through weakness, while at the same time devils increased the sufferings of others by mockery and insult.[1] The same is related in the life of St. Margaret Mary. During one of those extraordinary maladies to which she was subject, her angel said to her: "Come, let us walk in Purgatory." He led her into a place of fire, where she saw a great number of poor souls in human form, who raised their arms to her and implored mercy. She saw many angels there, consoling them, and she knew that they were the Guardian Angels."[2]

What is here revealed of the Guardian Angels can be piously conjectured of the other inhabitants of Heaven, even of those placed highest, and even of their King and their Queen, Jesus and Mary. Does not St. Thérèse tell us that Our Saviour visited Purgatory that He might bring a certain Jesuit Lay-Brother to Heaven?

IV.—Relations with the Church Militant

Visible relations of the souls in Purgatory with the faithful on earth have the character of miracles, and hence are rare. Earth is the realm of Faith. That such Faith may be meritorious, it must walk in the shadows, not seeing into object, but knowing it on the word of God. "Because you have seen, Thomas," said Christ to His Apostle, "you have believed; blessed are those who have not seen and have believed." That is why the mysteries beyond life remain hidden from us. We have seen that God, through compassion for these suffering souls, sometimes permits them to appear to the living, that they may ask for prayers or announce their deliverance. Here we speak only of that salutary action which the suffering souls can exercise in our favour, by the invisible means of prayer, for prayer is the line of communication between Purgatory, earth and Heaven. But the supernatural relations of prayer are invisible—they are the heart of a mystery. God alone, who hears their prayers for us, knows the secret.

---

[1] This intervention of devils is generally rejected by Theologians.
[2] Louvet, "Le Purgatoire" pp. 210—211.

Certain theologians, especially among the ancients, have questioned not only the existence, but even the possibility of this Purgatorial intercession for us. St. Thomas (IIa IIae q. lxxxiii, a. 11) places the objection: "Although the saints in Purgatory are superior to us by reason of their impeccability, nevertheless they do not pray for us, but rather it is we who pray for them. And his answer: "Although the souls in Purgatory are superior to us by reason of impeccability, they are our inferiors by reason of the pains they suffer; and from this point of view, they are not in a state which enables them to pray for others, but rather in a state where they have need of the prayers of others." These words must be carefully weighed. St. Thomas does not deny, as his objection does, that the souls in Purgatory pray for us; but he declares that, *from a certain view-point*, namely *inasmuch as they suffer the chastisement of divine justice*, they are our inferiors; and therefore—always from that view-point—they are constituted in a state where they plead for prayer rather than intercede by prayer. And, from this view-point, all that is very accurate. A poor person, inasmuch as he is poor, is not in a position to help others, nor is a sick person, inasmuch as he is sick, in a position to heal others. Such hair-splitting is the common way of theology, and very necessary for decerning truth from error. If therefore we consider the souls in Purgatory as suffering and given over to divine justice, it is evident that they are not in the position of the Blessed in Heaven, who, having abundance of all good things and no need to ask anything for themselves, think only of the good of those they love. These latter are truly in a position to intercede for others, for they possess an assured and perfect happiness which asks only to communicate itself.

But there are other aspects under which we can consider the souls in Purgatory. The theology of St. Thomas does not exclude these other aspects, but rather opens new fields of vision. Let us no longer contemplate the holy prisoners of Purgatory as wearing the mourning of penitents, but let us see them as dressed in the nuptial garment of charity. Let us consider them as making part of the immense Mystical Body of Christ, placed between the Blessed in Heaven and the exiles on earth, and let us ask ourselves if there could be any serious reasons for refusing them the power to intercede with God for those on earth.

Their ignorance of what passes on earth and of the particular prayers we address to them, has been put forward as an argument against their intercession. We have already shown that such ignorance does not exist. Even if such ignorance were admitted, it could still be maintained that these souls can pray for us, inasmuch as they have still the knowledge and the memories of earth. No soul in Purgatory but has spent a certain number of years on earth, and therefore no soul in Purgatory but knows the trials, temptations and miseries of poor human nature. The memory of relations, of friends, of companions will be kept fresh by each soul. What is required in order that a prayer for us may be born in the heart of Purgatory? Nothing else but charity—that fraternal charity, inseparable from the love of God, which unites among themselves the members of the Mystical Body of Christ. Were they to get no knowledge whatever of us from their entering Purgatory to their leaving it, the memory of the past would amply suffice to inspire them to pray for us and to recommend to God the affair of our salvation. The souls in Purgatory take their place in that great current of fraternal aid which unites the members of the three Churches. Granted, indeed, that these souls can neither merit nor satisfy for themselves nor for us; but this does not mean that they have not the power to intercede for their brethren in distress, for the benefactors who have assisted them.

Another possible objection—viz., that these souls are so absorbed by their pains that they can think of nothing else—need not detain us, since we have already sufficiently answered it at the beginning of this chapter.

The positive reasons in favour of the thesis we defend, are of weight. And of first importance, this doctrine is in perfect harmony with the state of grace and of charity in which these souls live. Their love for the neighbour matches their love for God. Now, love expresses itself in doing good. Here on earth, the most indigent, the most miserable, even sinners have the power to pray for themselves and for others. Are we to refuse a like power to the saints who live in Purgatory? Are *they* the disinherited of the Mystical Body, incapable of doing the least good to their benefactors and friends ? This, surely, is not the case.

Consider, moreover, that the most suitable way to expiate a fault is to practise the contrary virtue. Now, why does one go to Purgatory ? Is it not, in the last analysis, for having been wanting in charity ? This the soul expiates by a torrent of impetuous love and ardent desire which rushes without rest from Purgatory to Heaven—towards the Beloved, Who yet hides Himself and veils His face in impenetrable mystery. The soul also suffers from its lack of charity towards the neighbour, and this it expiates by the wholly disinterested supplication which it makes for those on earth—a supplication which rises without cease to the throne of the Father from the depths of the prison, and calls down on earth the rain of heavenly benediction. No, our dead—those at least who still live in God and have not suffered eternal damnation—do not forget us, and they will return us good for good. Not content merely to receive, they give. They give that which the most miserable can always give. They give *prayer*.

In fine, this is demanded by the doctrine of the Communion of Saints. In virtue of that communion, all the members of the Mystical Body share in the well-being of each, and each in the good of all ; for charity, its foundation, knows not ' mine ' or ' thine.' Every member receives and every member gives. If the souls in Purgatory could only receive, and found themselves wholly unable to give, it would seem the disruption of the rhythm of charity. Purgatory, therefore, must surely pay its debt of *suffrage* in the coin of *intercession*, while at the same time it repays the good offices of Heaven by ceaseless praise. Thus the balance is maintained.

A final consideration. It is a fact of experience that devotion to the souls in Purgatory draws down on us the Divine favour. In that case, God must intervene directly to reward our charity ; or He awaits their intercession for us, in order that He may accord the favour we have asked. Which is the more likely hypothesis ? Which is most in accord with God's ordinary manner of dealing with His intelligent creatures ? Is it not the second, or are we to banish from Purgatory the beautiful virtue of gratitude ? It would seem that the lovely flower of gratitude must surely open to full bloom in the soil of Purgatory, which receives daily the attentions of earth and Heaven. With a gratitude for what is past, the saints in Heaven remember those who have assisted them to their crowns, for now they do not receive assistance, but only compliments and praise. We can, however, heap our present assistance on Purgatory, and gratitude is its response. The only effective manner in which it can show its gratitude is by prayer and intercession for us.

V.—The Joys of Purgatory

Those who have written comprehensively of Purgatory, have spoken not only of its pains, but of its joys also. Some have underlined the pains, others the joys : and it is therefore important to strive for a happy medium. A fact which is certain, though at first sight rather startling, is that the joys of Purgatory, like the pains, are extreme. So, St. Francis de Sales :

" The majority of those who fear Purgatory, do so in view of their own interest and self-love, rather than of the interest of God ; and from this it arises that those who treat the subject ex professo, ordinarily represent only the pains of Purgatory, and not its happiness and its peace.

It is true that the greatest sufferings of earth cannot challenge comparison with the torments of Purgatory : but it is equally true that the interior peace of the souls is far above anything earth can give of prosperity and contentment. Though it is a kind of Hell, as regards its suffering, it is a kind of Heaven as regards the sweetness with which charity fills the soul ; a charity stronger than death and more powerful than Hell, of which the light is all fire and all flame. Happy state, therefore, more desirable than frightening, since its flames are flames of love and of charity. Frightening, however, because it postpones the end of all ends, which consists in seeing and loving God, and, by that seeing and that loving, of praising and glorifying Him for all eternity."

This coëxistence, in the same subject, of extreme joy and extreme suffering is evidently a mystery, but a mystery on which the life of Our Saviour and of some of the great saints can throw light. We know that the soul of Our Blessed

Saviour enjoyed, from the first instant of its existence, the Beatific Vision; and nevertheless that did not prevent it from suffering, during His whole life on earth, a long and severe martyrdom, culminating in the agony of Calvary. " I have a baptism," He said, " wherewith I am to be baptised, and how am I straitened until it be accomplished." These words give us a glimpse of the sufferings of the Heart of Christ before the glorification of His sacred Humanity. But these sufferings did not hinder his soul from enjoying an ineffable bliss.

The same phenomenon is seen in the lives of the saints. They suffer much, and they are filled with joy in the midst of their sufferings. St. Luke shows us the Apostles leaving from before the Sanhedrin, rejoicing that they had been found worthy to suffer an ignomenious scourging for Christ. " As much as in us abound the sufferings of Christ," said St. Paul, " by so much also shall our consolation in Christ abound " (II *Cor.*, I, 5.). The same apostle gives us a commandment of perpetual joy. " Rejoice in the Lord always: again I say it, rejoice. And the peace of God, which surpasseth all understanding, keep your hearts and your spirits in Christ Jesus " (*Phil.*, iv, 4, 7). All the saints, howsoever they suffer, enjoy an unspeakable joy of heart which nothing can take from them, and we see them devoured with a thirst for suffering. There is no such thing as a sad saint; for, as St. Francis de Sales put it, a sad saint is but a poor saint indeed.

This is precisely the reason why there is joy in Purgatory: for it is peopled with holy souls, inflamed with love for God and for the neighbour. Joy and charity go hand in hand. In St. Paul's list of the fruits of the Holy Spirit in the soul, charity comes first, with joy and peace following it: " charitas, gaudium, pax " (*Gal.*, v, 22). Joy is defined as pleasure in a good possessed. Now, whosoever loves God, the sovereign Good, already possesses Him in some fashion. This possession is not yet perfect for the Soul in Purgatory, because it does not see the Well-Beloved face to face. While its joy is not yet full, it is already immense, and overflows, like that of St. Paul in the midst of his afflictions. Let us attempt to explain further this their first and fundamental source of joy—viz., the Divine Love.

Whoever loves God is loved of God: or rather, it is God

Who has first loved, and has enflamed our souls with the love by which we love, according to those words of St. Paul: " The love of God has been spread abroad in our hearts by the Holy Spirit Who has been given to us." (*Rom.* v, 15). In Purgatory, the soul is loved by God, and it returns that love, so that it becomes impossible to banish joy. " If it is sweet to love and to be loved on earth," says Chollet in *La Psychologie du Purgatoire*, what must be said of Purgatory, where one loves with a purer affection, because one is holy and unchangeably holy ; with a more intense affection, since nothing can now distract the heart, but rather is love made tenfold by the perfection both of grace and of the natural life, enjoyed by these souls ; with a more enlightened affection, since the soul can see things now in their true perspective and estimate them at their real worth. Add to this that the soul is more loved, and *knows* that it is loved, for of what value is it to be loved if one is ignorant of it ? Through knowledge, we enjoy the affection of others. In Purgatory, the soul knows itself *clearly* as an object of love to God and to its brethren, and that knowledge gives birth to abundance of joy. Oh, the happiness of the souls who burn in Purgatory." Hell is Hell, because love has been entirely and eternally banished from it, to give place to eternal hate.

To love is to wish and to do good to the person loved. The souls in Purgatory are not deprived of that happiness as regards God. They wish Him all good, since He is the centre of all their affections ; they do him good, as creatures may, viz., in promoting His exterior glory by submitting themselves entirely to His Will. Their sufferings are a homage of praise to the holiness and the justice of God. In Heaven, God is praised with a full and unmixed joy. In Purgatory, God is praised with joy, but sorrow—the sorrow of the act of reparation—mixes with it. In Heaven, the saints do perfectly the Will of God, but it costs them nothing to do so. The souls in Purgatory, too, act in perfect conformity with the Will of God, but it costs them something to do so. There is no resistance to the Will of God either in Heaven or in Purgatory, and therefore peace reigns in both—for peace is the tranquility of order. Nothing could induce a soul in Purgatory to quit its prison cell before having fully satisfied its debts according to the regulations of divine justice. It is a source of joy and consolation to them that they can manifest their love for God by perfect submission to His Will.

Thus it is, that the love which these souls have for God is at once their torture and the principal source of their ineffable joy. To this fountain-source are joined the joys which they taste from their fraternal relations with the companions of their exile, with the Elect in Heaven, and with the faithful on earth. This latter is also based on the love which gives and the love which receives.

The soul in Purgatory gives its affection, its compassion, its prayer to each of its companions : and from each of them it receives a return. There is still another joy that is common to them all—the joy of seeing an incessant stream of their companions leaving for Heaven. Nor must we forget the joy that comes from mutual confidences, and from the revealing of the plan of divine mercy that has shaped the life of each holy soul.

The Blessed in Heaven also visit Purgatory, in order to bring consolation and efficacious aid to their brethren in pain. In return, these souls return thanks and praise. Here again we have the joy of loving and of being loved.

The same mutual love, the same exchange of benefits takes place between Purgatory and earth. An unceasing stream of suffrages—Masses, prayers, satisfactions of all kinds—arrives to Purgatory from earth, and in return, the suffering souls raise their supplication to God for the conversion of sinners, for the sanctification of the just, for the advancement of Christ's Kingdom on earth. What a source of joy to them to contribute, even in this manner, to the glory of God and to the salvation of their brethren.

These, then, are the many joys of Purgatory that stem directly from charity. But, as we have seen, the sister virtues of Faith and Hope, which are swallowed up in the glory of Heaven, have still their place in Purgatory, and they furnish other subjects of joy to the holy souls.

Faith, united to the new mode of knowing of the separated soul, gives rise to unspeakable intellectual joy of which earth can know nothing. In Purgatory, the soul enjoys a vaster knowledge without fear of error, and a clearer faith that knows no doubting. " We pass our lives in a series of enigmas," writes Chollet. " While we rejoice in a problem just now solved, another—darker and heavier often—has taken its place, and so we quit this life with many of our questions unanswered. In the next life, we find the greater part of our enigmas solved. We see the why of many things, and we know the pattern which before seemed an incomprehensible mass of tangled threads. It is a real joy to the spirit to be relieved of its sickness for certainties . . . The soul in Purgatory knows many things, but above all, it knows them with certainty. With axiomatic clarity, the soul sees and judges without the faintest trembling of doubt in the voice. How mighty is such knowledge compared to our so little sure and so hardly won knowledge. Beside himself with joy, Archimedes ran through the town shouting his immortal " Eureka." He had found! He had found! . . . All mysteries will not pass into knowledge for the soul in Purgatory, for there are yet shadows which must await the light of glory in order that they may be dispersed. One knows without knowing all: there is still ignorance, but there is no error . . . The soul in Purgatory knows itself to be immutably fixed on the rock of truth. Ask the savant, and he will tell you that no joy is comparable to that of surely walking in the light of evidence on the certain ground of truth."

Among the revelations which the exiled soul enjoys, must be placed its knowledge of its own destiny. On earth, we have but a fragmentary view of the benefits of all kinds with which God heaps our little lives, from our first breath to our last. In Purgatory, the book of our lives lies open before us, and we can read it all, piecing the fragments together into a splendid whole of goodness and mercy, which makes our souls tremble with joy in God our Saviour, as the soul of Mary did (*Luke*, i, 47). In their long hours of expiation, the souls can memorize this series of divine benefits, and its memories of them can sweeten its sorrow.

The gift of gifts in Purgatory which sets its seal on all the others, is certainly the grace of final perseverance, the confirmation in the love of God with the certainty of salvation. Comparing the joy of the soul in Purgatory to that of a sailor who has come safely through a horrible storm, Chollet goes on: "Saved! What joy there is in the word. And this is indeed the song of Purgatory. Saved! The soul has passed through the troubled waters of life, has been buffeted by the winds and waves of passion and temptation, and now it knows the great calm of being safely in port."

To this calm certainty, must be added the joy of hope, properly so called—the hope that is a forward look to an object one is certain to attain. On earth, hope has its alloy of fear and anguish. Fear is banished from Purgatory: there is only the joyful awaiting a certain reward. With full and certain joy, the soul can sing with the psalmist: " I rejoiced in the things that were said to me: we shall enter into the house of the Lord " (*Ps.* cxxi, 1). The house of the Lord: the soul rejoices because it knows that it already stands in the vestibule. Soon, to-morrow perhaps, that door will open, and the beauty of an earthly dawn, the pure azure of noon, the glories of a sunset will pale before the splendour that will open on the eyes of the soul. For the souls in Purgatory, more than for us, those words of the Apostle have their full significance: " We rejoice in hope " (*Rom.*, xii, 12): " Rejoice in the Lord always; again I say it—Rejoice, for the Lord is nigh " (*Phil.*, iv, 4-5).

Such, then, are the joys of Purgatory. " O God," we may well cry out, with Bossuet, " how mighty is Thy hand and how profound Thy wisdom, in that Thou knowest how to place such dire sorrows in a place where Thy peace reigns and the certainty of possessing Thee fills the soul! Where is the sage who will boast a knowledge of this wonder? For my part, I can but lift the corner of its veil."

Chapter VI

THE CHURCH TRIUMPHANT AND PURGATORY

IN THE PRECEDING CHAPTER, we have already said something of the reciprocal relations between Heaven and Purgatory. In particular, basing ourselves on private revelations, we have spoken of the visits of consolation which the angels and the saints sometimes make, by the permission of God, to the suffering souls.

I.—THE FACT OF INTERCESSION

The existence of these relations cannot be called in question. Although the magisterium of the Church has no definition on the point, one cannot deny that the Blessed have the means of coming to the aid of their brethren still in pain. The liturgy of the Church bears witness very clearly to this belief. Scarcely has the Christian closed his eyes, when she puts into our mouth this prayer: " Saints of God, come to his aid ; angels of the Lord, receive His soul and conduct it into the presence of God." Other prayers indicate the manner in which the saints can help those in Purgatory, viz., by way of prayer and intercession. In the daily Mass for the dead we find the following Collect: " God of bounty, Who dost wish the salvation of men, we beg Thy mercy for our brethren, neighbours, benefactors, who have departed this life, that, *by the intercession of the Blessed Virgin Mary and of all Thy saints*, Thou mayest allow them to enjoy eternal beatitude."

The early Christians chose their burial places near the tombs of the martyrs. Why this practice ? St. Augustine writes: " I do not see to what purpose this burial near the tombs of saints could serve, unless it was that those who loved them, seeing in whose vicinity they lie, recommended them to those same saints as to patrons who ought to assist them by their prayers before God."

II.—Mode of Intercession

The saints, therefore, intercede with God to obtain an assuaging and a deliverance from pain for the souls in Purgatory. But then, someone may object, all the souls will be very soon delivered, because the saints, on account of their compassionate charity, will not fail to recommend every soul to the Saviour, forgetting none. And as it is in the nature of things that God should hear the prayers of His saints and moreover that the souls in Purgatory oppose no obstacle to the efficacy of those prayers, it follows that Purgatory will continually empty itself according as souls arrive into it from earth. There will thus be no need for the suffrages of the Church Militant. Indeed, the intervention of the Blessed Virgin alone would suffice. The objection is a specious one. St. Thomas poses it in this form: " The saints who are in the fatherland pray for those who are in Purgatory, for the same reason and in the same manner as they pray for us. If, therefore, their prayer is efficacious for us, it will be so too for those in Purgatory and will deliver them from their pains—which in fact it does not; because, if it did, the suffrages of the Church would be redundant." And his answer: " The suffrages of the Church for the dead are satisfactions which the living make in the place of the dead: and that is why they deliver the dead from the pains which they have not yet paid. But the saints who are in the fatherland are not in the state of satisfaction. Therefore, it is not possible to equiparate their prayers with the suffrages of the Church."

Let us examine these words carefully. If we attend carefully to their sense, it becomes clear that St. Thomas holds that the satisfactions which the Church Militant offers for the dead have greater efficacy in delivering them than the simple intercession of the saints in Heaven. This is easily understood, if we remember that the saints are no longer in a state in which they can offer to God satisfactions, properly so called, to compensate for the pain which the souls in Purgatory ought to suffer for their sins. The word satisfaction, in effect, means a painful work, a work which costs suffering, expiation. Now, in Heaven there is no suffering; there, one can no longer satisfy for others or merit for oneself. To help others, one has only simple prayer, pure intercession, the credit that one has acquired before God by the saintly life which one has led on earth and which determines our eternal position, our rank in the city of God. God, taking that credit into consideration, could of course accept that prayer for diminishing the pain of the suffering souls; but one can conceive that His justice restrains the efficacy of that prayer so that it becomes limited, according to precise rules unknown to us. To substitute a simple intercession, which costs nothing, for rigorous pains, would be to ignore the claims of justice. Purgatory would be totally suppressed, and those on earth could say: "There is no great danger of going to Purgatory, since the saints in Heaven will quickly deliver us by their prayers." Reflecting on this question, certain theologians of note have come to the conclusion that prayer *alone*, independant of all satisfaction, is powerless, according to the laws of divine justice, to help the souls in Purgatory. If this opinion be admitted, the simple intercession of the saints in Heaven can have no direct effect in assuaging or delivering the souls in Purgatory. Its efficacy can only be indirect. If the prayer of the faithful on earth is useful to the dead, it is because it is always in some degree satisfactory, in the sense that it always costs some effort, some labour on the part of him who makes it. A prayer made among the harmonies of Heaven cannot serve to compensate for a pain of Purgatory.

We think, however, that the intercession of the elect can directly help the souls in Purgatory, but within very precise limits, and in given cases. Knowing the limits placed by divine justice, the saints have recourse to that means only which they see to be efficacious, because, as St. Thomas says, they conform their wills in all things to that of God and wish only the things that please Him. Though we are ignorant of these rules of divine justice, we can nevertheless, make some conjectures. We may think, for example, that the elect can efficaciously intercede for the souls in Purgatory on a title of gratitude, since any one of the elect may be a debtor to a soul in Purgatory for services rendered on earth. A soul in Purgatory may very well have aided such a one to sanctification, have directed him in the ways of sanctity, have shortened his Purgatory by its suffrages. In such a case, that saint may come to the aid of his benefactor, now detained in prison. His prayer, a simple intercession with no satisfactory value, will be acceptable before God in mitigation of the benefactors' pain, if not indeed for his complete deliverance.

Take another case. During his earthly life a certain soul in Purgatory has had a tender devotion to some saint or angel in heaven. This saint or this angel will have the power of using his influence in favour of his protégé. There are mysterious affinities of soul, inclinations of grace, special friendships which bud and blossom here below between a saint of earth and a saint in heaven. Call to mind, for example, the friendship of the Curé d'Ars for the martyr St. Philomena. If the saint of the earth eventually goes to Purgatory, how can we refuse to his friend in Heaven a certain direct power of showing his affection? One could imagine other cases in which the power of pure intercession could have direct force.

Confirmation of this view can be found in the writings of the saints. We will content ourselves with an example from the "Book of Foundations" of St. Teresa of Avila.

Don Bernardine De Mendoza, brother of the Bishop of Avila, spurred on by his love for the Blessed Virgin, offered to St. Teresa one of his houses near Valadolid for a Carmelite foundation. The offer was accepted. Now, two months later, Don Bernardine was struck down by a sudden malady which deprived him of the power of speech. He confessed only by signs. Some days later, he died in a place far removed from that in which the saint was at the time.

The Divine Master said to her: "My daughter, his salvation has been in great danger, *but I have had compassion on him, and have shown him mercy, in consideration of the service which he has rendered to My Mother*, in giving that house for the establishment of a monastery of her order. *Nevertheless, he will not leave Purgatory until the first Mass shall have been said in the new convent.*"

" From that day," continues the saint, " the great sufferings of this soul were ceaselessly presented to my spirit ; so much so indeed, that in spite of my great desire to make a foundation in Toledo, I lost not a moment in pressing forward to the utmost of my ability the foundation at Valadolid.

The execution of my design could not keep pace with my wishes; I was forced to remain for several days in the monastery of St. Joseph of Avila, of which I was prioress, and then at St. Joseph of Medina Del Campo, which was on my way. In this latter monastery, Our Saviour said to me one day in prayer: "Make haste, for that soul suffers greatly." From that moment nothing could detain me. Though I was short of many things, I continued my journey, and arrived at Valladolid on the feast of St. Laurence. When I saw the house where we were to live, I felt very displeased: the garden indeed was beautiful and pleasing, but the house, situated on the bank of the river, was unhealthy, and it was impossibile to make it habitable without incurring very great expense. Utterly wearied, I had to make a journey to a monastery of our Order at the entrance to the town—a journey so tedious that it doubled my pain. Nevertheless, I hid all this from my companions, lest they should be discouraged. What Our Lord had said to me sustained me in my weakness, and my confidence in Him made me hope that he would remedy all. On my return, I sent secretly for some workmen, and when they had built some cloisters I improvised cells in which we could recollect ourselves. One of the two religious who wished to embrace the reform—(St. John of the Cross)—and Julien of Avila were with us. The first made himself familiar with our manner of life; the second busied himself in obtaining, from the prelate, the permission for the foundations; since before my arrival, he had given us but good hopes. That could not be done immediately, and Sunday had come before the authorisation was given us. We were only permitted to have Mass said in the place destined to be the site of our church.

The Holy Sacrifice was offered. I was far from thinking that the prediction of Our Saviour in regard to Bernardine of Mendoza, would then be accomplished. On the contrary, I was convinced that the words, *at the first Mass*, referred to the Mass in which the most Holy Sacrament should be placed in our church. At the moment of Communion, the priest advanced towards us, holding the ciborium. I approached and at the very moment of receiving, Bernardine appeared to me with an all-shining countenance ... He thanked me

... I saw him ascend immediately to Heaven."

From this account, one can gather that Our Saviour takes account of the services rendered to His saints, and above all, to his Mother, when the soul faces Him at the moment of the particular judgment. By such services, both the duration and the qualities of its Purgatory may be affected. Doubtless, the Blessed Virgin prayed her Son to show mercy to Don Bernardine in consideration of the service rendered to her daughters. That prayer was answered, but on a condition which was relatively benign, when we remember that he had been in great danger of damnation. Thanks to the intercession of Mary, his Purgatory was in sum very short.

This example can very well be used as a foundation for another manner of envisaging the intervention of the elect in favour of Purgatory. According to that conception, the prayer of the saints in itself would have no efficacy in helping or delivering the souls. That prayer must rest on suffrages, on satisfactions offered by the faithful of the Church Militant. The angels and the saints themselves present these suffrages to God, and add to them the weight of their own merit. Their personal intervention increases the efficacy of these suffrages and augments their value in proportion to the degree of their own sanctity and glory. Thus the faithful on earth would furnish, as it were, the prime matter, while the presenting by the elect would bring, so to speak, the substantial form, which would render the suffrage of ten-fold value to the eyes of God. So does the solidarity which unites the members of all three parts of the Mystical Body, manifest itself in a tangible manner. P. Lamy, the Curé d'Ars of his diocese, has expressed this idea in his usual picturesque manner : " The Blessed Virgin offers our prayers to God. She embellishes them ... Divinely skilful, she knows how to make gold of our dross. The prayer, even when made with little attention, is always a prayer, and our Blessed Mother supplies that which it lacks ... She is ceaselessly busy in covering our weaknesses before the face of God. We feel her bounty, her charity. If she showed severity, we would be immediately overwhelmed ; we would disappear from before the face of God."

What P. Lamy says here of our prayers in general can be applied, of course, to the prayers which we offer for certain, particular souls. In the end, it is Mary the mediatrix who receives them; it is Mary who presents them immediately to God. It is she who renders them of value, who gilds them with her own merits and her own prayers. In this way, their efficacy is considerably increased, their value augmented in the eyes of God, far beyond anything we could guess. In fine, P. Lamy writes: " The Holy Virgin does not love Purgatory. It is a place of sorrow. I love to pray for the souls in Purgatory, and the most Holy Virgin chides me because I do not ask sufficient for them. She said: *I await graces for these souls*—the graces which I did not dare to ask."

This presentation of our prayers to God through Our Lady as Mediatrix is no pure fancy of P. Lamy. In many places of Holy Scripture, the same thing is affirmed of the angels and saints in Heaven. In the book of Tobias, the angel Raphael says: " When thou didst pray with tears and didst bury the dead; when, quitting thy meal, thou didst hide the dead in thy house in the day and bury them in the night, *I presented thy prayer to the Lord.*" In the Apocalypse, we see the four and twenty ancients, that is to say, on the best interpretation, the leaders of the Church Triumphant, prostrating themselves before the Lamb, each one having a harp *and phials of gold full of perfumes, which are the prayers of the saints*. Thus our poor prayers have been compared to perfumes received in the golden phials of the angels and saints. We supply the perfumes. The angels and saints receive them in their golden phials, that is to say, they augment the value, in refining the aroma so that, united to the perfume of their own intercession it may arise more sweetly to the throne of God. For our prayer, indeed, is so weak, and at the same time so strangely heavy, our perfume so full of impurity, that it is hardly presentable. The angels and the saints take this matter, more or less gross, more or less without form. They refine it, and when they have placed it in the gold of their censer, it rises easily to God. Apply that to the suffrages which we offer here below for the souls in Purgatory. The elect receive them, join to them the gold of their glory and of their intercession and thus greatly increase their efficacy. And it is the same current of prayer and supplication which, rising from the earth, passes through heaven, mounts to the throne of God, and from there descends as a soothing and extinguishing cascade on Purgatory. Bossuet has spoken of this supernatural phenomenon as follows :

"Why has it pleased God that our prayers should be presented to Him by the ministry of angels? This is a secret of His Providence which I do not attempt to explain to you; but it suffices for me to assure you that there is nothing which is better founded on the Scriptures. And finally that you may know how much this intercession of the heavenly spirits is useful for our salvation, I will add one word: while our prayers are of such a nature that they rise straight to heaven like an agreeable incense sprinkled on the fire of divine love, nevertheless, the weight of the mortal body retards them very much. See what I call the witness of your conscience. When you offer your prayers to God, what pain it costs your spirits! In the heart of what tempests have you forged your vows! How many vain imaginings, how many wandering and disordered thoughts, how many temporal cares have flung themselves continually in the course of your prayer! Thus soiled, do you think that they could rise to Heaven, and that that feeble and languishing prayer, which, amid all the checks that vex it, scarcely succeeds in crossing the threshold of our hearts, has power to pierce the clouds and to reach even into the heights of Heaven? Christians, who could believe it? Doubtless they would fall with all their weight if the goodness of God had not provided for them. He has sent His angel, whom Tertullian calls the angel of prayer; and the angel Raphael said to Tobias: *I offered thy prayers to God.* That angel comes to gather our prayers, and they mount, says St. John, from the hand of the angel even to the face of God. See in what manner they mount from the hand of the angel: wonder at how well it serves them to be presented by so pure a hand. They mount from the hand of the angel because that angel, joining itself to us and aiding our feeble prayers lends them its wings to raise them, its strength to sustain them, its fervour to vivify them."

There are also other ways in which the elect can contribute indirectly to the help and to the deliverance of the souls in Purgatory. Some authors think that they can pray Our Saviour to apply to these souls His own satisfactions, or those of the Blessed Virgin, or the surplus which they themselves have furnished to the Church's treasury, when they had paid their own debts here below. That hypothesis, however, appears scarcely probable : because it is hardly possible that Our Saviour would himself make a direct application of his satisfactions to the dead, even at the demand of his saints. The dispensing of His satisfactions has been confided by Him to the Church Militant and is limited to certain determined means, so that we have no serious reason to suppose that He will depart from that disposition of His providence. But it is probable that the saints in Heaven, by their intercession, obtain that the faithful on earth multiply their suffrages for the dead in general, or for such and such dead in particular ; that the Pope may delve more liberally into the treasury of the Church by according indulgences applicable to the souls in Purgatory. We may also suppose that the Blessed Virgin and the saints intervene in the distribution of vacant suffrages, that is to say, of those which are offered by the faithful on earth for souls who have no need of them, since they are in heaven, or who cannot profit by them, because they are damned. But these hypotheses appear to us to be much less satisfying than the first two modes of intercession of which we have treated. The second especially, that of the presentation to God of the satisfactions offered by the Church Militant, is worthy of our attention, because it is solidly founded on Sacred Scripture.

Chapter VII

THE CHURCH MILITANT AND PURGATORY

UNLIKE THE RELATIONS between the Church Triumphant and Purgatory, the magisterium of the Church has clearly affirmed that the members of the Church Militant can aid the souls in Purgatory by their prayers, good works and, above all, by the Mass. It is, therefore, a dogma of faith that we can be of service to our dead who have not yet attained to Heaven, but must expiate their sins in Purgatory.

I.—Foundation and Mode of our Power

Our power to aid the souls in Purgatory rests on the law of supernatural solidarity which we call the Communion of Saints. In virtue of that law, the Church, considered in its totality, that is to say in its three states together, constitutes one big family of which God is the Father and Jesus Christ the Elder Brother. This Elder Brother, made by God the New Adam, that is to say, the head and representative of regenerated humanity in place of the first Adam, offers Himself voluntarily as a victim of expiation to pay the debt of our sins, to reconcile us with God and to return to us the blessings lost by the disobedience of our first father. The treasury of satisfactions and of merits of our Elder Brother is infinite, inexhaustible. It is the property of the whole divine family in common. All the adopted brothers have the right to draw on it according to laws laid down by the Father. Christ has suffered and died for all. His sufferings and merits, infinite because of His infinite dignity, have been offered to the Father for all. But the application of these satisfactions and merits is made to each member of the family in different ways. In the Church, above all, this application is realised, firstly by way of the Sacraments, of which the greatest is also a sacrifice, a veritable memorial and mystic reproduction of the sacrifice of the Upper Room and of the Cross; then by prayer, that admirable and easy means given to all that they may gain access to the

THE CHURCH MILITANT AND PURGATORY

treasury of the Elder Brother. This means of prayer is at the disposal of all, that they may aid those in Purgatory. We have already shown in what manner the elect can aid these souls by their prayers. It is by the same method of intercession, that they aid us.

Besides prayer, the faithful have other means of aiding the souls in Purgatory, namely, works of satisfaction and indulgence. Properly speaking, works of satisfaction are acts of penance done in the state of grace with the idea of expiating sins already pardoned by contrition alone, or by contrition united to Confession. The work of satisfaction has for direct end the paying of a debt of temporal punishment left by actual sin. Indulgences accorded by the Church Militant to the faithful on the accomplishment of certain acts, which are always in some respects satisfactory, are uniquely concerned with the remission of this temporal punishment. It goes without saying that the efficacy of satisfactory works and indulgences has its primary and principal source in the merits and satisfaction of Christ. It is from Him that the power to liquidate our debt is given to our acts of penance. In the treasury of the Church are the inexhaustible merits of Christ, to which she adds the surplus satisfactions furnished by the saints, and it is on these that the Church draws when she accords indulgences. It is none the less true that the Saviour has willed to associate with Himself in some fashion, the faithful of the Church Militant in the work of expiation for sin. They can, by their satisfactory works and by indulgences, satisfy not only for their sins, but also for those of others. Like Christ, they can suffer in the place of their brethren, endure the chastisement merited by their brothers' sins, and thus become secondary and subordinate redeemers. That is what St. Paul meant when he said that he filled up in his flesh those things that were wanting to the sufferings of Christ in His body, which is the Church. (*Col.*, I, 24). " The sorrows and the torments endured by Christ during His mortal life, present, in spite of their infinite value, a kind of deficit, when viewed in a certain way. It belongs to men ... to complete the work of Christ ; and that is what Paul is proud and joyful to do by completing what is wanting to the sufferings of his Master " (*F. Prat.*). Doubtless, God could allow that the sufferings of the Saviour, which considered in themselves are of infinite value, should be amply sufficient to deliver us from sin, from the eternal punishment and the temporal punishment due to sin, without any cooperation on our part. This plenary pardon has been granted by Him for all our sins committed before Baptism; but He has willed, in His justice, to exact from us some contribution towards repairing the sins committed after Baptism. This is the deficit in the sufferings of Christ which we must make up by good works and penance. This completing must be furnished by us for our own sins, either in this world or in Purgatory. But we have the power to furnish it also for the sins of our brethren on earth and in Purgatory, by offering to God for this intention our satisfactory works, in stripping ourselves of them for the benefit of others. God accepts this supplication, as He accepted the great supplication of Christ, for all humanity. This is not surprising, when one remembers how, in a family, one member can pay the debts or endure the sufferings incurred by another. It is that law of solidarity which God has established in His supernatural Providence in regard to the Church.

But the limits of such substitution must be carefully noted. It does not pass beyond the limit of the satisfaction for the temporal punishment due to sin after Baptism. We can satisfy for others: but we cannot merit for others, in the proper sense of the word. Merit is an absolutely inalienable right to an augmentation of grace here below and of glory hereafter, which each acquires by his own acts done in the state of grace. It must always, therefore, remain with him who merits. But that in the act which has the character of satisfaction—the effort, the pain it costs—can be offered to God to liquidate the debt of temporal punishment due to the sins of others, whether those others be living or dead. In fact, every virtuous act accomplished here below by one of the faithful in the state of grace, has a double value: a meritorious value, which is inalienable; and a satisfactory value, which he can pass on to another. If the act is properly speaking a prayer, a third character of *impetration* is added. Considered in itself, prayer is neither a merit nor a satisfaction but a simple demand, or rather, the act of a beggar holding out his hand. Its proper force is founded on the goodness of Him to whom it is addressed.

That force, we have said, is at the disposal of every member of the Church. Each one of the faithful on earth, every soul in Purgatory, all the elect in Heaven can use it, if not always for themselves, at least for others. The question is whether, considered in itself and independently of all satisfactory value, it is pleasing to God in compensation for the temporal pain due to sin. If it is accepted for this end, its efficacy is certainly greatly restrained. Normally, according to the rules of divine justice, a debt of temporal punishment is liquidated by offering a satisfactory work, especially when there is question of discharging the debt of another.

This doctrine explains why, from a certain point of view, the Church Militant has a greater power than the Church Triumphant to help the souls in Purgatory. The blessed in Heaven can no longer accomplish works of satisfaction to compensate for the temporal punishment due to sin. Only by their prayer, resting on the glory which their past merits have gained for them, can they aid the suffering souls. On the contrary, *our* smallest prayer has a value of expiation and of satisfaction for sin, which we can use for their benefit; and we have the Mass and the numerous indulgences which are applicable to these souls. It is for us to furnish the prime matter by satisfactory works, which the elect can enrich by presenting them to God united to their own glory and intercession. It is easy to discover why divine Providence has willed that the assisting of Purgatory should be principally entrusted to the Church Militant. Firstly, the souls in Purgatory belong in some fashion to that Church, in the sense that they are still pilgrims on the road to the fatherland. They are, of course, sure of reaching the goal; but the last stage of the journey is rough and maybe long. They turn to us, whom they have just left, and say: Have pity on us, at least you our friends. We could have come without delay to our happiness, for we had all the means necessary in the holy Church. Alas! we have been negligent. Stretch forth a hand to us. You have all the riches around you.

This suppliant voice of our dear departed is for us at once salutary and consoling: salutary, because it inculcates the necessity of penance for our sins: salutary, because it invites us to acts of generous charity, acts which will increase our merit and cover the multitude of our sins ; consoling, because it is sweet to know that we are able to do good to those who have loved us here below and whom we will one day join. Yes, it seems that Purgatory, though placed so near to heaven, has its face towards the earth, from which its principal succour comes. That is why, as we have already said, it still takes part in our liturgy, in our offices, in our feasts, because it shares in the spiritual profit we draw from them.

Let us not forget, however, that we are totally ignorant of the measure in which we can aid our dead. We know that what we offer to God profits them ; but beyond that our knowledge does not extend. The Church Militant has jurisdiction only over the earth, and therefore its power to absolve does not extend to Purgatory. The good works, the indulgences, and even the Masses—in themselves of infinite and inexhaustible efficacy—which we apply to the souls in Purgatory, cannot be *measured* as to their efficacy by us. We cannot affirm that one Mass suffices to deliver such and such a soul ; that one plenary indulgence applied by us to a certain soul will completely wipe out its debt. This is a salutary ignorance which prevents us from forgetting our dead, which conserves in us the fear of the punishment beyond the grave, which augments the treasury of vacant satisfactory works to the great benefit of the forgotten souls, and causes us to multiply our acts of fraternal charity, to our own great benefit.

II.—Means of Helping the Holy Souls

The means by which we can aid the souls in Purgatory are as numerous as they are varied, since everything, in our virtuous and supernaturalised activity, can be turned to their profit. All the means are designated by the generic name of *suffrages*, that is to say, prayer and supplication offered to God for the souls in Purgatory. They can be ranged under three heads : (a) Prayers and indulgences ; (b) Alms and works of penance ; (c) the Holy Sacrifice of the Mass.

(a) Prayers and Indulgences.

We have placed special prayers for the dead and indulgences applicable to the dead in the same category, because the gaining of indulgences is nearly always attached to the saying of some vocal or mental prayer, and because the special prayers for the dead are usually richly indulgenced.

The Church herself places these special prayers on our lips. We have the Office of the Dead and the whole rite of burial, where the most touching prayers are found, for example, the De Profundis and the Requiem Aeternum invocation, which are themselves independantly indulgenced. Shortly after the Consecration at Mass, there is the Commemoration of the Dead, when the celebrant recommends not only those he names but also the whole population of Purgatory. A like general commemoration is made at the end of each hour of the canonical Office. It is found as the conclusion even to such a prayer as the Grace after Meals.

In thus keeping green the memory of the dead, the Church keeps Purgatory ever before our minds. We should join with the Church on every possible occasion in begging mercy for these souls, and a funeral or a cemetery should be for us the occasion of such a prayer.

One of the easiest means of helping the souls in Purgatory is indulgences. Let us sink our hands deeply into the treasury of indulgences, which the Church is daily augmenting, and draw them out, richly full. This is not the place for an expose of the theology of indulgences. Here we have only to remember that the majority of our prayers and good works are enriched with indulgences. Let us have the general and habitual intention of gaining all the indulgences we can and of offering them for the relief of the souls in Purgatory. In this practice, the distinction between plenary and partial indulgence is of no great moment, when there is question of their application to souls, since we do not know the degree of efficacy which God will allow them. In principle, however, and remembering the very difficult conditions the Church imposes for the gaining of a plenary indulgence, the latter must have greater efficacy for the souls than a partial indulgence.

The important thing in gaining indulgences is to fulfil strictly the conditions imposed by the Church. When kneeling is prescribed, we must kneel; or when six paters, six aves and six glorias are prescribed, we must not stop at four or five. How often has ignorance of the minutiae of the conditions, hindered the gaining of an indulgence.

Let us greatly value indulgences, since they have been bought with the blood of our Saviour. Let us not treat them with indifference, on the gound that they are numerous and easy to gain. Let us choose our favourites among the indulgenced ejaculations, and often during the day let us drop them on Purgatory like the petals of a refreshing rose. If ever we find ourselves in Purgatory, we will know the value of that rose.

(b) Alms and Works of Penance.

The giving of alms has always been considered, in the Church, a satisfactory work of the first importance. This is not surprising, seeing that the formal teaching of both the Old and the New Testaments stress it. " Alms," said the angel to Tobias, " delivers from death " ; and Daniel recommended Nabuchodonosor to repair his sins by alms. It would be entirely to misread this last passage if one were to read it as an invitation to the sinner to be of good cheer, since he can whitewash himself before God by flinging a largesse of alms. The covering of one's sins by alms, implies a previous renunciation of sin by sincere contrition and purpose of amendment, and has reference to the liberation from the *temporal* punishment due to sin. There is real penance in alms-giving, since our attachment to the world and our thirst for money is so insatiable, that when we deprive ourselves of our goods to give to others, it is often as if we tore off a piece of ourselves. That is why it is a work of satisfaction and of reparation for sin committed. If we give an alms with the intention of benefitting the Holy souls in general or some particular soul, God will set that sacrifice to the account of those we have in mind and will diminish their debt in proportion to our generosity.

It is easy to understand why the scripture so often and so magnificently eulogises alms-giving and attributes to it an efficacy which, at first blush, surprises us. A little reflection reveals its efficacy. Done in aid of the dead, it possesses a triple fecundity. It enriches the donor with merit, aids the poor, mitigates or even delivers the soul from pain, since it was for this intention it was given. Thus, from a personal and from a social view-point, it is an excellent work. All gain and no one loses, the greatest gainer being he who gives ; because—as we will demonstrate in the second part of this work—not only does alms increase our merit and thus gain an augmenting of glory, but it is also one of the surest means of anticipating our own Purgatorial debt, thereby assuring our speedy entrance to Heaven. It must be remembered, however, that our alms must be done with purity of intention, in a spirit of charity, and with that delicacy which charity suggests.

We speak here of material alms bestowed for the benefit of the dead. But there is no question of limiting the alms merely to the poor and the miserable. Apart from needy persons, there are charitable institutes, and there are good works of every kind which are in constant need of help: vocational works, mission work, orphanages, associations of Catholic Action, etc. There is a wide choice, and care in choosing can often augment the merit of the gift. This merit does not necessarily depend only on the quantity of the thing given, but also on the financial situation and the interior dispositions of the donor, as is clearly shown by Christ's words about the widow's mite.

Poverty may prevent the giving of material alms, but the spiritual alms of penitential and satisfactory works are at the disposal of all. At the head of these spiritual alms, are the voluntary penances, great or small, which one imposes on oneself for the expiation of sin, and which may be applied to the souls in Purgatory—such as fasting, small privations in eating and drinking, renunciation of a permitted curiosity or of an innocent pleasure, and an occasional self-denial in the small luxuries of every-day life. But the great penance for all men is work, the duty of one's state in life, and offered in a spirit of penance, it can be of great help to the souls in Purgatory. The degree of efficacy will be proportionate to the vexatiousness of the work and to the degree of sanctity in the worker.

It is of faith that the trials of life, which we call providential crosses, when borne in a christian spirit, can pay the debt of sin. These crosses, chosen by God and not by ourselves, are more often the most salutary penances: physical or moral suffering, bereavement, poverty, etc. The important thing is not to neglect this treasure of suffering, which is really a mercy from God, since it is given in place of future punishment for ourselves, and in order that we may have spiritual alms for the dead. There is no one of us but has something to suffer, and therefore something to give to the Holy Souls.

(c) The Holy Sacrifice of the Mass.

The most excellent and most efficacious of all the suffrages for the dead, is the Holy Mass.

It must be carefully noted that every Mass, offered for the souls in Purgatory, profits every soul there, but in a measure known to God alone. The Mass, indeed, is the common good of the universal Church, because it is the memorial and mystic reproduction of the Sacrifice of the Cross. It brings to every member of the Church, whether of the Church Militant, the Church Suffering, or the Church Triumphant, benefits according to the state and the needs of each. "When a priest," says the Imitation, "celebrates Mass, he honours God, rejoices the angels, edifies the Church, gains repose for the dead, and makes himself a participator of all good things." The Mass honours God, because it is a sacrifice of adoration, of praise and of thanksgiving. It rejoices the angels and all Heaven, because the Blessed, animated with the purest charity for God and men, thrill with pleasure in seeing God honoured and their brethren of earth and Purgatory aided and laden with blessings. It edifies the Church Militant, on which it pours a rain of all graces. It procures rest for the dead, because it is a sacrifice of propitiation and impetration. In the Mass, the Church, in liturgical prayer, offers sacrifice for all the faithful departed and begs that they may be introduced into the place of refreshment, light and peace. It is certain that every soul in Purgatory receives some diminution of its debt by the celebration of any Mass, even though we cannot measure that diminution precisely. This is very consoling for us all. After death, our relations, our friends, our contemporaries may forget us, but the Church will never forget us. Christ will never forget us, and every Mass, which is at one and the same time, the action of Christ and of His Church, will bring us refreshment, consolation and, finally, deliverance. Thus, no soul is completely forgotten and each one participates, in a measure fixed by the just mercy of God, in the treasury of common suffrages accumulated by all the Masses which are celebrated each day in the world.

But that the Mass may have a special efficacy for some soul or group of souls, we may ask the celebrant to apply the

Holy Sacrifice to this soul or to these souls. God habitually keeps count of such special intentions, all the more so because they are asked, according to traditional usage, by the offering of an alms to the Church and to her minister. These stipends are in no sense the price of the Mass; to think so would be simoniacal and mercenary. The stipend is an alms made to the Church in the person of her minister, for his support and for the expenses incurred. That alms, like all alms, constitutes in itself a satisfactory work, which can be used for the benefit of the souls in Purgatory. In this case, we are justified in thinking that the alms has a special efficacy with God, for it concurs directly with the celebration of Mass. Joined to the special intention of the celebrant, it procures for the souls a greater participation in the satisfactory fruits of the Mass. Other things being equal, a Mass specially applied to a soul will profit that soul more than it profits the rest of the souls. We may also say that a High Mass or a long Office has a greater satisfactory value than a Low Mass or a short Office, because the action of the Church and her ministers are here taken into account. As the satisfactory value of an act depends, in the last analysis, solely on the will of God, we can also affirm that the generosity of the alms made to the Church can incline the Saviour to accord to it a greater satisfactory value. A poor man who has a Mass celebrated for his relations at a great pinch to himself, can by that act secure for them aid every bit as powerful as a rich man for whom the arranging of many Masses means no personal sacrifice. We can go even farther: a generous alms offered for the celebration of one single Mass can, in a given case, be so pleasing to God that the single Mass is of more value to the soul to whom it is applied, than many other Masses for which one has paid the simple stipend fixed by the Bishop of the Diocese.

These and other like cases can be explained by the fact that God reserves the application of the satisfactory or impetratory value of the Mass to the Holy Souls. He has His secrets of which we know nothing. Thus the vulgar and ridiculous objection is exploded, which says that in the Church as in the world, riches are the all important thing, and that if you have money you can buy yourself out of Purgatory. Each one is treated by God according to his own worth, and there is no exception of persons. What is certain, is that the rich man who has numerous Masses celebrated for his dead is the common benefactor of the whole Church, since every Mass profits the whole Church. He not only assists those of his dead who have need of help, but also the whole population of Purgatory.

There is another manner of augmenting the efficacy of the Mass for the help and deliverance of the souls. It is to assist at the Mass, and uniting oneself therewith, to pray fervently for the dead. One cannot directly profit the souls in Purgatory by one's Communion. Communion, like all the Sacraments, is directly ordained to the spiritual good and sanctification of the recipient. But one can associate the Holy Souls with one's Communion, by praying for them in the Thanksgiving. Our prayers at such a time have a special efficacy, and moreover, the reception of Holy Communion is one of the habitual conditions for the gaining of plenary indulgences which may be applied to the dead.

It is, therefore, very true that the Mass is the great means of aiding the souls in Purgatory—a fact that is not to be wondered at when it is remembered that the Mass is the application of the fruits of Calvary.

(*d*) Permanent Works of Assistance.

Because there is no moment of the day or night in which Mass is not being celebrated, the Mass may be regarded as a work of permanent assistance to the souls in Purgatory. But besides the Mass, there have been established in the Church, especially during the nineteenth century, a certain number of pious assiciations and a religious congregation, having for direct end the organising of help for the Holy Souls, and known as the Black Cross. We can only hope to enumerate the principal of these pious works.

The first in order, was an archconfraternity under the patronage of Our Lady of the Assumption, founded at Rome in 1841. To this was affiliated another which was founded in the church of Notre Dame de France at Jerusalem, established by a Brief of Leo XIII, in 1896. In 1865 the "Archconfraternity of St. Joseph, Protector of the Souls in Purgatory and Patron of a Good Death," was established in the diocese of Langres. In 1884 came the well-known "Work of Expiation for the Deliverance of Abandoned Souls in Purgatory," which has for its end the celebration of many Masses for these souls.

All these associations have their particular statutes and demand from their members prayers and some form of alms, by means of which they can participate in the spiritual favours with which the Church has enriched them. These spiritual favours consist above all in various indulgences applicable to the souls in Purgatory. These souls are thus doubly helped : by the Masses which each association causes to be celebrated for them, and by the works of satisfaction performed by the members. The assisting of the souls in Purgatory has been organised in a manner more continuous and more efficacious by the establishment of a religious congregation of women entirely devoted to the helping of the Holy Souls— the "Institute of the Helpers of Purgatory," founded in Paris in 1856 by Eugenie-Marie-Joseph Smet (in religion, Mere Marie de la Providence), who is today among the Venerable of the Church. The cause of her beatification has been recently introduced.

Considering that there was not in the Church, any religious institute for which the principal end was the relief of the Holy Souls, she set herself to work with zeal, after much prayer and prudent consultation. The Curé d'Ars encouraged her by telling her that it was the will of God and " a realisation of the love of the Heart of Christ." With five companions she pronounced her vows and launched her work in Paris on the 27th December, 1856.

She herself, by her whole life and conduct showed to her spiritual daughters the way that must be followed in order most efficaciously to aid the Holy Souls. She offered herself as a victim of expiation for these souls. All her prayers, all her mortifications, all her heroic acts were offered for them. She gave proof of real genius in the exercise of charity towards the neighbour, in finding the secret of working at the same time and by the same acts, for the relief of the souls in Purgatory and of the poor on earth. The secret consists in offering to God for the Holy Souls the spiritual and corporal works of mercy done for the living. That is why the Institute devotes itself to all kinds of work.

God ratified the act by which she offered herself as a victim of satisfaction for the souls in Purgatory. Terrible trials came to her; spiritual anguish, physical sufferings, calumny, mockery—nothing was spared to her. "Among things that are not sinful there are five which I dread," she said, "namely, to be separated from my relations, to found a religious family, to starve, to be overwhelmed with debt, to contract cancer. By the grace of God I have been inflicted with all five." At the age of scarcely forty-six she died in 1871 after a cancer-torture of two years.

Her children have followed in her footsteps and, by their life of charity and of reparatory suffering, they have preached to us our duty to the Holy Souls.

III.—The Reasons for Helping the Holy Souls

Having treated of the means of helping the Holy Souls, we now pass on to consider the reasons for helping them. Some reasons that suggest themselves are: the love of God; the love of the Church Triumphant; the various titles which the dead have to our assistance; our own interest.

If we truly love God, we ought to wish to please Him and to do Him good in what measure we can. Can we do good to God? Many deny that we can. This is an error since Christ Himself has said that whatsoever is done to the least of His, will be considered as having been done to Himself—a statement all the more arresting when it is considered in its Gospel context, for it comes immediately after the description of the Last Judgment. On the eve of His Passion He repeats His doctrine that the resume of the whole law is the loving of one's neighbour as oneself, and He adds: If you love Me, keep My Commandments. Now, what do the inhabitants of Purgatory mean to Christ? They are, after the Blessed in Heaven, the choicest portion of His flock. They are the predestined, the saints, the elect who will soon take their place in the heavenly Jerusalem. It can be said that Christ, Head of the Mystical Body which is His Church, suffers in some way in each of His suffering members; that He is, so to speak, an exile in Purgatory in the person of each soul there. To visit, to console them, is to visit and to console Him. Undoubtedly, His justice has obliged Him to deliver to the severe torments of Purgatory these elect souls. But we cannot please Him more than by delivering these exiles, when we take their place and liquidate the ransom fixed by justice. Can we claim to have a true love for the Saviour if, when we can easily help Him in the person of the souls dear to Him, we yet neglect to do so?

That which pleases God rejoices also the angels and saints. If there is great joy in Heaven upon the conversion of one sinner on earth, how much more so when a new saint makes his entrance there. When Beatrix entered the second Heaven, Dante tells us, the planet became more resplendent for her. "And I saw a flock of heavenly splendours which moved towards us, each one crying: behold who comes to augment our love." By delivering the souls in Purgatory, by hastening their entrance to Heaven, we draw on ourselves the gratitude of all Paradise; we forge bonds of friendship with all its inhabitants. Happy he who lays up for himself the patronage of his brethren in Heaven, for the day of his own departure from earth.

If now we turn our eyes to the inhabitants themselves of Purgatory, how many titles to our assistance may we not find there?

First, there is the common title of fraternal charity, for they are all our brethern in distress, to whom the precept of loving our neighbour as ourselves has full application. It is an error to think that charity towards the Holy Souls is merely a work of supererogation, which concerns only the saints and the perfect. The limits of our world are not the limits of christian charity. Charity extends to all places where we have brethren. It mounts to Heaven, and descends to Purgatory and stops only on the borders of Hell from which love has been for ever banished. In the name of our brotherhood in Christ, every soul in Purgatory has a right to our assistance; and so the Church prays for all those who rest in Christ, without exception. And we have seen in our own days how the Holy Spirit and the Blessed Virgin have drawn attention to the forgotten souls in Purgatory who receive no personal prayers.

Some among these souls may also have a title of justice,

because of some prejudice which we have done them on earth and which has not been repaired, either because we did not wish it, or because circumstances have rendered the reparation impossible. The forms that injustice can take are very numerous : we can injure a person in his soul, in his reputation, in his health, in his social position, and in a hundred other ways. They are condemned to a long Purgatory, of which we have been the occasion, and perhaps to a large extent the cause. And who can number the sins we may have occasioned to such-and-such a soul by our injuries, our complaints, our impatience, our roughness of character? All that requires restitution, reparation, satisfaction. An easy method of discharging this debt of justice is by offering many suffrages for the departed soul.

Among those who have the right to our suffrages in strict justice, should we not include those who have sacrificed their life for the common good, those who, by their devotion to the common good, have given their lives in the defence of the fatherland? The poet had every reason to write that those who have filially died for the fatherland have the right to see their people gather round their bier.

Besides strict justice, there is the justice of honour or gratitude. No one on earth can exempt himself from all gratitude to the dead. Every man has benefactors who have preceded him to the tomb, and many of whom are doubtless still in Purgatory. No man is sufficient unto himself. We owe to the dead, whether directly or indirectly, the better part of that which we are and have, and the most indebted are not the poor but the rich and the fortunate in every domain. The fable of the goose plumed with a peacock's feathers has its lesson for all. We are not the heirs of all the ages without being their debtors, too. Let us, therefore, pay our debt to Purgatory by gratitude, and not appear before the Sovereign Judge with the mark of ingratitude stamped on our foreheads. Our Heaven will then be more blue and our eternal joy more full.

Who among us has not seen many we called our friends depart from this life? In all probability, many of them are still in Purgatory. True friendship survives the grave, for it triumphs over death, the enemy of man, the fruit of sin.

Let us remember that those we have loved on earth are always living, that we will soon join them and they will be our companions for eternity. If we have forgotten them, we will have proved the proverb : out of sight out of mind—and how we shall blush to meet them. Let us spare ourselves these humiliations. But if we have not forgotten them, our reunion will be without a shadow. It will be soldered for eternity.

Then, there are strong bonds of gratitude and obligation which bind us to our dear ones. A father, a mother, a brother, a sister, a wife, a husband, children dearly loved, how can we forget them, when they have passed to the next life ? And let us not forget the bond of spiritual paternity which community of life and ideal creates among the members of the same religious family, or the sacerdotal paternity that exists between the priest and those souls who have been born again in Christ through him. All those who have been in any sense our spiritual fathers, have a special right to our suffrages, and we should not forget them.

We will here pass lightly over the last reason we have cited, namely, our own interests, the well-regulated love of ourselves ; for we will treat of it at length in the second part of this work. We will there show that one of the surest means to secure our own final perseverance and even to obtain Heaven immediately after death, is the constant exercise of mercy towards the suffering souls. For it is written : " Blessed are the merciful for they shall obtain mercy."

IV.—Prayer to the Souls in Purgatory

May we pray to the souls in Purgatory ? May we recommend ourselves to them as we recommend ourselves to the saints in Heaven and to the prayers of the faithful on earth ? May we ask for spiritual and even temporal favours through their intercession ? We have indeed already answered that question when we affirmed above that they can pray for us and do so pray. If they can pray for us, it is logical that we should be able to pray to them. Certain theologians, especially among the ancients, have declared that the invocation of the suffering souls rests on no serious theological foundation. In doing so, they based themselves on the silence of the Church in her liturgical prayers and on two phrases of St. Thomas, which he uses en passant and indeed indirectly corrects in other passages. But when carefully examined, it is found that not the invocation, but the objections to it, lack foundation.

In the first place, the silence of the Church in her official prayer is no great argument, for, even though she has given no lead in the invocation of the souls in Purgatory, she has allowed the habit of such invocation to grow freely among her children for many centuries. Great saints, who were certainly in harmony with the spirit of the Church, have often had recourse to these souls. The Roman catacombs bear unequivocal testimony to the antiquity of such invocation, as, to take but two, the following inscriptions show: "May thy soul rest in peace! Pray for thy sister" "Pray for Celsinian, thy spouse." Notice that the first inscription unites prayer for the dead with prayer to the dead. In fact, is it not in this form that the invocation of the souls in Purgatory is habitually practised? We invoke them in praying for them. In reality, the two formulas are equivalent. Our invocations become a kind of contract with these souls. We begin by giving to them prayers, sacrifices, satisfactions, indulgences, which, in virtue of the Communion of Saints, alleviates and sometimes terminates their pain. We ask, in return, that they should remember us with God, and should concern themselves with our interests, according to the designs of divine Providence and the order of charity. This is the method of invocation which is backed by the authority of the practice of the saints. "If we only realised," said St. John Vianney, "the power of the souls in Purgatory ... and what they can obtain for us by their intercession ... We must pray much for them, that they may pray much for us."

Needless to say, all the delicacy of fraternal charity must be observed, and every hint of sordid avarice excluded, when we make our little contracts with the souls in Purgatory. One must not say: "I offer so many Masses for the souls in Purgatory, on condition that they obtain for me the grace I seek." The suffering souls must be foremost in our minds, and we must heap suffrages on them with a lavish hand—ever heaping and heaping, with no thought of weighing and huckstering. This is the truly fraternal manner of invoking their intercession.

"Everything," writes Henri Bolo, " ought to be serious, and have something of the eternal about them, in our relations with those holy souls, who are living the most solemn and most terrifying drama that could be imagined. Foolishness and puerility, between them and us, can easily cross the line into sacrilege, and small higgling can spell cruelty. Does the suppliant realise that he is asking beings in pain, to obtain for him a paltry piece of this world's goods, a miserable handful of money, a vainglorious success: and that he makes the satisfaction of this miserable request, the absolute condition of his helping them? Even granting that the holy souls could hear such bill-of-exchange prayers and ridiculous vows, and that they could answer them, such conditional propositions would still remain a contemptible exploitation, which, if it occurred between the living themselves, would cause a blush of shame on every decent cheek. Faced with the thought of such harrowing pain, many will think that it is monstrous even to think of oneself, and not to devote oneself entirely to alleviating it."

We come now to the objections drawn from St. Thomas. Two passages in the Second Part of the " Summa " are in question. " The souls in Purgatory," he writes, " because they do not yet enjoy the vision of God, cannot know what we think or say. That is why we do not implore their suffrages by prayer; but we ask, viva voce, the suffrages of the living " (IIa IIae, q. lxxxiii, *Art.* 4, *ad* 3). These words seem to proclaim the futility of our prayers to the holy souls, on the ground that these souls cannot know the requests we make them. But it must be noted that St. Thomas speaks here merely en passant, in order to reply to an objection which was raised against invoking the saints in Heaven. His answer is of value in establishing the thesis that the saints in Heaven can be invoked, and it must be remembered that his ' en passant ' reference to Purgatory does not accord with his ' ex professo ' treatment of the subject in the Prima Pars, where he speaks of the knowledge of souls separated from their bodies (Ia *q.* lxxxix). St. Thomas attributes a double knowledge to these souls—a natural knowledge and a supernatural knowledge. By the first, not only do they preserve the memories and the knowledge they have acquired on earth, but they also acquire, by virtue of an infused light adapted to their new mode of existence, an imperfect and confused knowledge of all the things of nature, and a distinct and detailed knowledge of a certain number of beings and of objects. The extent of this particular knowledge varies with each. It is determined by knowledge previously acquired, or by a special tendency or affection, or by a natural aptitude, or finally by a particular disposition of Providence. As to events among men, to which category prayers to the holy souls belong, the separated souls know nothing, according to their natural knowledge; but they can get to know them, either from the countless throng of souls which arrives constantly to Purgatory, or from the angels, or from a special revelation of the Holy Spirit. This last mode of knowledge is evidently supernatural; but, then, the souls in Purgatory are wholly supernatural. When separated from their bodies, they do not lose the supernatural gifts with which God has adorned them here below. Their love of God and their neighbour is very perfect. God loves them as daughters and cherished spouses, and He is not a Judge who is always irritated with them. He remains for them a Father and a Spouse. and everything leads us to suppose that He allows them to know what the Church Militant is doing for their release, either by giving them an interior illumination, or by the ministry of angels.

Finally, the Thomistic objection is purely of the philosophic order, and arguments of this kind are always subject to revision. In our day, some excellent Thomists hold that the natural knowledge of separated souls, prescinding entirely from the supernatural, is very much greater than was heretofore thought. If one presses rigorously the consequences of the Aristotelian theory of human knowledge, one arrives at the conclusion, reached quite logically by the Nestorians, that after death the human soul is incapable of all intellectual and moral activity, but remains in a profound sleep, awaiting the general resurrection. Logically, too, according to these principles, all reward for the good and punishment for the evil must begin only after the general resurrection. One error breeds another. Philosophy has but the rôle of a handmaiden to Theology, and must be rigorously checked with the doctrines of Revelation and with Christian practices connected with dogma. We have seen above that the objection against the invocation of the suffering souls, drawn from their ignorance of our prayers, is not tenable, since these souls, both in the order of knowledge and in that of love, are placed in a supernatural condition which postulates for them normal and continual relations with the other members of the Mystical Body of Christ.

PART TWO

THE MEANS OF AVOIDING PURGATORY

Chapter the First

GENERAL CONSIDERATIONS

I.—Is it Possible to Avoid Purgatory?

Before discussing the means of avoiding Purgatory, we must first answer the question—is it possible to avoid Purgatory? To avoid Purgatory one must have that purity which is worthy of seeing God face to face, and which of us is unspotted from sin? Even if a person dies with a deep contrition extending to the smallest faults, there is still the question of the temporal punishment due to sin after the sin itself has been remitted. Short of a special revelation, one cannot know whether one's debt of punishment has been sufficiently paid. All this is indisputable, but it does not prove the impossibility of paying here below one's debt to divine justice. By a rigorous and prolonged penitence, one can furnish a superabundant satisfaction, and even add in one's degree to the great treasury —the satisfactions of Our Saviour, of the Blessed Virgin and the Saints—on which the Church draws for her Indulgences. Doubtless, one dies without seeing one's balance-sheet: but what a joyous surprise to meet the hand of Christ stretched out to us with an unreserved Come. To propose the avoidance of Purgatory, then, is not a chimera. It is a generous and perfectly realisable object.

Many consider Purgatory as a necessary stage on their journey to Paradise. You would scandalize them, almost, if you announced an ambition of going straight to Heaven. They would see in it the mark of presumption, and a danger to the virtue of humility. They consider that they themselves sound quite the right note when they say: " If only I succeed in getting to Purgatory!" But is Purgatory the only ideal for the Christian soul? Is an immediate Heaven the privilege of an elite ? Is it foolish presumption to hope for it ? On the contrary, is it not the natural desire of a soul, supernaturally aflame with the love of God ? God has prepared all things that we might pass directly from earth to Heaven. In His plan, immediate entry to Heaven after death is the rule : it is Purgatory which is the exception, because it is an invention of the infinite mercy of God for those who are tardy, whose number, though it may well exceed that of the punctual, does not affect the plan of God. It is, therefore, no presumption or lack of humility to thus desire to conform oneself to the plan of God, in avoiding Purgatory. Rather is it an ambition which honours Christ.

We find in the holy Catholic Church, the Spouse of Jesus and Mary, a superabundance of means for the avoidance of Purgatory. These means have increased and multiplied, so that we have greater opportunities of paying our debts than had the early Christians. Progressively and under the inspiration of the Holy Spirit the Church has used, In favour of her children, the infinite treasury of the merits of Our Saviour, confided to her. As " the first, fine, careless rapture " of charity cooled with the passing centuries, the Church has sunk her hands deeper and deeper into that treasury. Besides, it must be remembered that there is a law of progress in the Kingdom of God on earth. At first, it was the grain of mustard seed : now, it is already the great tree, which will continue to put forth many branches with the passage of time. Our times abound with the means of salvation : the river of grace has swollen its banks : the fountains of the Saviour are opened. Those, therefore, who will not pass to Heaven, except through the severities of Purgatory, can blame only their own negligence and sloth.

II.—IN FACT, THERE ARE SOULS WHO PASS STRAIGHT TO HEAVEN

That there are a certain number of souls who have passed immediately to Heaven, without having tasted the exile of Purgatory, cannot be seriously contested. Of course, private revelations concerning Purgatory must be received with very great reserve. But it would be unreasonable to dismiss them all as fables, just as it would be unreasonable to dismiss, a priori and en bloc, all the miraculous events recorded of the saints. Example of blessed deaths are not wanting in Catholic hagiography. It has often pleased God to reveal to His servants, or to manifest in a sensible manner, that a certain soul has been received immediately into Heaven. Testimony to this would fill many pages. It will suffice to refer to the Autobiography of St. Teresa.

In this work, finished by the saint in 1565, she speaks of three religious who entered Heaven immediately after death. The first was a Dominican, P. Pierre Ibanez, a man of great virtue. Of the second, a Carmelite, she writes that, while in a state of profound recollection during Mass, she saw this priest render his spirit to God, and saw the soul ascending immediately to Heaven. It was revealed to her that he had won this privilege by fidelity to his religious observances.

St. Teresa speaks only of one other such revelation, that concerning the immediate entry of St. Peter of Alcantara. " Among the many souls whose lot was revealed to me," the saint adds : " I have seen but three who did not have to pass through Purgatory on their way to Heaven " : from which one may conclude that the number of those who go directly to Heaven is relatively small. But two things must be borne in mind : first, that the saint speaks only of those whose lot God had revealed to her ; and, secondly, that these lines were written seventeen years before her death. In " The Book of Foundations " (Chapter 7), composed between 1573 and 1582, she speaks of certain religious, " whose life is a veritable martyrdom and who, suffering their Purgatory in this world, will have none to suffer in the next " : which seems to suggest that blessed deaths are not so rare.

In fact, St. Teresa, on the very day of the foundation of the monastery of the Carmelite Reform of St. Joseph of Avila (24 August, 1562), gave the habit to four religious, who appear to have been all four of the number of those who entered Heaven immediately after death. The first, Ursula of the Saints, was called to the nuptials of the Lamb, after twelve years of religious life. The very day she died, St. Teresa, who was then at Alba, saw her mount to Heaven in splendour and glory. The second, Marie of St. Joseph, a pillar of the

Teresian Reform, was favoured by God with an earthly Purgatory, in the form of very great sufferings during the last years of her life. Bereft of speech, and in a state of terrible suffering, she wrung the hearts of her Sisters who assisted by her bed-side. One of them whispered to her to make an act of complete resignation to the Will of God. She did so, and kept doing so till she died. To the Sister—M. Isabella of St. Dominic—who had counselled her in her last moments, God revealed that she had passed directly to Heaven. The deceased Sister revealed herself to M. Isabella, and thanked her for suggesting those acts of resignation which had merited for her a great reward in Heaven and an exemption from Purgatory.

The third Sister, Marie of the Cross, also endured much suffering; but her death was so tranquil that it was impossible to say at what moment she died. Her passage to Heaven was indicated by a sudden change in her, for death transfigured her body with a beauty it never had while alive. An ineffable whiteness, like the reflection of eternal beatitude, shone in her—symbol of the purity of her soul.

Not less edifying was the death of the fourth, Antoinette of the Holy Spirit, to whom St. Teresa appeared after her death. Her last years were passed in continual ecstasy. For her also, it seems certain, her last breath coincided with her entry to Heaven.

All this is very consoling, because it shows that a soul can attain without delay to Heaven. But it must not be supposed that such blessed deaths are the exclusive property of religious. There are also holy souls in the world who die in the kiss of the Saviour, after having obtained the grace of a blessed death. Which of us has not known such souls, who have spent their lives giving good example and sowing seeds of good around them? At the moment of death, they were truly ripe for Heaven, and there seemed no reason why they should have been detained, for even a moment, on their passage to Heaven.

III.—THE BEST MEANS OF AVOIDING HELL

Christ has said: " Enter by the narrow gate, for large is the gate and broad is the way that leads to perdition, and many are they who pass that way ; but narrow is the way and strait the way that leads unto life, and few there are who find it" (*Matt.*, vii, 12-14). These words serve well as an introduction to our subject. To seek to avoid Purgatory is indeed to seek the narrow gate and to turn one's back on the large and broad way. He who proposes as his aim the mere avoidance of Hell, has already set his feet on the broad way, for, in effect, he says : " Provided I attain to Purgatory, I am content. I shall avoid mortal sin, which leads to Hell,; but, for the rest, I shall enjoy the taste of living, and not concern myself with peccadilloes : " the unmistakable voice of spiritual lukewarmness. " I know thy works," is the awful warning of the Lord in the Apocalypse " that thou art neither hot nor cold. I would that thou went hot or cold. But because thou art lukewarm, and neither hot nor cold, I will begin to vomit thee out of my mouth."

This sentence is realised every day, They who seek only to avoid Hell and have no care for venial sin are quick to fall into grave sin and take the road to perdition. This should not astonish us, for it is a fact of experience in the moral order, that one almost never arrives at the end which one proposes. One always falls short, and hence it is with caution that a man is to be judged strictly by the better of the resolutions he makes. Resolutions represent the ideal. The reality, very often, is quite another matter. It is very easy to sketch a magnificent plan : the difficulty is to put it into execution. It follows from this, that the best means of avoiding Hell is to propose to oneself the avoidance of Purgatory. In doing so, one stands a double chance : 1° perhaps the complete avoidance of Purgatory ; 2° so arranging one's debt, that the sojourn in Purgatory will be shortened and made less rigorous. To sum up, then : in making every effort to avoid Purgatory, one will at least reach Purgatory ; but in proposing the mere avoidance of Hell, one is already on the way to it.

IV.—Why One should Strive to Avoid Purgatory

The least notion of Purgatory should suffice to give a first answer to that 'why,' viz.—because therein one suffers unspeakable torment. This is the spontaneous cry of self-love —legitimate, certainly, but unworthy of being the unique or the principal motive for a soul that loves God. The love of God, the love of the Church—this is the dominant motive. These two loves, in reality but one love, open new horizons to the eyes of faith, and inspire us with more worthy answers to that ' why.'

The love of God proposes the answer : " I must strive to attain immediately to Heaven, because God desires it as part of His plan." According to that plan, the period on earth constitutes the normal time of trial. This does not mean that God, so to speak, has created Purgatory against His Will. Purgatory may be called a concession wrung by His justice from His mercy. So much does He love us, that His paternal Heart wishes to avoid inflicting Purgatory on us, but would rather welcome us without delay into His home. To give pleasure to our Heavenly Father, to satisfy His love, to avoid inflicting the pain on Him—pardon the expression—of having to punish us after death, we must strive to avoid Purgatory.

Another consideration. Whosoever loves God should have at heart the deep desire to participate as soon as possible in the eternal feast of the Lamb. Heaven is the place of full and perfect praise. On earth, and in Purgatory, God is but imperfectly praised. In particular, the praise that mounts from Purgatory is a sorrowful praise. The two words, praise and sorrow, clash a little, for praise is the flower of gratitude, of joy and of perfect happiness. This is the perfect praise which God loves to receive from His creatures. It is impossible to give it to Him in Purgatory. The time spent in Purgatory will be time lost to perfect praise, for it will mean an absence from the choir of the Elect, where our place is marked.

To avoid Purgatory is to honour, to magnify the redemption of Christ, in saying with the psalmist : " Copiosa apud Eum redemptio " : which is to say, in effect to Our Saviour : " You have placed a superabundance of means for the complete attainment of our salvation. You have multiplied remedies against sin. Where sin abounds, Lord, Thy grace does superabound. There is nothing wanting to Thy redemption. You have done all things royally, magnificently, and I cannot tell how Thou couldst have added to Thy benefits." Let us have at heart to give this testimony to Christ, and thus to manifest to Him our gratitude.

If we love the Church, we will strive to give her joy and to render service to her. The death of a saint ripe for Heaven is a day of joy to the universal Church.

The Church Triumphant acclaims the new arrival with cries of joy and triumph, for is there not now a new sun in that world of light, a new guest at the banquet, a new brother in the family ? If there is joy in Heaven on the repentance of a sinner, how great must be the joy at the entry of a saint ! On the contrary, the death of an imperfect Christian would be a day of mourning in Heaven, were sorrow possible there. Let us be more charitable to our brethren in Heaven, and let us procure for them the joy of seeing us immediately after death.

Tears of a divine joy are shed on earth at the death of a saint, for there is one gone before who will plead for us. The petals of their prayers will be scattered on us, spreading joy and consolation in our valley of tears. Tears of sorrow, tears heavy with anguish are shed at the death of the lukewarm. One wonders if they have attained their end, and a shroud of sorrow is heavy on the souls of those who have known and loved the departed.

Purgatory rejoices at the entry of a saint to Heaven. Doubly do they rejoice : because they love God and the neighbour ; and because one more intercessor for them has gone before the throne of God. Purgatory does not rejoice at the coming of another soul to its place of punishment. The new arrival is received with that shake of the hand that speaks one's sorrowful inability to help a sufferer.

Is it not terrible, after the sufferings of this life, to have still to suffer in the next ? It is in our hands to avoid this. Let us live in such a manner that our death will rejoice the whole Church and procure our entry into Heaven.

V.—Various Means of Avoiding Purgatory

Since sin is the cause of Purgatory, it is evident that the radical means of avoiding the one is to avoid the other. Whoever, after Baptism, keeps himself from sin, even from what are called semi-deliberate venial sins, need have no fear of Purgatory. But is such a purity of conscience possible to poor human nature? Yes, it is possible for some elite souls to attain to it for a short time; no, if there is question of the general run of men; and an unqualified no, if there is question of a long space of time, of a whole lifetime, short of a special privilege such as was given to the Mother of God for the whole of her life. This is the formal, dogmatic teaching of the Council of Trent. Certain great saints have enjoyed the privilege in question for a period of their life, but this is not so for the ordinary mortal. All must strike the breast and make their own, in very truth, the fifth petition of the *Pater*: " Forgive us our trespasses as we forgive them that trespass against us." From this it emerges that the use of reason entails also the risk of going to Purgatory.

This risk, we have seen, can be averted, for we have at hand the means of attaining to Heaven immediately after death. These means are many and varied. Some are of an infallible efficacy, as martyrdom, properly so-called, or a plenary indulgence *in articulo mortis*. Other means, objectively very powerful, are efficacious according to the manner in which we use them, and in proportion to the greatness of our debt, as frequent Confession and Communion, the spirit and practice of penance, etc. In general, every good work of charity brings with it the power of preparing for a happy death.

We will pass in review these many means, without any claim to exhaust the list. We shall commence with those of which the efficacy is infallible. It is difficult to establish a hierarchical order with reference to their efficacy, among the others. It is evident that any one of the means, well used, will suffice to preserve us from Purgatory. Each of them, of course, supposes the state of grace, or looks to our being in it at the hour of death. Some are not available to all, but those available to us are sufficiently numerous to satisfy all tastes, according to the impulse of the Holy Spirit. Let us choose that means or those means which best suit our own spiritual temperament.

Chapter the Second

THE SACRAMENTAL MEANS

I.—Baptism

AMONG THE MEANS of avoiding Purgatory, pride of place must be given to those which immediately or from afar, draw their efficacy from the Sacraments instituted by Christ.

The first of the Sacraments, Baptism, effaces all sin and all punishment due to sin. Thus, baptized infants who die before attaining the use of reason, and adult neophytes who die so soon after Baptism that they have not committed the least sin, will not know Purgatory, but will pass straight to Heaven.

Knowing this sovereign power of Baptism, and affrighted by the awful penances imposed by the early Church for sins committed after its reception, many catechumens of the first centuries put off their Baptism as long as possible. They waited almost till the moment of death. Against such a gross exploitation of the divine mercy, the Fathers of the Church often protested in their homilies. There is a remarkable similarity between the discourses which they directed against such laggards, and those which we hear to-day directed against the faithful who attempt to defer their confession or their reception of Extreme Unction till the last minute. In both, the reasoning put forward is almost the same.

To-day, in the mission countries, where catechumens abound, Baptism can send directly to Heaven a certain number of privileged souls. Surprised by a mortal sickness before having finished their instruction, they receive the Sacrament *in extremis* with the right dispositions, and their souls appear before the sovereign Judge in all the purity of baptismal innocence. For them, there is no Purgatory.

Those who have kept themselves from all mortal sin after their Baptism and come to the end of their lives with simple faults and the sins of human frailty, may very well escape Purgatory, because the punishment incurred by the faults is light and can easily be set aside by the reception of the

Sacraments, the gaining of indulgences, and by acts of the love of God.

II.—MARTYRDOM

To die a martyr is an infallible means of reaching Heaven without having to pass through Purgatory, The Church has always prayed *to* the martyrs, never *for* them. Martyrdom—or Baptism by blood, as theologians call it—produces the same effects as the Sacrament of Baptism itself, at least as regards the remission of sin and of all the punishment due to sin. Just as the newly baptized who dies without committing sin, sees the gates of Heaven open immediately to him, so also he, who suffers martyrdom with the required dispositions, is received without delay into the choir of the Elect.

We say *with the required dispositions*, for St. Paul writes: " And if I shall deliver my body to be burned and have not charity, it profiteth me nothing." Exterior death—the death of adults, we mean, for the case of the Holy Innocents and of infants is different—is of no value before God, unless it is accepted for His love. True martyrdom is not solely an act of the virtue of endurance. It supposes also an act of perfect charity, and indeed of the most perfect charity, according to those words of Christ : " Greater love than this no man hath, than that a man lay down his life for his friends.

The true martyr, then, is he who suffers death—or receives a mortal wound—through love for God, in order to remain faithful to the truth revealed by Him, to the moral law in His Commandments. Violence must not be met with violence. If he defends himself, he may have great merit before God, according to the motive which inspires him, and if that motive is perfect charity—as, for example, to safeguard the faith of a whole people—his death may have the same efficacy as that of a martyr ; but in the Church of God, that title will not be given him, and theologians will commonly refuse him that special accidental glory, known as an aureola, which they reserve to Martyrs, properly so called, to Virgins and to Doctors. The soldier who dies fighting for a just cause is not a martyr ; but before God, on account of the dispositions of his soul, he may make of the sacrifice of his life a perfect holocaust, which will open to him immediately the Kingdom of Heaven. So, too, the soldier, dying for his fatherland, who offers his life principally for the triumph of the Kingdom of Christ in that fatherland, may have before God a merit equivalent to that of the martyr, even though he will have no chance of being ever named in the martyrology by a solemn decree of the Church.

In his First Epistle, St. John says: " Jesus has given His life for us." We also, we should give our lives for our brethren. To give one's life for one's brethren through love for God, to contract a serious malady in nursing the sick, to expose oneself and suffer death in order to administer the Sacraments —this is not canonical martyrdom, but is martyrdom by analogy, which is of the same value before God.

What a splendid death is martyrdom, for it is the paying of Christ in kind, in thus dying for Him who died for us! To wash one's sins in one's own blood in order to present oneself before God in the immaculate robe of Baptism—what a splendid grace ! What glory can compare with that of shedding one's blood as a testimony to truth, thereby becoming a living apologetic of the religion of Jesus ! " If the grain of wheat falling into the ground," says Christ, " dieth not, itself remaineth alone ; but if it die, it will bring forth much fruit. Whosoever loveth his life shall lose it, but whosoever hateth his life in this world shall preserve it unto life everlasting ... and I, when I shall have been lifted up from the earth, shall draw all men unto myself " (*John*, xii, 24, 25, 32). Martyrdom participates in this fecundity of Our Saviour's death, for the blood of the martyr is the seed of Christians.

All that is very beautiful, you will say, but of what value is it for me as a means of avoiding Purgatory. It is quite remote from my life. But take a glance at the map of the world and perhaps it will not seem so remote. Think of Mexico, of China, of Russia ; hear the mutterings and attend to the atrocities of atheistic Communism. The time is indeed ripe for nourishing a martyr's soul within us, for we know not what to-morrow may bring us. The enemies of God increase and multiply on all sides. Hell rages everywhere. Was there ever a more quicksand epoch than that in which we live.

The warning is—Be ye ready—for a half-paganized world is returning to the era of the martyrs.

And, further, if martyrdom proper is not our lot, there still remains martyrdom by analogy. Let us be martyrs of duty, for duty is never done, and it can involve a slow and hidden martyrdom. It were easy to cite a dozen cases—the struggle to keep pure, martyred hearts, victims of betrayal and brutality, and in general, the weary weight of all this unintelligible world. Of all these pains before God, we can earn for ourselves the equivalent of martyrdom, and thus avoid Purgatory.

III.—FREQUENT CONFESSION

An almost infallible means of avoiding Purgatory is frequent Confession, faithfully practised.

In the first place, it prevents our debts from accumulating, in this sense that it is a potent preservative against new sins. If it does not immunise against all sin, still it is a fact of experience that it diminishes the number of sins and prevents evil habits from taking root in the soul. It makes us practise that great precept of vigilance: " Watch, for ye know not at what hour the master will come ... What I say to you, I say to all: Watch ! " (*Mark*, xiii, 27). " Be ye ready, because at an hour ye know not, the Son of Man will come " (*Mat.*, xxiv, 44).

Frequent Confession liquidates, little by little, the debt of our past sins, for we may always accuse ourselves anew, according to the prayer of the Psalmist: " Wash me yet more from my iniquities, O Lord " (*Ps.*, 1, 4). It produces this effect in two ways; for every Confession augments habitual charity or sanctifying grace in the soul. A greater habitual charity gives power to produce a greater act of charity, and the fire of this charity consumes sin and tempers the soul to its pristine beauty. Moreover, the penance imposed by the confessor, however light, has for its proper efficacy to diminish, and even to entirely cancel, the debt of sin. A long series of well-made Confessions is thus an assured means of arriving at perfect purification and avoiding Purgatory.

Add to this, that frequent Confession facilitates the gaining of plenary indulgences. Whoever confesses at least each fortnight, can gain all the ordinary indulgences for which Confession is required. And, as we shall see, indulgences are the precious coins which the Church puts in our hands that we may liquidate our debts to divine justice.

A final reason for the efficacy of Confession, in our context, is that it is itself a work of penance, a work of satisfaction. Many pious persons experience a repugnance to this practice. It suffices that it is commanded by the Church, or prescribed by the rule, in order that this repugnance may grow: curious attitude, indeed, of a sick person towards the remedy that will heal him. To surmount that repugnance is itself a true penance, the effect of which will be added to that of the Confession itself. It is clear, then, that frequent Confession is an excellent means of avoiding Purgatory.

IV.—INDULGENCES

We have in Indulgences, so liberally granted to us by the Church, a means at once easy and efficacious to wipe out the debt of our sins. This means is attached directly, by its origin, to Sacramental penitence, which requires of the penitent contrition, confession and satisfaction.

Satisfaction is represented by the penance imposed by the confessor. This has for its end, to satisfy divine justice for the sins committed after Baptism. In the early centuries of the Church, long and hard penances were imposed on those who confessed grave sins, and only after the performance of these penances did the penitent receive *full* absolution, that is to say, not only the absolution of sin itself, which can be had immediately by Confession, but also the total absolution of the temporal punishment due to sin. In other words, to that final reconciliation, the Church attached what we call to-day a plenary indulgence. The Church has received from Christ the full and entire power to absolve the faithful, not only from the sins themselves, but also from the punishment due to sin. "Whatsoever thou shalt bind upon earth, shall be bound also in Heaven; and whatsoever thou shalt loose upon earth shall be loosed also in Heaven," said Christ to St. Peter.

The same words were spoken, on another occasion, to all the apostles together (*Mat.*, xviii, 18). The temporal punishment due to sin is a binding chain, which prevents our entry into Heaven unless and until we have been delivered from it. It is in our hands, then, to have ourselves delivered from these chains by those who, in the Church, have received the power to do so. But it is understood that this deliverance must respect the requirements of equity. Divine justice demands a compensation commensurate with the sin. Formerly, the Church demanded far more from the penitent than it demands to-day. It is true that our confessors impose very light penances on us, even for mortal sins, if one compares them to those which were in use in the early Church. What is a chaplet or an entire Rosary, or a Way of the Cross, or a day's fast, or a small alms, beside whole years of austerities, of fasts on bread and water, or long pilgrimages on foot ? However, divine justice remains ever the same : its tariff has not changed. One must pay the price. What does the Church do in order to aid us ? Knowing our weakness, and the frayed health of these latter times, she dips her hands deep into her treasury—the treasury of the satisfactions of Christ and His saints, of which she is the dispensatrix.[1] We call this divine coinage by the name—indulgences. An indu'gence is a ransom from the temporal punishment which we owe to divine justice for our sins, even after we have repented of them and obtained absolution. It does not concern *the remission of sin*, but *the remission of the pain due to sin already pardoned*. This must not be forgotten.

How can we acquire this precious currency ? We have only to observe the conditions which the Church very wisely imposes, whether there is question of plenary or partial indulgence. These conditions are not Draconian, for they contain nothing that is beyond the power of goodwill, and they are easy to fulfil. For a plenary indulgence, which remits all debt and makes the soul immaculate for Heaven, there is

---

[1] On this idea of our worn-down health, compare Francis Thompson's magnificent *Health and Holiness*. He writes : " The pride of life is no more ; to live is itself an ascetic exercise ; we require spurs to being, not a snaffle to rein back the ardour of being . Man is his own mortification. Hamlet has increased and multiplied, and his seed fill the land."—*Translator's Note.*

required a full repentance for all sin, both mortal and venial, without wilful attachment to the least of them. The soul must renounce all that displeases God, and unite itself with all its powers to His will. In a word, it must love God, according to the first and the greatest commandment. Is it so difficult to love in this way an all-good and all-lovable Father?—especially when we are aided to this perfection by Confession and Communion, which are ordinarily (not always) required for the gaining of a plenary indulgence. Add to this, usually, a visit to a church with prayers for the Pope's intentions, and you are delivered from the heavy weight of your sins, in their pains as well as their culpability. If we were to make this exercise every day, or at least once a week, we would stand a very good chance of escaping Purgatory.

Perhaps you find that, now, it is all so easy that you are inclined to be sceptical about it. But ask yourself the question : what have I done more difficult than this, to obtain a remission incomparably greater than that of the temporal punishment, the remission of the mortal sin itself and of the eternal pain it entailed ? You went and knelt at the feet of a priest who represented Christ, and you said : ' Father, I have sinned ' ; and he raised his hand over you, forgiving you in the Name of Jesus Christ. What more simple in its means, what more marvellous in its effects ? Do you forget that the love of God for us knows no bounds ; that He has given us His Only Son, and has allowed Him to offer Himself as a victim for our sins, that the rights of justice might be fully satisfied ? What God asks of us is faith in His love and a return of love. If we give that return of love, He will forget all. " For charity covereth a multitude of sins " (1. *Pet.*, iv, 8).

V.—Frequent Communion

As we have already said the two *raisons d'etre* of Purgatory are unpardoned venial sin and the temporal punishment due to mortal and venial sins already pardoned. Suppress venial sin ; remove the temporal punishment : Purgatory disappears, and there remain but Heaven and Hell. Now, frequent Communion is one of the most efficacious means of getting rid of venial sin and of being liberated from the temporal punishment due to sins already confessed.

The Blessed Eucharist, our spiritual food, produces in the supernatural order, parallel effects to those produced by material food in the natural order. One of the functions of food is to repair the losses of the body, and to recuperate the forces spent in everyday living. In the spiritual order, our souls are weakened by those daily sins which escape our most vigilant watch; more so, by the wounds of deliberate venial sins; and by those same wounds, our debt to divine justice mounts higher and higher. If, every morning, we make a fervent Communion, receiving Our Lord with sincere sorrow for our sins; if, like Magdalene, we wash His feet with our tears; if, growing bolder, we make Him an offer of all that we have and are, in an act of perfect charity—surely our venial sins will melt as the snow does in the warm summer sunshine. And when we have risen from our divine tête-à-tête with Divinity, Purgatory will not threaten us. We will be rightful citizens of Heaven, and Heaven would surely be open to us, were we to die on a day of many days thus begun.

This is further strengthened, when it is remembered that, when we possess Our Saviour thus in Holy Communion, we can plead with Him for a plenary indulgence, granted as a pure gratuity of His love. Between Him and us, there is not then the thinnest wall of separation. The time is then ripe for asking.

Death has often been compared to a painful journey, to a dark and gloomy passage through a tunnel. The metaphor is very suited to those whose journey is to Hell, and to those also who must pass to Purgatory. The souls who go to Purgatory are still, in some way, on the journey: they have not yet reached their destination. But for those who are ripe for Heaven, death is not a journey. It is, rather, a simple raising of the curtain, a charge of décor. It is a wall which crumbles, in order that we may see the face of God, and the splendid assembly of His Angels and Saints.

Fervent souls, who communicate frequently, such is the destiny which awaits you. And you also, who have not the opportunity you so ardently desire of communicating often, be consoled. The Lord is nigh unto them that seek Him.

He will take up His abode, with the Father and the Holy Ghost, in the soul of the just, Do you desire this Heavenly Bread with a hunger of soul ? He will refresh you, even though you are unable to eat. Do you thirst for this Wine ?—He will refresh you, even though the cup is far from your lips. Only hunger and thirst for this nourishment, and He will nourish you as He nourishes those who have the happiness of assisting at His Sacramental Banquet by frequent Communion.

VI.—The Sacrament of Extreme Unction

At all the most important stages of life, God has placed the Sacraments for our strength and our comfort. It is, above all things else, by the *Sacraments* that the faithful are privileged above the infidel and the heretic, for the Sacraments are the abundant channels of grace. To prepare the soul for its entry into eternity, the Catholic has " the last Sacraments," as he calls them, that is to say, a last absolution which cleanses his soul from all stain of sin, and resurrects it to grace, if it is dead in sin. Moreover, the Viaticum of the Body and Blood of Christ strengthens his faith, raises his hope to such strength that only the thin veil of weak flesh prevents it from changing immediately into vision. Finally, there is Extreme Unction, which in the divine plan is, so to speak, the finishing touch to the toilette for the nuptials of the Lamb—the final cleansing of sin.

. . .

It is certainly a great grace for the Christian to be privileged to receive the last Sacraments worthily before appearing for judgment ; it is a choice grace, a certain sign of predestination if it crowns a virtuous life as a gift desired, and not merely accepted through the insistence of those who stand around the deathbed. When we ask, as we should do very often, for the grace of final perseverance, we should add a prayer asking for the grace of the last Sacraments. If we ask that grace often and fervently, with a full appreciation of its value, God will accord it to us. If, however, He does not accord it, because in His mercy He foresees that we shall die a death incompatible with the reception of the last Sacraments, He will give us its equivalent. There are they who die in making an act of heroic charity or in suffering martyrdom for the faith ; others die suddenly, after gaining a plenary indulgence, when the eye of God sees no stain of sin on their souls, nor any debt of sin. Such as these have no need to regret their not being able to receive the last Sacraments, even if they have spent their lives of prayer in asking for this gift ; for God has answered them in His own way. Abandoning ourselves entirely to the will of God, we ask constantly for the gift of the last Sacraments. If we do not obtain the grace of receiving them, God will so arrange things that we shall receive the grace attached to their reception, namely, the ultimate preparation necessary for immediate entry into the Kingdom of Heaven.

We shall speak only of the last of the last Sacraments—Extreme Unction—and that for several reasons. Firstly, because it is a Sacrament of which many people are afraid, and every effort must be made to banish from among Christians this diabolically-inspired fear. Secondly, because it is the Sacrament most directed intended to preserve us from Purgatory. Thirdly, because it is often the only Sacrament which dying people can receive in a surely efficacious manner, at the hour of death. Finally, because it is the source of special graces to enable us to support our sickness, and to accept our death if our last hour has come.

Why is Extreme Unction feared ? Is it because of the epithet *Extreme*, in the sense that the receiving of this Sacrament means a kind of capitulation—an admission that this is the end and that there is no longer any hope of recovery ? "You ought to receive Extreme Unction" becomes their equivalent of " you are finished ; you are dying." This is the unfortunate idea which is at the root of the detestable abuse, so common in many places, of not calling the priest until the patient is in his last agony, and of not even mentioning the last Sacraments to him until he is on the point of rendering up his soul. Even then, how many relations and friends will not dare to warn the patient and will not send for the priest, thereby stupidly allowing the soul to enter eternity without preparation. Know then that this misunderstanding is something gross against which the Church energetically protests. *Extreme Unction* means *the last ritualistic and sacramental* unction which the Church administers to her children. Many anointings are made at Baptism. The unction of holy Chrism is given at Confirmation. Finally, *in a case of grave sickness*, and not merely at the *last* moment of one's life, the Church gives another sacramental unction, different from all the others, which we call *Extreme Unction*, formerly known as *the holy oil, the oil of benediction, the sacred unction*. The Orientals have a lovely name for it. They call it *the oil of prayer—Euchelaeon*.

If you would know how false and how fateful this misreading of ' Extreme ' can be, turn to the words of St. James: " Is any one sick among you ? Let him call the priests, and let them pray over him, anointing him with oil in the name of the Saviour. And the prayer of faith will save the sick man, and the Lord shall deliver him, and if he has committed any sins they shall be pardoned unto him " (*Epis*. V, 14-15). You see that in this text there is not question of the moment of death. There is question of sickness—not an ordinary, light indisposition, but—which is serious enough to be able to cause death. In such a sickness, one has the right to ask for Extreme Unction, and well-regulated self-love counsels us to do so, even if those about us think that it should be deferred. A well-instructed Christian will not hesitate to ask, as soon as he feels that his malady is a serious one, or when he has received mortal wounds. Far from being fearful, he will see in this sacrament that best of remedies, not only for the soul, but also for the body.

This Sacrament was instituted specially for the sick. Sickness is a consequence of sin, and leads to death. We have need when we are seriously ill, of special graces to help us to patience and resignation. It may happen, too, that the sickness is an obstacle to our spiritual good. In that case, Extreme Unction is a divine remedy to deliver us from that consequence of sin and restore our health. " The prayer of faith," St. James says explicitly, " will save the sick man and the Lord will deliver him." This is a clear allusion to the restoring of bodily health, at the same time as the Sacrament helps to the eternal salvation of our souls, and should help to add to our crown in Heaven by prolonging our sojourn on earth. And if, according to God's plan, our end is approaching, this Sacrament will not give us bodily health, but it will comfort us and give us a foretaste of the serenity and peace to come.

But it must be carefully noticed that this Sacrament, in so far as it is a remedy against bodily sickness, acts after the manner of a remedy and not by way of instantaneous miracle. Hence, even from this point of view as well, one should not defer the reception till the moment of death, for it would be rash to expect quasi-resurrections. Its healing power consists in the aid it renders to natural causes, in sustaining the reserves of the sick person that are not yet exhausted. This is certainly the reason why cases of healing by Extreme Unction are so rare. Under the pressure of a ridiculous fear, the Sacrament is not asked for until the doctor has declared that there is no further hope ; and it would then require a miracle, outside the ordinary Providence of God, to effect a cure. However, in spite of this fear, who among us has not heard of wonders wrought by this Sacrament in rallying the sick ? How often, indeed, do we not notice the sensible betterment, physically and morally, in the patient, after the reception of this Sacrament. In serious sickness, we should be eager to receive this Sacrament. We should thank God for His mercy in giving it.

. . .

The spiritual efficacy of Extreme Unction is infallible, if the subject places no culpable obstacle.

That obstacle would be mortal sin not repented of, or not confessed when one could have confessed it : for Extreme Unction is a Sacrament of the living. A sick person is still a living person. To be curable, he must not be dead. To receive worthily the Sacrament of Extreme Unction, one must be in the state of Grace ; one must have spiritual life within him. There is a Sacrament—Penance—that is destined for the resurrection of the spiritually dead. Penance restores life to those who have forfeited it ; but, usually, it does not restore the perfection of life one received at Baptism. Sin has trodden on that life, and the imprint of its passing is still on the soul., The mortal wounds are gone, but the scars remain. The guilt of sin is gone, but the soul is not completely free from its debt to divine justice—the debt of temporal punishment remains. God is more pleased with us if we pay that debt here below, because of his Paternal desire to receive us without delay into his home. Therefore he has instituted the Sacrament of Extreme Unction, in His mercy, that those who have been remiss in gathering the worthy fruits of penance, of which the Gospel speaks, may have this opportunity of recovering the spotlessness of their baptismal robe. Theologians express this truth by saying that this Sacrament is destined for the removal of the relics of sin, of all that could be an obstacle to our entering Heaven. "Extreme Unction," says St. Thomas, "achieves the spiritual healing of man, and by removing all that could impede his entry into Heaven, perfects his preparation for eternal life." Of all the means of avoiding Purgatory, it is the most authentic. Only one other surpasses it : the avoidance of all sin.

Extreme Unction thus shows itself as a kind of complement of the Sacrament of Penance. Penance removes sin : Extreme Unction, the relics of sin. That is why, in the order of the last Sacraments, Penance comes first in time. Viaticum follows. Then Extreme Unction, as the ultimate preparation for eternity.

. . .

But what is to be understood by the term—*relics of sin* ? Among them must be primarily counted that terrible chastisement, that awful relic of sin—death of the body. Extreme Unction can at best deliver us for a time from this death, by the restoration of health, but it can deliver us from the fear of death. The fear of death is natural to us all : we put the thought of it from us. The sinner, more than all others, dreads it. The memory of past sins, the time lost and squandered, the uncertainty of the future, all cast about the sinner the gloom of the fear of death. Extreme Unction can lessen, if indeed it does not totally supress, its terrors by reviving faith and hope in the soul, so that the sinner, thus armed, can meet the diabolical suggestions to despair. One of the effects of Extreme Unction is certainly to strengthen us against the exaggerated fear of death, to calm our souls with the perspectives of the divine mercies and the desire of eternal life, where we shall see God face to face, in the company of His angels and saints, and in the company of those holy souls we have known on earth.

Another relic of sin is that kind of grovelling which makes prayer and God and the things of God so irksome to us, and which binds our spirit to things of earth, to regrets for cherished persons and things that are loved, which must now be left aside for ever. Extreme Unction efficaciously combats this attachment to the ephemeral, by giving to our souls a grace of supernatural illumination which makes us see all things in the shadow of eternity. It has been well said: " The true outlook on human life is that which the soul knows when it is on the point of quitting that life." Extreme Unction gives us that true life, before which the phantoms and the illusions disappear, which have been all too powerful as will-of-the-wisps to keep us to the cowardly and ordinary ways of least resistance to the world and most resistance to grace. The patient who has received Extreme Unction has lost all interest in the seeming-important trifles of life. The look which he has turned to eternity, has forever unmasked the foolishness of earth, for now he understands the word of the Apostle : " The shape of this world passes " (1 *Cor.*, vii, 31).

The *relics of sin* mean, above all, the temporal punishments due to sin ; which temporal punishments are the great *raison d'etre* of Purgatory. Extreme Unction has for its special end to deliver us from these punishments. It provides this effect both directly, in virtue of its proper efficacy, and indirectly, by causing us to accept with resignation and in a spirit of expiation, all the sufferings of the last illness and of death itself. Death, courageously and Christianly accepted, in a spirit of all-submissive penance, in union with the suffering Christ, is a most efficacious means of satisfying divine justice and obtaining the remission of the debt of sin.

Extreme unction not only removes the relics of sin : it removes also the sins that still remain. The Apostle St. James affirms expressly, and Trent defines against Protestantism : " If the sick person is in sin, it shall be forgiven him." Of what sins is there question ? First and before all—venial sins, which are so easily committed when one is sick, and that multitude of small faults of which one is made culpable by force of habit and of which one has not yet properly repented ; and finally, those oft-repeated sins told in Confession after Confession without a really thorough purpose of amendment. The grace of the Sacrament inspires regret for these innumerable faults, and that rite of anointing all the different senses seems to be designed expressly to invite the patient to a universal contrition by recalling to his mind the memory of all his sins.

There are also the sins, even grave ones, inadvertently omitted in Confession. Extreme Unction sponges away all the sins of our life. It is like a new Baptismal cleansing, which should leave us quite prepared for Paradise.

It happens often enough that the sick man, surprised by the sudden approach of death, can neither confess nor receive the holy Viaticum. It is of course quite lawful for the priest to give absolution to such a one, but it can be only *conditional* absolution, the efficacy of which is a matter of doubt to theologians. One only resource is left—Extreme Unction. Suppose that the unfortunate person is in a state of mortal sin. This Sacrament can, in such an extreme case, restore to him the life of grace, if he makes an interior act of repentence, even though that repentence be one of attrition only.

Such, then, are the benefits which this Sacrament of the sick can bring us. Such is the great means divinely prepared for the avoidance of Purgatory and the immediate gaining of Heaven. Happy those to whom God gives the grace of being able to receive this Sacrament with the full use of their senses! Happy those who, so far from entertaining a silly fear, ask for this heavenly remedy the moment they feel themselves in serious danger of death! Happy those, who, in this matter as in all others, practise the precept: " Love thy neighbour as thyself," and procure for their relations, friends and acquaintances, the divine gift, by calling the priest to the bedside in good time, instead of leaving it till the sacred rites are a blameworthy and undignified comedy of silence! This is the best way of obtaining for ourselves the grace of receiving this Sacrament, for God usually treats us as we have treated others. Turn a deaf ear, in such circumstances, to the voice of carnal love. " The sacraments have never caused a death. The sick person often reads in your eyes, your face, and even in the sound of your voice, the emotion which you fear to cause him. He watches for an opportunity of speaking; but he too fears to alarm your tender love, if he asks. This fatally discreet fencing goes on between you and him, which can only be terminated by a frank declaration of the danger which he runs—a declaration to which he will respond, perhaps, by a generous acceptance which will turn his agonized life towards God and eternity." (*Monsarbé*).

VII.—THE MASS OF THE LIVING

While one hears often of the Mass for the Dead, it is only of recent years that the term *Mass of the Living* has come into use. But it is the term only which is new, for the practice is as old as the Church.

What, then, do we mean by the words? Very simply, it is the Mass which is celebrated for the living, just as the Mass of the Dead is that celebrated for the dead. Many pious persons, in pursuance of the maxim—" Well ordered charity begins with oneself "—reserve a certain sum in their wills for the celebration of Masses for the repose of their souls: a wise and commendable precaution, which will insure a more prompt release from Purgatory. The question is, however, whether it would not have been more profitable for them to acquire, during their lives, the benefit of the Masses which they wish to have celebrated for them after death. There can be no doubt as to the answer, for it has been given by Pope Benedict XV. He writes: " Why do not the faithful, who wish to secure a rich and holy death, have Holy Mass celebrated for that intention? Applied to the living, the fruits of the Holy Sacrifice are much more copious than when applied to the dead. Their application to the former, supposing their intention and their dispositions to be as they ought, is *more direct, more certain and more abundant* than their application to the latter."

We shall expound these words of the Sovereign Pontiff.

Firstly, the application of the special fruit of the Holy Sacrifice to the living is made in a more direct manner. Why is this so? Because the Church has jurisdiction over the living, while she has not such jurisdiction over the dead. The priest, at the altar, is the representative of the Church. He acts in her name. If he celebrates Mass for a certain member of the Church Militant, the fruit of that Mass is *infallibly* applied by God to that person, if the latter does not oppose an obstacle to the reception of the divine benefits. In effect, God has left the faithful to the jurisdictional authority of the

Church, and He concerns Himself with keeping a check on their wills. The priest, minister and official representative of the Church, says to the Saviour: " I wish to apply the fruits of this Mass to this particular person." And God obeys the voice of the Minister of His Church. Infallibly and immediately, the fruit of that Mass goes to whom it is destined, just as a Sacrament, administered by the priest to a certain person, is really, infallibly and immediately conferred on that person and not on any other. With the dead, things are otherwise. On leaving this world, the soul falls into the hands of the living God, and must now deal solely with Him—with His justice, be it remembered, for the reign of His mercy is now over. God has, as it were, contracted no obligations towards the Church with regard to the dead. He has not bound Himself with a promise by which He must necessarily take account of the will of the Church, as regards particular souls of the dead. She cannot command Him in virtue of a power mercifully given to her, as she can in the case of the living faithful. As a humble suppliant, she prays for the particular soul of the dead. She offers the Holy Sacrifice for the soul, and begs the Saviour to deign mercifully to apply the fruits to that soul. God *habitually* takes cognisance of that desire and supplication of His Church, but we do not know in what measure. And, for just reasons known to Himself alone the fruits may be applied to another soul.

Let us consider the case of a rich man who has led a very lukewarm life, who has had little charity towards the poor, and has reasoned more or less like this: " Short of mortal sin, I intend to enjoy life. Of course, I shall expose myself to a long Purgatory by doing so, but I have a means by which I can shorten it. I shall provide for a large number of Masses to be said for me within a certain time after my death, and I shall thus look to my best interests." This risky calculation is in great danger of being upset by divine justice. Of course, the Church on earth will celebrate the Masses as required. The good curé of the parish will bless his late parishioner who has left such a good foundation. He will speak in his panegyric, of the spirit of faith of the deceased, who has been perhaps a little worldly during his life, but has looked to his best interests in the end—by supplementing the curé's meagre income. In spite of this praise rising from the earth, however, God may apply these Masses offered for the rich man to the benefit of some souls of the poor. The soul of the rich man, now wholly converted, will applaud this and say that he is getting his deserts from a just and good God.

Suppose, on the contrary, that the same rich man had caused the same number of Masses to be celebrated for himself during his life. The Church, having jurisdiction over him, could make a direct application of the special fruit of the Mass to him, and God would be infallibly bound by the wishes of the Church in the matter. This would be the source of many actual graces for the soul, urging it to repentance if in mortal sin, or to a better life if lukewarm: graces of preservation against the dangers of the world: choice graces, causing the soul to believe in the love of God and of its neighbour. With a greater goodwill, such a man might have won the grace of a complete change of heart, by having Masses thus offered while he still lived. Thus it is that the Church can apply the fruits of the Holy Sacrifice in a more direct and surer manner to the living than to the dead, because the Church has jurisdiction over the first, but not over the second. For the latter, she can use only the voice of supplication, or as theologians call it, the *voice of suffrage*.

It remains to establish that the fruits are also *more surely* applied to the living than to the dead. This is easily done.

The lot of the deceased for whom Mass is offered remains always more or less uncertain for the inhabitants of the earth. Has he been judged worthy to enter Heaven immediately? Then he has no need of the suffrages of earth. Has he been condemned to Hell? Our prayers and our good works are eternally useless to him. Is Purgatory his lot? Only then can he profit by the satisfactory fruit of the Mass in the measure willed by God and *if God wills its application to him*; for, as we have seen, God may apply it to another soul.

This uncertainty concerns ourselves as well as others, so that the Masses which we provide for ourselves in our wills, may be useless to us, for the reasons indicated. On the contrary, the Masses which we cause to be offered for ourselves, while living, cannot fail in their effect, if we do not culpably place an obstacle to it. If our intention is right and our dispositions good; if even, while we are in sin or in spiritual laxity, we desire to escape from this sad state and we solicit the grace of conversion or fervour, these graces will be surely given to us, because, as long as we are on earth, we can pass from sin to grace, from lukewarmness to fervour. The way is open to us to make progress in virtue, to acquire new merit, to augment our degree of glory in Heaven. We may do so for our friends, as well: for we cannot offer them a more precious gift than to have a Mass said for them, while yet they live. After death, it may perhaps be too late to pray for them. Let us try to make certain their and our own salvation, while there is yet time.

There are other causes of incertitude than those arising from the mysteries of the beyond. Can we be certain that our last testament will be scrupulously respected? One must reckon, too, with thieves, spoilers, and all the hazards that hedge around money.

Certainly, these considerations ought not to diminish our charity for our dear departed, nor prevent us from doing all in our power to help them, nor discourage us from founding Masses for their intention. But they should usefully clarify our devotion, and open our eyes to the needs of the living and to our own interests. We have in the Mass, a real and infallible means, if we place no voluntary obstacle, of assuring for ourselves a good and holy death. Let us profit ourselves and others of the living by it, while not forgetting the souls in Purgatory.

Finally, the participation in the fruits of the Mass is normally more abundant with the living than with the dead.

When the Mass is applied by a priest to one of the living who is in the state of grace and places no obstacles, by interior discordance, to the reception of the divine benefits, the Mass exercises freely in his regard its triple efficacy of *impetration, propitiation,* and *satisfaction.*

Its impetratory power is that which is based on the prayer of Jesus, the principal Priest, though the invisible One, of the sacrifice. Jesus offers to His Father, for us, His infinite merits, and asks that all things necessary to our salvation should be given to us, in consideration of these merits. Help of the temporal order, which aids to our salvation, enters into the object of that prayer, as well as the spiritual graces of sanctification. That invisible prayer of Christ, to which is joined the supplications of the Church Militant, in the person of the visible minister, is infallibly applied to the person for whom the Mass is specially offered, if his lack of proper dispositions does not place an obstacle to it. On the contrary, the impetratory power, properly so called, of the Mass for the dead, is very difficult to define. The inhabitants of Purgatory can no longer receive graces of sanctification because they are incapable of all spiritual progress, and benefits of the temporal order are useless to them. One thing only closes Heaven to them: the temporal punishment due to their sins. Does the Mass obtain for them *directly*, by way of simple request, the diminution of that punishment? There are theologians who deny this, and say that such impetration can only be *indirect*. In consideration of the Sacrifice offered for a soul in Purgatory, God inspired the living to pray and to offer satisfactions and indulgences for the help and the deliverance of that soul. In every way, as regards its power of impetration, the Mass is much more abundant in its fruits for the living than for the dead.

The living only can profit by its propitatory power. This power is exercised towards the remission of mortal and venial sin, not by the way of immediate absolution, as in the Sacrament of Penance, but by means of the graces of conversion, of contrition and of perfect charity, which God gives to sinners in consideration of the merits and the satisfactions of Our Saviour. The souls in Purgatory cannot sin. The venial sins which have disfigured them at the moment of death, have been wiped away by the intense contrition which the first sight of God's holiness caused in them. There remains only the temporal punishment due to them, and to the others, which have been forgiven, as to their guilt, while they were still on earth. Happy souls who cannot offend God! They certainly do not regret their inability to participate in the propitatory fruit of the Mass. But for us, poor sinners still on our journey to eternity and uncertain of reaching our goal, this propitiatory fruit is an inestimable prize.

As regards the *satisfactory* power of the Mass, which has reference to the temporal punishment due to sin, it would seem, at first sight, that the souls in Purgatory are in a state in which they can profit by it more fully and more surely than the living. They are, indeed, always in the required dispositions for assuring the effect of this satisfaction. The faithful on earth can render it useless by their attachment to sin : but, so far from opposing the least obstacle to the payment of their debts, the souls in Purgatory sigh ardently for their deliverance. It is thus that they who are in mortal sin cannot benefit by the satisfactory fruit, for the punishment due to sin cannot be remitted before the guilt of the sin is forgiven. From this point of view, the situation of the souls in Purgatory is incontestably superior to that of the living faithful. But from another point of view, the advantage is reversed. Sin and dispositions being equal, the punishment demanded by divine justice is greater for the dead than for the living. It must not be forgotten that the present life is the reign of mercy, and beyond the grave is the reign of justice. It is easier for us to pay our debts here below than in the next life. A single Mass offered for us while we live on earth can suffice to discharge our debt, if it is small. After death, many Masses may not suffice, perhaps. We add that *perhaps*, because our ignorance of the divine scale in the next life, is absolute. All that we know is that divine justice is less exacting *before* than *after* death.

We conclude from all this, that we have in the Mass an inexhaustible source of all graces and benefits ; that in offering it for ourselves or for our earthly friends, not only are we using a very efficacious means of avoiding, or at least shortening our Purgatory and theirs, but we are also enriching ourselves and them with the graces of sanctification, which, if we use them properly, will augment our degree of glory in Heaven. What must *not* be concluded from all this, however, is that we should diminish our liberality towards the dead, and have less Masses celebrated for them, and more for ourselves. It would be cruel to turn to the detriment of the souls in Purgatory, this very true doctrine of the superiority of the Mass of the living over that of the dead. We must not forget that the act of fraternal charity which we accomplish in having a Mass celebrated for the dead, renders us very agreeable to God, augments our merit before Him, draws His mercy on us and serves to cover the multitude of our sins and our debts. There is an equitable way of using the doctrine in question: it is simply to enlarge the domain of our charity, by thinking of the living, and of ourselves especially, while not forgetting our dear deceased. To have a Mass celebrated, from time to time, for the special intention of our sanctification and perseverance in grace, instead of postponing the Masses till after our death, is to take a clearer view of our own best interests. The precaution we show in providing for Masses for ourselves after death, is certainly not blameworthy: but it would be a miscalculation to give it the preference over the more sure and more efficacious practice which the theology of the Mass of the living reveals to us. Like charity towards the neighbour, the love we bear to ourselves ought to be enlightened. When the choice is between the good and the better, ought we not choose the better?

VIII.—The Religious Life

An excellent means of attaining salvation and of anticipating one's Purgatory, is to practise the Evangelical Counsels, or in other words, to embrace the religious life, the life of perfection. "If thou wouldst be perfect," says Christ, "go, sell all that thou possessest and give to the poor, and thou shalt have treasure in Heaven; then come, follow me." ... "Amen I say unto you, that whosoever shall leave house, or brethren, or sisters, or father, or mother, or wife, or children, or lands *for my sake*, shall receive a hundredfold and shall possess life everlasting." (*Mat.*, xix, 21, 29). These texts do not refer to Purgatory, but it is evident that Purgatory, was not made for the perfect. The perfect—meaning those who have followed the counsels just quoted, by living a life of Poverty, Chastity and Obedience, and persevering therein till death—need have no fear of Purgatory. They are living images of the Son of God and their life is fully conformed to His. Nothing can prevent their entrance into Heaven.

You will answer, perhaps, that before embracing such a life, a person may have committed grave faults—even crimes: for there are always the workers who come at the eleventh hour. Will not a past like that merit some sojourn in Purgatory. The answer to this is, that according to the opinion of theologians, the religious Profession, by which a soul devotes itself entirely to the service of God, is a perfect holocaust, and is every bit as efficacious as Baptism for the cleansing of all sin and of the debt of sin. It is the equivalent of an act of most perfect charity, which entirely purifies the soul of the professed and gives to it its first innocence. We take for granted, of course, that he who consecrates himself to the Lord, does so with interior dispositions which are in harmony with the sublime act of which the ceremony is the exterior manifestation. If such is the case, the religious need have no fears concerning the past. The day of his profession marks the beginning of a totally new life. As on the day of his Baptism, Heaven shines around him, and were he to die on that day, Heaven would be immediately opened to him.

Begun with an act of perfect charity, the whole life of a religious, truly faithful to the spirit of his vocation and to the new obligations which he has contracted, is a continuous act of perfect charity. Having given himself wholly to God, he continues that giving at every moment of his life. His life of charity grows as from its dawn to the fullness of its noon.

. . .

But where is such an ideal religious to be found? "Where is the valiant woman?" says the Wise Man. "Her price is above that of pearls." The same can be asked of the perfect religious. Where shall we see the marvel? Or how may we convince ourselves that such a one, who has sinned in Adam like all his kind, can maintain himself in sublime heights without ever stumbling?

Let us agree that sin—and even mortal sin sometimes—can penetrate the cloister. But let us remember, too, that in the religious life, it is more difficult to sin than in the world; that one repents more easily; that one can do penance more efficaciously; that one dies with greater serenity; that one dies with the hope of more speedy succour.

In the convent, one sins with greater difficulty, because the occasions of sin, which abound in the world, are very rare. The whole at the religious life is planned to turn the soul to God, to unite it to Him, and to detach it from the earth. The three vows of Poverty, Chastity and Obedience cut the three great cables which prevent our frail skiff from setting sail on the sea of perfection. If some smaller ties remain, they will be cut through in time, and superiors and brethren will aid in this, often without sparing us. For in the relgious life, one is never alone. Our brethren's eyes are always on us. What a safeguard this can be!

In the convent, one rises more promptly after a fall, for one must return to the soul of one's religious family or become a monster. Everything preaches tears and repentence and the *Miserere*. The means of sanctification are immediately at one's hand. A religious receives more graces in a day than many of the faithful in a whole year.

In the convent, we have said, one does more efficacious penance. The observance of his Rule alone is for the religious a daily penance, a penance hard on nature, which regulates all activity from morning till night and brings all the virtues into active play. That severe legislator of the beatification and canonization of the servants of God, Pope Benedict XIV, said: "Give me a religious who has always faithfully observed his Rule, and I shall canonize him immediately." And St. John Berchmans wrote these words in his notebook of resolutions: "My great penance will be the common life." In this crucible of the common life, of the daily penance, the soul purifies itself easily of light faults, of which even the most fervent are guilty, and it has an abundance with which to pay its little debts to divine justice.

As a religious, one dies with greater serenity. The religious soul is detached from all earthly things and has its treasure in Heaven. Death is more a gain than a loss to it, so that many die even in transports of joy. Their joy, at this hour, is in proportion to the fervour of their life. They see that the little pains of this life, are not worthy to be compared with the weight of glory to come. God is already in their hearts, and in a few moments the glory of Heaven will open on their eyes. The founder of La Trappe has written: "The pain of living without pleasure is worth the pleasure of dying without pain." The religious dies with full confidence in Him who said: "He that believeth in me, although he be dead, shall live; and whosoever liveth and believeth in me shall not die forever."

But suppose that the religious departs from this life with

serious debts to the justice of God, Who is of course much more exacting where grace has more plentifully abounded. See the advantage of the religious life even after death. That religious is one of a numerous family of brethren, who will all aid him by their prayers, their sacrifices, their suffrages of all kinds. It is the custom for all the priests of the same Order, of the same Congregation, or of the same Province to offer a Mass for the deceased relgious; while the others recite offices and receive Holy Communion for his intentions. All that supplication follows immediately on the death of the religious. While remembering the impenetrable secrets of God, we may yet have excellent reasons for believing that the good religious —we do not speak of the bad or the doubtful—will not remain long in Purgatory. We have established, therefore, that one of the great means of avoiding Purgatory or almost doing so, is to become a religious and to observe faithfully to the end, all the obligations of that state.

It is clear that this means cannot be employed by all. But the proverb has it that the habit does not make the monk. One can wear the heart of a monk beneath fashionable trappings, as witness the multitude of tertiaries of all Orders, who vie with the religious in fervour. On the day of judgment, many of the faithful living in the world, will put the lukewarm and lazy religious to the blush. They will not have taken a vow of Poverty, but they will have practised poverty of spirit —the first of the Beatitudes to which Heaven is promised. They will not have taken a vow of Chastity, but they will have observed, with a fidelity passing over into heroism, the sacred laws of marriage and of conjugal chastity. They shall have used this world as though they used it not *for the shape of this world passeth* (1 *Cor.*, vii, 31), and their heart shall have remained pure, and they shall see God. They will not have made a vow of Obedience, but they will have had a constant care to do in all things the Will of God, and adore His designs in trial and suffering. These, of course, will not have the special merit attached to the religious life, but these religious in spirit can make their Purgatory in this world, and they will be placed higher in Heaven, than the lukewarm and negligent religious; for God knows no caste, and makes no exception of persons.

CHAPTER THE THIRD

HOLY DISPOSITIONS AND SALUTARY PRACTICES

APART FROM THE SACRAMENTAL or quasi-sacramental means of avoiding Purgatory, there are other means which consist of virtuous dispositions, or in practices which are particularly efficacious in helping us to acquire a perfect purity of conscience and in delivering us from the debt of sin. Many of these means are clearly indicated in Holy Writ. We shall treat of a few.

I.—THE SPIRIT OF PENANCE

To cultivate in oneself a spirit of penance is one of the surest ways of avoiding Purgatory.

To define the spirit of penance, we must first be clear on what penance itself means. It is a hard word to our ears: its content is rigorous fasts, bloody disciplines, hairshirts, ashes, chains—and in thinking of these, we tend to forget that penance is above all an interior virtue, directly pertaining to the cardinal virtue of justice, and inseparable from the love of God.

The virtue requires that one have committed at least one actual sin. In his original innocence, Adam had not the virtue of penance. The good angels, who never committed a sin, have no need of penance. Our Saviour and the Blessed Virgin could not be ranked among the penitents. The same must be said of infants who have not yet attained to the use of reason, for they are not responsible for the stain of original sin with which they were born. Original sin is our sad heritage from Adam. The virtue of penance and the act itself of repenting cannot enter the soul till after the first actual sin, mortal or venial, has been committed.

Would to Heaven that we had no need of the virtue of penance, which we all do so need. Penance is an essentially human virtue. Both St. John the Baptist and Our Saviour began their preaching with the words: " Do penance, for the kingdom of God is at hand," and Our Saviour added : " Unless you do penance, you shall all likewise perish." And St. John the Evangelist wrote : " If any man believe himself to be without sin, he deceives himself, and the truth is not in him."

Penance consists essentially in three acts, which we express when we make an act of contrition. We must first detest sin because it is an offence against the all-good and all-amiable God. That is contrition properly so called, the true movement of conversion by which we change our interior dispositions. We have loved that which displeased God, and by penance we renounce it. Were it in our power, we would annihilate the evil we have done. We efface the past sin as much as we are able ; we fling it towards nothingness with all the force of our will. What wonder, then, if the all good and all-merciful God effaces that sin as the sun does the clouds ? (*Is.*, xliv, 22).

It is an excellent thing to detest sin, and to put it from us with all the face of our will. But that alone does not suffice. The sin has had its effects : it has left traces of its passing. Like a deadly missile, it has been directed against God Himself. It constitutes a full insult, and reparation is due for all insult. Penance, the daughter of justice, is not confined to the mere detestation of sin, and its rejection. It wishes also to destroy the evil effects of sin. Hence the sincere desire to make satisfaction to God and to men ; hence the serious efforts to produce those " fruits worthy of penance," which the holy Precursor recommended to the multitudes on the banks of the Jordan.

Nor is that yet all. If the soul is sincere, penance implies also the firm resolve not to sin again. If one truly detests sin, how can one retain the intention of sinning again ? The unworthy penitent can deceive the priest by a seeming act of contrition, but he cannot deceive God, to Whom all things are open.

Such, then, is true penance. Those frightening practices which the word, penance, brings to the imagination, are unworthy of the name, if they are not inspired by the triple interior sentiment of contrition which we have outlined.

• • •

Having clarified the meaning of penance, it is easy now to speak of the spirit of penance. Every virtue worthy of the name has its own spirit. The word *spirit* means *breath*. The spirit of a virtue is that which the virtue breathes in the ear of the heart. As a light breeze bends the flower, so the spirit of a virtue inclines the will to the performance of acts which are proper to that virtue. The spirit of penance inclines us to contrition, to satisfaction and to a purpose of amendment. When that breath moves habitually in the soul, and the soul bends spontaneously to its sweet motion, that soul can be said to have the spirit of penance.

Whence is that breath? It comes, without doubt, from justice, of which penance is an authentic daughter; but it comes above all from charity. It is a breath that is redolent of noon and of the Holy Spirit. And where shall we find the spirit of penance at its highest? We find it in the souls of those great servants of God, who were all heroes of penance, each in his own manner and according as the Holy Ghost inspired him. The reason is not far to seek. Detestation of sin is proportionate to the love which one bears to God, and the measure in which one's knowledge of the majesty of the Person offended and of His infinite amiability grows in the soul will augment the vehemence of one's desire to repair one's sins. The tenacity of the resolution to avoid sin will be measured by the strength of the chain which attaches us in love to God. This is the secret of the saints' penance, and of the hatred they bear to sin and the trappings of sin. Hence the terrible vengeance which they take on themselves for their least faults, and that ardour for penance which has sometimes to be moderated by the confessor. Hence, too, that constant vigilance, accompanied by extreme distrust of self and profound humility, which cause them to flee the least occasion of sin. This is certainly no servile fear of Hell or of Purgatory, but divine charity and that gift of filial fear, which is the seventh of the gifts of the Holy Spirit.

We have seen the admirable effects of the spirit of penance in the souls of the saints. With us, in whom the love of God is still feeble, the same spirit will not show itself by heroic deeds; but, if it is really there, it will not remain inactive. Every spirit tends to breathe, every habit to pass into act.

The spirit of penance ought to remain in every Christian soul until the last breath of life. St. Augustine used to say that even those who have no crime with which to reproach themselves, should take care to leave this world with sentiments of true penance; and St. Paul wrote: " It is little that I am judged by you or by any human tribunal; for though I should be guiltless of anything, yet should I not by this be justified" (I *Cor.*, iv, 3-4). There may come a time when, by reason of age or infirmity, one may not be capable of doing *penances;* but one is never dispensed from the *virtue of penance* or from the *spirit of penance.*

Practically, the spirit of penance can be developed in every Christian by the following acts:

1° THE CONSTANT REMEMBRANCE OF PAST SINS

When God, in His mercy, has pardoned our sins in Confession and our souls have become joyful and free, we are inclined to forget the past, and soon begin to consider ourselves as little saints. This is not the effect of the spirit of penance, The soul that is penetrated with this spirit, says on the contrary: " Wash me yet more from my iniquities "—asking again and again for a fresh pardon, with growing repentance and warmer tears. It is certainly an excellent habit to accuse oneself again in Confession of sins already confessed, in general, however, and with a prudent care against arousing dangerous memories. By doing so, one can guard against null, and even sacrilegious Confessions, and also relieve the priest from the doubts that may arise when a penitent has only a swirl of venial sins and imperfections of which to accuse himself: which accusation often savours of pure routine.

2° FLIGHT FROM THE OCCASIONS OF SIN

This flight is the touchstone of true repentance, and a fortiori of the spirit of penance; for how could the spirit of penance exist when, with lightheartedness and with at least a confused knowledge of the danger, one exposes oneself to the danger of committing the sin again. Whoever is influenced by the spirit of penance has a very clear knowledge of his fragility. He knows that our enemies are stronger than us and that God does not aid the foolhardy, who run into danger by ignoring the requirements of elementary prudence. The foolhardy have already gone over to the enemy, in their hearts.

3° *The accomplishment of the penances prescribed by the Church :* salutary penances, which are of a light kind, except for the long fast of Lent. From these, our state of health or our duties may dispense us at times. But neither our state of health nor our duties can ever dispense us from the spirit of penance. When a person with this spirit finds himself unable to fast, he will discover other means of doing penance. If he cannot do all the fasting, he will do some of it. There are hundreds of ways by which he can substitute for his inability to fast.

4° *The joyful, or at least the calm and resigned acceptation of the penances of the good God*—the pains of life, the crosses of Providence, the daily cross we must shoulder if we are to follow Christ. The daily cross, the dull routine of duty—that is the penance that is nearest to our hand, and which is all the harder for having nothing of heroic glamour about it.

5° *Immediate detestation of sin committed and promptitude in confessing it.* Alas, there are none free from being surprised into sinning. It may happen that even a person who has lived for many years in a spirit of penance may fall into a fault more or less grave. But the spirit of penance immediately breathes its detestation of the sin, and hastens to free the soul by a prompt Confession. Sin and the spirit of penance cannot live long together, for one expels the other.

. . .

At first sight, this programme might seem calculated to keep the soul in a state of continual sorrow, and to kill all joy. In reality, this is not so. The spirit of penance is the brother of that solid Christian joy which is born of the love of God, and to which St. Paul gives the second place in his list of the gifts of the Holy Spirit. It is the same Holy Spirit, indeed, who produces the sorrow according to God (II *Cor.*, vii, 10), which is the source of the spirit of penance and of the joy according to God—the fruit of charity. The Church knows well how to unite the tears of penance with the sweetness of holy joy, just as in the middle of Advent she places *Gaudete*

Sunday, and *Laetare* Sunday in the middle of Lent. She is ever mindful of the third beatitude : " Blessed are they who weep, for they shall have their consolation " (*Matt.*, v, 5), and she has composed a special prayer asking for the gift of holy tears. A perfect spirit of penance is the source of these tears. Mingling with tears of love, they constitute the beatitude of penitents and exiles—the beatitude proper to this valley of tears.

"Among all those who weep," says Bossuet, "there are none who will be more quickly consoled than they who weep for their sins. In all other sorrows, tears are merely an added evil; sin is the only evil which one can heal with tears ... But what shall we say of those who weep with love and tenderness? Happy are they—a thousand times happy! Their heart melts within them, as the Scripture says, and seems as it would flow through their eyes. Who will explain to me the cause of these tears? They who have experienced them often cannot explain what it is that so touches them. Sometimes, the goodness of a Father; sometimes, the condescension of a King; sometimes, the absence of a spouse; sometimes, the darkness which His sensible withdrawal causes, and sometimes the joy of His voice when He calls His spouse; but, more often than not, the cause remains obscure " (*Med. sur Evan.*, iv° *jour.*).

The penitent psalmist knew that the tears of penance are united to the holy joy of love; and the Apostle certainly did not wish to kill the spirit of penance in souls when he called unto all Christians: " Rejoice in the Lord always; again I say it, rejoice. That your sweetness may be known to all men: the Lord is nigh " (*Phil.*, iv, 4-6).

. . .

True joy, the joy that is according to God, the beatitude of blessed tears, is not the only effect of the spirit of penance. It produces other marvellous fruits in the soul which it possesses.

First of all, humility, true and sincere: humility before God and men. The true penitent, *having his sin always before him,* has no difficulty in recognising his misery, for there is no trace of the proud and arrogant pharisee in him. He prefers himself to nobody, and places himself last of all. The hardness of pride can find no place in the penitent soul. The tears of penance have softened it to wax, on which the Holy Spirit can breathe.

Sweetness and benevolence towards others are inseparable from true humility. The penitent soul is sweet to persons, sweet to things. It is never angry, never impatient, bears with all. It is very happy to find occasions of satisfying for sin, because it knows its own demerits. In short, there is nothing so calculated to transform a soul and to give it the character of Jesus, than the spirit of penance. Jesus has described Himself as meek and humble of heart. The penitent soul has this character. It is stamped on the soul of every saint.

With the virtues we have named, there is allied a certain serene and sweet gravity—that supernatural gravity which reveals the presence of God and has its source in an intimate and habitual commerce with Him. In detaching itself from sin, the penitent soul has severed itself from the world and its vanities, and therefore its gaze is fixed more on Heaven than on earth. It has had a glimpse of the beauty of God, and it is filled with home-sickness for Heaven. It groans in exile, and realises that beautiful thought of St. Augustine: " He who does not groan as an exile, will not rejoice as a citizen." The spirit of penance matures a man and gives him the true sense of life. It breathes into his soul those austere and salutary thoughts and sentiments which one associates with a visit to a graveyard.

How can a complete idea be given of a penitent soul ? It is like an apparition on earth of an inhabitant of Purgatory. Consider the attitude, the conduct and the sentiments of a soul in Purgatory. There, the spirit of penance flourishes and is found in its full purity. Supreme detestation of all sin, warm tears of love-inspired repentance, ardent desire to satisfy divine justice by joyful acceptance of awful suffering, perfect humility without a grain of hardness or pride—such are the dispositions of Purgatory.

But earth can afford us perfect examples of the spirit of penance. There was David, the author of the canticle of repentance ; there was Magdalene, whose tears washed the feet of the Saviour ; and are we not told that Peter's ceaseless tears wore furrows in his cheeks? Read the "Confessions" of St. Augustine—the saint who used to repeat: "Even if your conscience reproaches you not, take care that you do not leave this world without striking your breast."

. . .

We have not yet shown that the spirit of penance is an excellent means of avoiding Purgatory: but surely there is no need to do so. The opposition between the spirit of penance and the 'raison d'être' of Purgatory is full and complete. Why does one go to Purgatory? Because there are venial sins unrepented of, or because one has not sufficiently discharged one's debt of temporal punishment, or for both reasons. Now, consider in the first place, that venial sin cannot remain in a soul that has the spirit of penance. It may indeed make a surprise entry into such a soul: but it will be immediately effaced by the tears of penance which ceaselessly flow. As regards the debt of sin, habitual perfect contrition is a sacrifice of agreeable sweetness before God, for "a contrite and humble heart he will not despise" (*Ps.* l, 19). Sometimes, the vehemence of repentance suffices alone for the debt of the greatest sins, as we gather from Christ's words to the penitent thief. If to interior repentance, you join fruits of penance which are indeed but the proper movement and natural tendency of the spirit of penance—fruits, be it remembered, which God estimates less by quantity than by the spirit of love which inspires them—it is a clear conclusion that a soul, in which this spirit dwells, is assured of a holy and a happy death. Once delivered from the shackles of the body, its flight to Heaven will be a straight one.

The spirit of penance is, therefore, a very desirable thing. It is a marvellous effect of the grace of God which transforms souls. We must ask it " with confidence and without fear from the Lord, who gives directly to all and refuses none " (*Jas.*, I, 5), for it is one of that category of spiritual and supernatural goods, necessary to salvation, which God does not refuse to those that ask with insistence. The spirit of penance, or of compunction as the ancient monks called it, is very rare to-day. Nevertheless, it makes an integral part of the Christian spirit, and the word of the Saviour remains:

"I say unto you: unless you do penance, you shall all likewise perish."

II.—The Loving Acceptance of an Earthly Purgatory and of Death

Because we are all sinners, we have need of purification; we have all debts to divine justice which must be discharged in this world or in the next. Most of us discharge a part on earth, and the rest in Purgatory, thereby doing a double Purgatory. But in the divine plan, Purgatory on earth ought to suffice for our perfect purification. Our Saviour has given us, in His Church, the means by the use of which we can attain to Heaven immediately after our death, and divine Providence aids us towards this by putting trials and sufferings in our way. The Holy Trinity, living in the just soul as in a temple, the object of knowledge and love, does not remain inactive, but sweetly and gently pursues the work of transforming us into the divine. Happy those who do not hinder this work! Sacrifices are required of them, for the transforming of a son of Adam into the divine, the stripping off of the old man (as St. Paul put it), cannot be done without suffering. Holy Scripture teaches this truth in various ways. Our Saviour tells us the Heavenly Father is the husbandman of the mystic vine which is the Christ, and of which we are the branches: "Every branch that bears fruit, he will prune it, that it may bring forth more fruit" (*John* xv, 2). These curbings on the natural are painful. St. Paul puts it in another way: "For whom the Lord loveth, he chastiseth; and he scourgeth every son whom he receiveth. Persevere under discipline. God dealeth with you as with his sons; for what son is there whom the father doth not correct? But if you be without chastisement, whereof all are made partakers, then are you bastards and not sons. Moreover, we have had fathers of our flesh, for instructions, and we reverenced them: shall we not much more obey the Father of spirits, and live? And they indeed for a few days, according to their pleasure, instructed us: but he, for our profit, that we might receive his sanctification. Now all chastisement for the present indeed seemeth not to bring with it joy, but sorrow; but afterwards, it will yield to them that are exercised by it, the most peaceable fruit of justice" (*Heb.* 12, 6-11).

How great soever our pride would make us, we are but little children as regards the supernatural life. Christ has indicated this expressly: " I say unto you in truth: whosoever shall not receive the Kingdom of Heaven as a little child shall not enter therein." We must make ourselves little children under the hand of God the Father, and receive His Paternal corrections with a filial heart and with the spirit of a child.

If the Father prunes, chastises, corrects, the only Son made man presents Himself to us as the model of the life we ought to lead. He is the Way Who indicates the strait way that leads to life: " I have given you an example, that as I have done unto you, so do you also." He is the Truth Who instructs and illumines us: " He who follows me does not walk in darkness, but has the light of life." He is not only the light of life, but Life itself; for Christ is the true Life, Who comes to communicate Himself to us through the Blessed Eucharist: " As I live by the Father, so he that eateth me, the same also shall live by me." To be saved, we must model ourselves upon Christ, " that he may be the first-born of many brethren " (*Rom.*, viii, 29).

The rôle of the Holy Spirit is like that of a mother. He is the Paraclete, that is to say the Intercessor and the Consoler : " Likewise the spirit also helpeth our infirmity. For we know not what we should pray for as we ought; but the Spirit himself asketh for us with unspeakable groanings. And he that searcheth the hearts, knoweth what the spirit desireth ; for he asketh for the saints according to God " (*Rom.*, viii, 26-27). By the sweet unction of His presence, He consoles us in our childish sufferings. He helps us to endure the hardships of paternal correction, and inspires us to kiss the hand that strikes us for our good.

Thus, then, is the education of a child of God, of a future citizen of Heaven, effected on earth. Those who docily submit themselves to this regime can have the assured hope of being received without delay into the paternal house, when the end of their Purgatory on earth shall have come.

* * *

This Purgatory is not necessarily the same for all, even though there is a fund of suffering common to all. This fund is constituted by the three great penances inposed by God on man after his sin : the passibility of the body, which suffers from heat and cold, from hunger and thirst, and the thousand natural shocks that flesh is heir to ; hard and painful work, which bathes the brow in sweat or torments the brain ; death, finally, the penance of penances which none can escape. There are those who avoid the first in great measure ; there are the great number of those who lazily avoid the second ; but all must endure the third. It is the debt of nature which must be paid and which no hand can cancel.

Apart from this common lot of suffering, there are the providential crosses which the Lord has lovingly measured to each of us. For some, it is the crucible of interior suffering, of those mysterious and terrible sufferings through which the majority of the great servants of God have passed, and which are known as mystical trials. For others, it is the burden and the trammel of affairs, from which they cannot escape because they are part and parcel of their duty in life. This man has lost a loved one : this other has met with financial ruin ; a third has had his health shattered for life. There are greater crosses and small crosses, and the small cross may cause great suffering to him who meets it, than does the great cross which is measured to the shoulders of one of God's heroes. And the hero, who bears the heavy cross, may come to his knees under the light one. The all-good Father Who is in Heaven, does well that which He does. He knows each of His children, and He prepares for each, the cross which best suits him. The important thing is for each to take up his cross and follow Christ, because " it is through many tribulations that we must enter into the kingdom of God " (*Acts*, xiv, 21). If, at our death, we find ourselves condemned to Purgatory, it will be because we did not know how to profit by a purgatory on earth.

. . .

We have just said that death is the great penance imposed by God on man because of sin ; " the wages of sin is death," says St. Paul. It is a terrible penance from which our whole being shrinks, but from which there is no shrinking. If we accept it in a spirit of repentance and reparation, at the very moment when it comes upon us, it can take the place of all the other penances which we could have accomplished and which we neglected ; of all the trials which we have badly borne ; of all the Providential crosses against which we have chafed. In imitation of the penitent thief, we might make our deathbed prayer, and speak to God somewhat like this : " The law which Thou hast imposed is just. Death, which is already my heritage as a son of Adam, is due to me on account of my personal sins. I accept it with all my heart to repair the outrages to Thy divine majesty, I accept it to honour Thy justice and Thy holiness. Lord, have mercy on me, according to Thy great mercy ! "

Death can be viewed from another angle. It can be made into a sacrifice of love, in thanksgiving for the love with which Christ has first loved us. " Lord," we might say, " Thou Thyself hast passed by the way of death. Thou didst die for love of us, that we might learn to die for love of Thee. One dies for love of Thee when one accepts death in order to accomplish Thy Holy Will. Lord, for Thy Will, I accept my death."

Thus offered, as a sacrifice of love, death may efface all sin and all the debt of sin, for it is an act of perfect charity which must surely open Heaven to us. If this sacrifice of love is possible when death is already pressing our eyelids, how much more is it both possible and doubly meritorious, when it is made in full health and in full liberty, by offering one's life as a holocaust for the triumph of a noble cause. Thus, the missionary who exposes himself to death to extend the Kingdom of God on earth ; thus, too, the Christian soldier who dies to defend his country from unjust aggression and to guard the sacred patrimony of the Catholic Faith.

III.—To Do All for Love

Being a simple substance, the human soul tends naturally to simplicity, to unity. In the order of knowledge, it seeks instinctively to bring back all things to one first principle, which gives the key to all the rest. In the order of virtue and piety, it also seeks for unity. Faced with a multitude of duties, of precepts, of practices, it seeks to discover the secret that simplifies all. It has a horror of the multiplied and the complicated, which confuses it. It seeks the one thing necessary, in which it will find its repose. That one thing necessary is God Himself and His love, because the human soul is made for God and can find its rest in Him alone. Our Saviour Himself, who knows what is in man, since He created Him, alluded once to that innate tendency of the human soul towards unity, when He said to Martha : " Martha, Martha, thou art troubled and art busy about many things, but one thing only is necessary " (*Luke*, x, 42).

Pious souls, animated by a perfect good will to serve God, but tormented and confused by a multitude of precepts, of means of sanctification, of pious practices, must be reminded that one thing only is necessary in matters of piety, of spirituality, of perfection : the practice of the first and the greatest of the Commandments, which directs that we must love the Lord our God with our whole heart and with our whole soul, and with all our strength and with all our mind (*Luke*, x, 27). Life, therefore, can be simplified, by carrying all things back to the love of God, by informing and penetrating with this love all the other precepts and counsels. In a word, it is possible to make of life a continual exercise of the love of God.

This is not a high mystical secret reserved to certain of the spiritually initiated. It is a very simple truth, a fundamental and elementary principle of the spiritual life, since it concerns the first Commandment of God. Why, then, is it forgotten in practice ? But it is a fact of daily experience that one is most inclined to lose sight of elementary and fundamental principles. There must be a constant hearkening back to this truth, if one is to avoid taking a wrong road, or a road which, though very laborious, is more or less a dead end.

To do all for the love of God : to seek to please Him in all : what could be easier or sweeter to the heart ? A great and noble love is necessary to the human soul to energize it. Now, the greatest and most noble love, which cannot deceive and which has power to fill the great void of our longing is the love of the Infinite, the love of the Holy Trinity, One God in Three Divine Persons. To this unique and primary love, all other loves ought to be subordinated, and that subordination is easy and natural, when one truly loves God, when one is possessed of a passionate desire to please Him always and before all. It is for this reason that Christ says that His yoke is sweet and His burden light, for the love of Christ makes all things sweet and light. The Beloved Disciple, St. John, wrote : mandata ejus gravia non sunt (1. *John*, v, 3). Why, then, do some find them insupportable ? Because they are lacking in the love of God. And why are they so lacking ? Because they will not use the means of cultivating that love : to renounce sin and to pray for the gift of love. God commands us to love, and He does not command the impossible. He cannot, therefore, refuse the love we ask. " The love of God," says St. Paul, " is spread abroad in our hearts by the Holy Spirit which has been given to us " at Baptism, and which returns to us through the Sacrament of Penance when we have had the misfortune to lose the Divine Presence.

That all the commandments and precepts may be reduced to this master one is clearly taught by Christ. " Master," the doctor of the Law said to Him—" Master, which is the great commandment of the Law ? Jesus answered him : Thou shalt love the Lord thy God with thy whole heart and with thy whole soul and with all thy mind : this is the first and the greatest commandment. The second is like unto it : Thou shalt love thy neighbour as thyself. To these two commandments the whole law and the prophets can be reduced " (*Matt.*, xxii, 35-40 ; *Luk.* 20, 41-45 ; *Mk.*, xii, 28-38). Christ spoke of a second commandment, but He hastened to add that it was like unto the first, that it reduced in practice to the first and was inseparable from it. For we love our neighbour because God has willed and commanded it. When one truly loves a person, one loves also the friends of that person. Our neighbour has an equal title with ours, to be called the child of God. Love must exist between the children of the same father.

Listen to St. Paul's paean on charity : " Charity is patient, is kind ; charity envieth not, dealeth not perversely ; is not puffed up ; is not ambitious, seeketh not her own, is not provoked to anger, thinketh no evil ; rejoiceth not in iniquity, but rejoiceth with the truth ; beareth all things, hopeth all things, endureth all things" (1, *Cor.*, 13, 4-7).

"Whether you eat or drink," the same Apostle says, "or whatever else you do, do all to the glory of God." This is to make the first commandment enter into daily life: into the accomplishment of all the other commandments, into the practice of all the virtues; in short, it is the easy means of simplifying the religious life and of giving it a unity. It is, also, of all ways the most direct way of arriving immediately to Heaven without having to pass through Purgatory.

This practice makes easy the accomplishment of all Christian morality, even when most austere. Love banishes pain, St. Augustine says, or if the pain persists, it is softened by love. The true love of God gives a ten-fold energy to the soul in face of a duty to be performed. Because so many neglect this motive of love, because they do not see duty from love's angle, therefore are so many lukewarm and remiss in the service of God.

The habit of doing all for love places the soul in a state which is a kind of moral impossibility of committing mortal sin and even deliberate venial sin, for how could such a soul lightheartedly commit even a venial sin, when it truly loves God and seeks to please Him in all things. Hence, St. John in his first Epistle, writes: "Whosoever abideth in him, sinneth not; and whosoever sinneth, hath not seen him nor known him. He that commiteth sin is of the devil: for the devil sinneth from the beginning. For this purpose, the son of God appeared, that he might destroy the works of the devil. Whosoever is born of God, commiteth not sin: for his seed abideth in him, and he cannot sin, because he is born of God. In this, the children of God are manifest, and the children of the devil" (1 *John*, iii, 6, 8-10).

It is evident that, so long as we are in this mortal flesh, we will be guilty of certain faults of surprise, certain indeliberate venial sins. But in such a soul as that of which we speak, these will soon be burned up in the warm flame of love which continually fills it. Bitterly regretted and repaired, almost as soon as committed, these faults leave no trace on the soul and are often the occasion of a more fervent love.

It is hard to see how a soul which lives continually in the love of God, need have any fear of Purgatory, above all of a long Purgatory. There is, of course, the question of the temporal punishment due to all sin, however light : but a sane theology teaches us that the love of God, when it is perfect and intense, can suffice to wipe out this temporal punishment. Love feeds and grows on acts of love. Our charity, ceaselessly fed by new acts of charity, can rise to such a pitch of intensity that it takes the place of Purgatory, and prepares the soul for the immediate vision of God.

IV.—The Remission of Debts

Purgatory can be compared to a debt which we owe to divine justice for our sins. Now, Our Saviour, in the Gospels, has taken care to show us the means of being delivered from our debt to the Heavenly Father. Since our debt accumulated daily, He thought it necessary to expressly recall that means in His own Prayer, the ' Pater Noster ' : " Forgive us our trespasses as we forgive them that trespass against us." Though there are more profound requests in this prayer, Christ passes over them, and singles out this one for special underlining. " If you will pardon men their offences, your Heavenly Father will pardon you your offences," He adds, assuring us that this demand of ours, when sincerely made, will be infallibly heard. Our lot is therefore in our own hand. Why seek afar for the means of avoiding Purgatory ? It is to our hand. It is in this phrase of the ' Pater.' Perhaps, so far from using it, we rather expose ourselves to a long Purgatory, and even to Hell, were God to take us literally at our own word. For what else is such a prayer from a heart filled with deliberate and nourished hate, than a prayer for the damnation of the soul that prays.

Our debt to God is immense, and it grows daily more and more. As we grow older, our debt grows with us, if we do not employ the means of liberation given to us in the ' Pater.' What terrible and long Purgatory rancour prepares for itself, supposing that it does avoid Hell ! It is of rancour, the daughter of hate—of the rancour that kills the soul—that the Apostle St. John speaks ! " Whosoever hateth his brother is a murderer, and you know that no murderer hath life everlasting dwelling within him " (1 *John*, iii, 15). A soul soaked in gall and vinegar will never taste the sweets of Paradise.

But suppose that the resentment which we nourish does not amount to the mortal sin of hate, that it is simply a little drop of vinegar hidden in the depths of our heart. " I pardon him," one says, but the former cordiality is gone and a glacial politeness has taken its place. If the drop of vinegar is not completely rejected, one cannot be received into the kingdom of full charity, where the elect love each other with all their heart. The drop of vinegar must be expiated in Purgatory ; because, in order to enter the Kingdom of Heaven, one must become as a little child. There is no vinegar in the heart of a child.

Christ has clearly indicated the necessity of pardoning offences if we wish to obtain mercy before God. This pardon must not be on the lips only, with reservations in the heart, but sincere and full. This is the condition, which if fulfilled, will be rewarded by the remission of our own debts to God. To a soul that comes before Him, free from bitterness, filled with sweetness, benignity and love for its neighbour, Jesus will say : " I have blotted out thy iniquities as a cloud, and thy sins as a mist " (*Is.*, xliv, 22). As the summer sun, gathering its heat, dispels the mists that film the fields like milk-spray, so will God dispel our sins : not the least vestige of them will remain. But if we wish to obtain this pardon, we must give a like plenary pardon to our brother who has offended us.

V.—To Avoid Judging Others

Besides the full and sincere pardon of offences, Our Saviour indicates in His Sermon on the Mount another infallible means of obtaining full mercy in our last hour. " Judge not and you shall not be judged. Condemn not and you shall not be condemned, for with what judgment you judge you shall be judged."

The particular judgment awaits all at the hour of each one's death. The just and the sinner must suffer it, but what a difference there is between the judgments : for one, a sentence of approbation and reward, with no hint of condemnation which the word itself would seem to imply ; for the other, a sentence of condemnation to Hell or to Purgatory, according to the state of the soul. Thus, when Our Saviour says: " Judge not and you shall not be judged," He means that if we refrain from condemning others, we shall not ourselves be condemned. For the man who does not rashly condemn his neighbour; who does not attribute malicious motives to him; who puts a good complexion on all that his neighbour says and does; who pleads extenuating circumstances, even when his neighbour stands openly convicted; who is not suspicious or censorious—for such a man, says Our Saviour, there is no judgment in the sense of a condemnation, which is to say plainly that such a one will taste neither Hell nor Purgatory. Such a soul will be measured by the measure with which it has meted. You have been merciful to your neighbour; you shall obtain mercy, for " Blessed are the merciful: they shall obtain mercy " is the Beatitude of the Mount. In the inner forum of your mind, in your conversations with others, you have not condemned your neighbour: now you yourself will meet the same kind judgment you have given.

Such is the unvarying practice of the divine mercy towards us: God is the Father, and all men are His children, and He wills that all men should love each other as Jesus has loved each. In His teaching, Christ uses every inducement to lead us to the observance of this essential precept. What is done to the neighbour, He takes as done to Himself. If we pardon others, He will pardon us. If we refrain from condemnation, we ourselves shall not be condemned. Mercy shall meet with a return of mercy. Thus are promises heaped on the observance of this precept.

In the observance of this precept, as in all others, Jesus Himself has willed to be our model. He, " to whom the Heavenly Father had given all judgment " (*John*, v, 27) abstained, during his life here below, from severely judging and condemning sinners. Where the scribes and Pharisees were severe and merciless, He was indulgent and merciful. He says: " And if any man hear my words and keep them not, I do not judge him: for I came not to judge the world, but to save the world. He that despiseth me, and receiveth not my words, hath one that judgeth him: the word that I have spoken, the same shall judge him in the last day " (*John*, xii, 47-48). All this is beautifully realized in Christ's conversation with the woman taken in adultery.

To refrain from condemning others is, therefore, an easy means of avoiding condemnation—that is to say, of being admitted immediately to Heaven. This means becomes all the easier when we reflect that we are incapable of forming a true and just judgment on the conduct of others. Knowledge, integrity, impartiality, legitimate authority—we are lacking in all these essentials to judgment. When we call up our neighbour before the tribunal of our mind for criticism, for judgment, for condemnation, we usurp a divine function, we trespass on the rights of God. " He that judgeth his brother judgeth the law," says St. James. God has very good reason to forbid us to do that of which we are incapable, for we have neither the integrity nor the impartiality requisite for doing so. " O man, whosoever thou art that judgest, thou art inexcusable. For wherein thou judgest others, thou condemnest thyself. For thou dost the same things which thou judgest " (*Rom.*, ii, 1-2). But, above all, how can we judge without knowledge. To judge, we would need to be able to read our neighbour's conscience like an open book, and that is the privilege of God alone.

Everything urges us not to judge, and yet how widespread is the mania for judging. Those who wish to curb that mania in themselves, and by repairing false judgments in the past to avoid Purgatory, should listen to the words of St. Paul : " Put ye on, therefore, as the elect of God, holy and beloved, the bowels of mercy, benignity, humility, modesty, patience ; bearing with one another and forgiving one another, if any have a complaint against another . . . But above all these things have charity which is the bond of perfection " (*Col.*, iii, 12-14). Charity is the unique resource : it covers a multitude of sins and holds the key to Paradise.

VI.—Spiritual Infancy

Infants do not go to Purgatory. If they have been baptized, they enter Heaven. Our Saviour Himself has canonized them, when, having embraced a child and set him in their midst, he said to them : " Amen I say unto you : unless you be converted and become as little children, you shall not enter into the kingdom of heaven. Likewise, whosoever shall humble himself as this little child, he is the greater in the Kingdom of Heaven " (*Mat.*, xviii, 1-5). On another occasion, He said : " Suffer the little children to come unto me, and forbid them not, for of such is the kingdom of Heaven."

These words of the Saviour are for all Christians, for they do not contain a counsel for the generous of soul, but are an indispensable condition for entering Heaven. If, in our passage through life, we fail to acquire that infancy of soul which opens heaven, we shall find ourselves eternally condemned to Hell, or to Purgatory where we must remain till we have acquired it. What, then, is this blessed infancy which is so powerful in aiding us to avoid Purgatory ? There has been much discussion of it, especially since the time of St. Thérèse of the Child Jesus, who showed in her own life a sublime example of this infancy. The fact that they are in Heaven is a proof that all of the saints practised it, but it is in the life of the Little Flower of Lisieux that it shines most brilliantly, because her whole life was a living of this precept. The " little way " of this lovable saint is nothing else than a very simple form, accessible to all, of that spiritual infancy recommended by Our Saviour.

Spiritual infancy is not a simple virtue, but an ensemble of virtues and a particular attitude of soul. It consists in two things : to practise by will and by choice the virtues natural to infancy ; and to take up towards God the attitude of an infant towards its father or mother.

" God," says Proverbs, " has made man right." Sin twisted him. God made man simple, tending straight towards his Creator and God. Sin complicated him and turned him back on himself. Without completely escaping the dire consequences of Original Sin, infancy has the privilege of preserving something of the primitive integrity and simplicity. Pass in review the numerous faults and vices opposed to integrity and simplicity of heart : you will find that none of them have a place in the child's heart.

The child is naturally humble. He knows his weakness and quickly calls for help. He knows his need, and his most frequent gesture is one of spontaneous asking. He is without pride or pretention. If he is forgotten and no attention is paid to him, he accepts that as the natural state of affairs, and he knows nothing of vanity. Ambition means nothing to him, for with a little he is content.

Avarice has not part in the child, and he practises unconsciously the evangelical counsel: " Be not solicitous for tomorrow : sufficient for the day is the evil thereof." Neither is there rancour or malice in his heart. His language is a true speaking of his thoughts, for he has not learned to dissimulate : unconsciously again, he fulfils the recommendation of Our Saviour that our language should be " Yea, yea and nay, nay." The child is innocent. His gaze is pure and his eye is limpid as a source. He is a child of light who knows nothing of the works of darkness. He is a star at its rising, a flower of spring, a diaphanous crystal untarnished by the least breath of impurity. As in a mirror, the Holy Trinity is reflected in his soul, and the angels call him brother.

But above all, the child is loving and confiding. He loves his father and mother and abandons himself entirely to their care. His father and mother are all in all to him. Their love is sufficient for him. A kiss from his mother dries his tears, chases his little worries, is the sovereign balm for all his sorrows.

Such is the natural infant, and such we must make ourselves, spiritually, if we wish to enter Heaven. To avoid Purgatory, to be worthy, at death, to enter into the eternal company of God, of His angels and His saints, we must cultivate the souls of children, by having towards God a truly filial spirit, and a truly fraternal spirit towards our neighbours, with humble sentiments in regard to ourselves. We must detach ourselves from all things created, place all our hope and confidence in God, totally abandoning ourselves to His Providence, believing always and in spite of all in His ineffable love. We must be "children in malice" (1 *Cor.*, xiv, 20) and, "laying aside all malice, and all guile, and dissimulations, and envies, and all detractions, as newborn babes, desire the rational milk without guile, that thereby you may grow unto salvation : if so be you have tasted that the Lord is sweet" (1 *Pet.*, 91, 1-3). We must endure in a filial spirit the corrections of the Father Who is in Heaven, "for whom the Lord loveth, he chastiseth ; and he scourgeth every son whom he receiveth

... for what son is there, whom the father doth not correct" (*Heb.*, xii, 6). Nothing could be more contrary to spiritual infancy and the filial spirit which animates it, than want of resignation in trials, murmurings against Providence, chafings at the daily cross. Impatience with oneself after a fault is also out of keeping with spiritual infancy, for we should turn to God with love and confidence, and ask for pardon. A little act of humble and peaceful repentance, of childlike confidence and filial love is more powerful for the cleansing of a fault, than a mountain of bitter contrition and crushing impatience with self, which merely hinders the soul in its flight to Christ.

A final trait of spiritual infancy, and one which has great bearing on our subject, is drawn from the parallel with the child who hands his little treasure of halfpennies and pennies to his mother. So too, do we hand the satisfactions we offer for sin, confidingly, to God, to dispose of them as He wishes. "I hoard nothing," says St. Thérèse. "All that I earn is for the Church and for souls." This is a mighty means of touching the Heart of Jesus and of obtaining from Him the great alms—Paradise.

VII.—Detachment from Earthly Things

It can be said that the eight Beatitudes of the Sermon on the Mount constitute so many means of direct and immediate entry to Heaven. When one of the Beatitudes is truly established in a soul as in a fixed abode, Heaven is already begun for that soul. This is true of all the Beatitudes, but especially of the first, to which the Kingdom of Heaven is expressly promised: "Blessed are the poor in spirit, for theirs is the Kingdom of Heaven."

The sense of these words must be carefully noted, for Christ does not say "Blessed are the poor." Such a formulation would be open to a double mis-interpretation. Thus worded it would seem to open Paradise in an automatic fashion to all the poor, even to those among them who spend their lives kicking against the goad and railing against God for the hardness of their lot. Thus worded, it would also seem a condemnation of the rich, and even their exclusion from the Kingdom. Now, the Beatitudes are for all classes, and no one is excluded from availing of them. Riches, of course, as we know from Christ's words about the eye of the needle, constitute a serious obstacle to entrance into Heaven. But it is not the mere fact of being rich that is dangerous, but the kind of heart that goes with it. For the heart of a rich man can be centred in his riches, and in them he can place his confidence, as did the man of whom Our Saviour spoke in the parable:

"The land of a certain rich man brought forth plenty of fruits. And he thought within himself, saying: What shall I do, because I have no room where to bestow my fruits? And he said: This will I do: I will pull down my barns and will build greater; and into them will I gather all things that are grown to me, and my goods. And I will say to my soul: Soul, thou hast much good laid up for many years, take thy rest; eat, drink, make good cheer. But God said to him: Thou fool, this night do they require thy soul of thee: and whose shall those things be which thou hast provided? So is he that layeth up treasure for himself, and is not rich towards God." (*Luke*, xii, 16-21).

St. Paul denounces the same evil: "For they that will become rich, fall into temptation, and into the snare of the devil, and into many unprofitable and hurtful desires, which drown men into destruction and perdition. For the desire of money is the root of all evils; which some coveting have erred from the faith, and have entangled themselves in many sorrows" (1 *Tim.*, vi, 9-10).

In our day, when the golden calf has so many adorers and the love of money so many victims, we cannot question these words of Christ or of the Apostle. It is certain, therefore, that the possession of riches constitutes a source of temptations, a real peril to salvation. But it is clear that the evil lies *not* in the possession of riches, but in the love and attachment with which they are possessed. The temptation can be surmounted and the peril avoided, by the grace of God. "Who therefore can be saved?" asked the astonished apostles, when they heard Christ's words about the rich. And the answer came: "With men these things are impossible, but not with God, for all things are possible to God" (*Mark*, x, 27). He Himself indicated to the rich Pharisees the means of escaping the wrath of God : " But yet that which remaineth, give alms ; and behold, all things are clear unto you " (*Lk.* xi, 41), that is to say, give alms and you will appease the justice of God ; you shall " buy back your sins," according to the vivid expression of Holy Writ ; you will detach yourself little by little from the love of money. St. Paul exhorts Timothy : " Charge the rich of this world not to be highminded, nor to trust in the uncertainty of riches, but in the living God, (who giveth us abundantly all things to enjoy), to do good, to be rich in good works, to give easily, to communicate to others, to lay up in store for themselves a good foundation against the time to come, that they may lay hold of the true life " (1 *Tim.*, vi, 17-19).

Christ spoke of the poor *in spirit*. A man can be poor in spirit, while possessing great riches ; and another, in direst poverty, can be rich *in spirit*, because his heart is firmly fixed on the little he has, thirsts after gold, would sell itself for filthy lucre, and is filled with envy of all who are richer in the world's goods. But a rich man may keep his heart detached from his riches and attached only to the Soveriegn Good—God —and know how to become rich before God by generous almsgiving. Thus will he make unto himself friends of the mammon of iniquity, that at the hour of death, he may be received into everlasting dwellings (*Luke*, xvi, 9).

The true Christian spirit is inseparable from this poverty of spirit. The words of Christ to his apostles : " Whosoever among you does not renounce all that he possesses cannot be my disciple," are simply another formulation of the first Beatitude. These words evidently refer to renunciation in spirit, to interior detachment, which makes a person seek his happiness in God alone. Again, His words : " No man can serve two masters, You cannot serve God and mammon " (*Mat.*, vi, 25) point to the same truth, and the words which follow contain this remarkable advice : " Be not solicitous for to-morrow, for to-morrow will be solicitous for itself." This is not a condemnation of a moderate care for one's future and for the future of that extension of one's personality—one's children. Christianity is not a school of sloth. In bidding farewell to the Ephesians, St. Paul wrote : " I have not coveted any man's silver, gold or apparel, as you yourselves know :

HOLY DISPOSITIONS AND SALUTARY PRACTICES 165

for such things as were needful for me and them that are with me, these hands have furnished. I have showed you all things, how that so labouring, you ought to support the weak, and to remember the word of the Lord Jesus: It is a more blessed thing to give than to receive" (*Acts*, xx, 33-35).

What is certainly opposed to the Christian spirit is the state of habitual inquietude, which arises from being continually absorbed in the pursuit of things which rivet the heart to earth, and leave no room for God and the things of God in the mad pursuit of riches, as though man's highest end was to pile thousands on thousands. "Therefore," says St. Paul, "if you be risen with Christ, seek the things that are above; where Christ is sitting at the right hand of God: mind the things that are above, not the things that are upon the earth. For you are dead, and your life is hid with Christ in God" (*Col.*, iii, 1-3).

All this amounts to saying that to be truly detached from things of earth, one must be attached to things of Heaven. Man cannot find his true happiness in himself. His heart, his affections, his thoughts, his desires, turn of necessity to where his treasure is. For the Christian soul, that treasure is God Himself. To God he tends; for God he longs. "What have I in Heaven besides Thee? With Thee, I can desire nothing on earth" (*Ps.*, lxxii), the Christian soul cries out with the Psalmist. With such detachment from earth and attachment to God, the soul cannot but be happy on earth.

Such, then, is the state of poverty in spirit, which Christ beatified and to which He attaches the Kingdom of Heaven as the reward. Indeed, such a state anticipates Heaven for the soul: "The soul of the just is in Heaven," says St. Gregory. The Holy Trinity dwells therein. The treasure is, in some fashion, already found and taken possession of, so that only a light veil prevents the full enjoyment of the bliss of eternity. When the shape of this world shall have passed for this soul, the veil will be rend, and Heaven will fill it with its unspeakable joy. There could be no question of Purgatory for such a soul. The joyful acceptance of real poverty and of all the sacrifices and penances which it inevitably imposes, or the generous practice of poverty in spirit in the midst of an abundance of this world's goods, will surely leave no debt of sin to be expiated in Purgatory ... " And the peace of God, which surpasseth all understanding, keep your hearts and your thoughts in Christ Jesus," is the prayer of St. Paul for the Philippians. The poor in spirit know that peace, and the ear of God is turned to their prayer : " Clamorem pauperum exaudivit Dominus." Let us listen again to the words of Christ, heavy now with all the thoughts we have been considering : " Blessed are the poor in spirit, for theirs is the Kingdom of Heaven."

VIII.—The Constant Remembrance of the Last Things

Find a means of avoiding sin, and you have found a means of avoiding Purgatory, is so incontestable as to be axiomatic, for Purgatory exists because of sin.

Now, this means exists. " In all thy works," says Holy Writ, " remember thy last end, and thou shalt never sin." This does not mean that the constant remembrance of our last end—death and what follows after death—will necessarily preserve us from all those sins of human weakness, which even those of highest virtue can avoid only by a special, extraordinary grace : it means, rather, that such remembrance will preserve us from full and deliberate sin, whether mortal or venial.

By purely human reasoning, Plato arrived at the conclusion that the only true philosophy is the constant thought of death, and the Fathers of the Church have commended him highly for this wisdom. Indeed, from a purely natural viewpoint, nothing is more calculated to inspire a man with true wisdom, and to keep his feet in the way of duty and virtue, than the habitual thought of death. But the teaching of Revelation and of the Christian faith on death and what follows death are much more powerful to aid us towards leading a good life, than the flickering light of ancient wisdom. The dogmas of Christianity give us light on the gravity of an offence against God, which no human reasoning could ever throw. In revealing the existence of Heaven, Hell, and Purgatory, they furnish us with motives for the avoidance of all sin, and make us anxious to set our feet firmly on " the strait way that leads to life."

Meditation on death and on the last things is not a merely intellectual venture into the knowledge of the beyond. It brings grace with it, to sustain our weakness in the hard combats which we must wage against ourselves, against the devil, against the allurements of the world. We cannot doubt that grace accompanies such meditations. By affirming that the thought of death will preserve us from sin, Christ has implicitly obliged Himself to give us the necessary grace to avoid sin, if we keep our minds on our last end.

There is a mediaeval tale of a merchant who confessed such grievous sins that the priest felt constrained to give him a long and arduous penance. The penitent refused to accept it. He repaired to other confessors, but found them not a whit less indulgent. He decided, for he was a man of means, to make a special journey to Rome and lay his case before the Holy Father. Through the mediation of a powerful protector, he obtained a private audience with the Holy Father. He made a full and complete confession, and explained why he had appealed to Rome on the whole matter. The Pope listened to him, and in the end, gave him as penance to bestow a big alms on the poor. He was up in arms immediately, declaring that his business was not flourishing, that there was an economic crisis : and such was his eloquence, that the Holy Father saw that his purse was the neuralgic point with the good man, and decided to change the penance. He proposed a Wednesday and Friday fast every week for a year. But the merchant protested that he had a bad stomach and that his digestion left much to be desired. The Pope saw very well that there was no hope of imposing a penance commensurate with the sins confessed, but he remembered the words about not quenching the smoking flax, and decided to try a better means. He had a ring, which had been given him as warning against the dangers of his high dignity, and the posy of which read : " Memento mori " : Remember that thou must die. Taking it, he put it on the finger of his penitent, saying :

" For your penance, you will wear this ring, and you will

read the words upon it twice daily, once on rising and once on retiring."

"Most Holy Father," the merchant answered, "this penance I can surely perform."

"Well, then," said the Pope, "make your act of contrition, and I shall give you absolution."

A fortnight had not passed since his return from Rome, when, having faithfully performed his penance, he began to reflect seriously that he must die some day, and that that day might not be far distant. He thought of his ill-gotten gains and of how little they would avail him in that day, and these reflexions led on to a firm resolution. He would take from his profits only what was necessary for himself and his family and give the rest to charity. Some time later, he died. If this man did not immediately enter Heaven, his sojourn in Purgatory was a very short one. The constant remembrance of death had worked wonders in his soul.

Let us use that panacea against sin, and remembering that death comes like a thief in the night, let us remember also that warning of Our Saviour: "Take heed, watch and pray. For ye know not when the time is. Even as a man who going into a far country, left his house . . . Watch ye therefore, (for you know not when the lord of the house cometh: at even, or at midnight, or at the cockcrowing, or in the morning), lest coming on a sudden, he find you sleeping. And what I say to you, I say to all: Watch" (*Mark*, xiii, 33-37).

"Wisdom," says an author of our day, "is a flower which comes to blossom on the tomb, and the living have but to stoop and gather it . . . What is death ? . . . It is a witness.

It attests, not now by words which can deceive, nor by protestations which can be interested, that the present life is but a poor thing. Pleasure, sorrow, riches, passion, glory, beauty, and all the objects for which one toils and suffers, lies and does evil, end in a corpse, a few bones, a pince of dust, nothing . . ."

. . .

The thought of death and what follows death can be not only salutary, but even sweet and attractive, by linking it with the thought of our deceased ones—parents, relations, neighbours, friends. When a person is advanced in years, he can count more friends beyond the grave than this side of it. It is sweet to live in memory with them, to pray for and to them. When our conversation is with them, as St. Paul might put it, we learn to see the things of this life in their proper perspective. The soul turns from things of earth, and unites itself with God, and longs for the day when they shall receive it into everlasting dwellings, where it will be united to its friends. The invisible and beneficent presence of our departed friends is about it. Whether they are in Heaven or in Purgatory, they pray for us. When the soul has tasted the sweetness of this company, it cannot be separated from it, because the world holds no charm for it and a heavenly nostalgia fills it to the overflow.

"This profound joy which living with the dead gives to us, appears to be composed of two very distinct elements. Living with the dead is a fact of an essentially delicate and elevated nature : and every act of superior morality is per se a principle of beatitude for the conscience.—To live with them is to live with a purer, better and happier humanity. We can hope for no material advantage from them : our fidelity to them is essentially disinterested and on a higher plane " (*H. Bolo*).

"Show me your company," says the proverb, "and I'll tell you what you are." The blessed dead—for it is of them only we speak—no longer sin. They love God with their whole heart and they do all the good they can. They are perfect. They are the cream of humanity.

Frederick Ozanam has written many beautiful pages on this subject of commerce with the dead. He says : " I seem to see, gathering about me in a better world, those dear and holy friends who have been with me from my cradle, and who now await me beyond the grave. I have a habit of conversing with them ; by their aid, my mind rises more easily towards those invisible regions where God dwells. If God dwelt there alone, we could perhaps forget Him : but when we recall, one after another, the good friends who have preceded us to the grave, we are strongly enticed to follow in their footsteps towards our heavenly home. Blessed be our holy mothers, who first set our feet in the way of holiness—in the way that will lead us to re-union with them, now that they have left us for a better world . . . As the number of our friends beyond the grave increases, the attraction which draws us to their happy home will increase with it, and as death breaks, one after another, the bonds of friendship that bind us to earth, our thoughts and our conversation will be more and more in Heaven. It is a consolation to those parents who lose their children when but infants, to know that they have little angels watching over them and their family—angels who are their own children."

The belief that our dear ones do not forget us in the region of glory, but are rather our assiduous protectors, who, by the permission of God, can sometimes give us the impression of their mysterious presence, is something that is firmly fixed in the human soul. This is how Ozanam describes the feeling he had of the presence of his mother, after her death: "Many moments have come, when I began to have a presentiment that I was not alone; when something of an infinite sweetness passed in the depths of my soul, like an assurance that she had not left me . . . like the glance of a passing wing caressing my face. Then I would seem to hear the footsteps, the voice, the breathing of my mother—and that breath would warm and vivify my soul . . .

Thinking of their union in eternity, he adds: "Even in my actual solitude, the remembrance of the august scene of my mother's death came back to sustain and to raise me up: and the consoling thought that a very short time kept me from her, cheered me . . . "

He objects to the expression: "He is no longer," as both untrue and unworthy a Christian's speech. "On the contrary, we should say: He has left us, but we have not lost him. He is not lost to friendship: the tomb of a Christian is like one of those commemoration stones which the patriarchs raised where they were obliged to separate for a time. It should symbolize a short separation and an eternal re-union. Above all, he is not lost to the Church, for the Church is a society which is not rent by death. It has a law which unites those who have passed to their reward with those who are still in the conflict: earth is but its vestibule, and Heaven is its sanctuary, into which are gathered the pure and the best of mankind."

We ought to imitate Ozanam and taste, like him, the sweet and profound joy of living in company with those we have loved, and who await us in a better world. We shall thus be able, through this holy commerce, to avoid all sin, and, in consequence, to avoid Purgatory.

IX.—To Ask for One's Purgatory on Earth

The easiest and most accessible means of avoiding Purgatory is sincerely to ask of God the grace to suffer our Purgatory on earth.

Such a prayer must not be from the lips only, but should be made with an ardent desire to be heard. Sometimes we have a secret fear that God will take us at our word and answer our prayer, and therefore, in this as in all other things, let us have the courage to really mean what we ask in prayer. To ask for one's Purgatory on earth is equivalent to asking for sufferings, for crosses, for trials of every kind, for one cannot escape atoning for one's sins. " It is through many tribulations," says St. Paul " that we must come to the Kingdom of God." God, who sees the secrets of our hearts, will hear us, if we truly desire that which we ask.

This sincere desire does not necessarily exclude all irrational fear. Our sensibility may fret at the thought of suffering. We must meet this fear of suffering by recalling to mind that He Who punishes us is an all-loving Father, Who wills only our good ; that He will give us the grace to support our trials with resignation and even with joy, if we ask it of Him ; that here on earth, His justice is always tempered by His mercy, so that—other things being equal—His chastisements are less rigorous than in the next life.

Our attitude under trials will be the test of the sincerity of our prayer. If, remembering our prayer, we accept with sweetness and resignation the crosses which Providence sends us ; if, at every blow, we sincerely kiss the hand that strikes, then indeed have we proved the sincerity of our prayer, then indeed have we entered on the strait way that leads to life. Like the souls in Purgatory, we shall experience a sweet joy, in conforming ourselves to the will of God.

This prayer should be made with full filial confidence,

because "he that wavereth is like a wave of the sea driven with the wind and tossed. For let not that man think that he shall receive anything of the Lord. A double minded man is unstable in all his ways" (*Jas.*, i, 6-7). We shall certainly be heard, because our prayer is fully conformable to the will of God, which is that we should avail of the time of this life to prepare ourselves for immediate entry into Heaven. "And this is the confidence we have in him," says St. John, "that if we ask anything according to his will, he heareth us" (1 *John*, v, 14).

To confidence, we must add perseverance, which will be another certain witness to the sincerity of our prayer. If we insist that we desire our Purgatory on earth; if we triumph over our fear of the cross, Our Lord will surely be touched. In some way or another, He will arrange that all our accounts shall be settled at the moment of death. And perhaps those accounts will not be so terrible, particularly if we take the following precautions:

1. We should be careful not to augment our debt by new sins. The sincere request to be allowed to do one's Purgatory on earth can be a powerful check on all sin. One says to oneself: "The more I sin, the more I shall have to suffer, and that in the near future. By multiplying my offences, I prepare for myself a very hard trial, a long and terrible sickness, perhaps a veritable martyrdom for my last days." Fear is the beginning of wisdom. This thought of an immediate sanction in this life can certainly be very salutary to turn us from lukewarmness to a fervent and perfect life.

2. We should take the initiative on divine justice, by voluntary penances. There is no better means of disarming the hand of our Father and softening His chastisements, than to raise our own hand in punishing ourselves.

3. We should beg God fervently for the grace of receiving the Last Sacraments, unless indeed we are to die a martyr's death; as also for the grace of a plenary indulgence at the hour of death. We have no certainty that God will hear us by granting us these two graces; but, if our prayer is well made, He will give us their equivalent.

4. Finally, an infallible means of mitigating our Purgatory on earth, is a great charity towards the souls of the dead, be-

cause God has a habit of treating us as we treat others. But this is a matter of which we shall treat at length in the next chapter.

Chapter the Fourth

OF CERTAIN EXCELLENT AND SALUTARY ACTS OF CHARITY

CERTAIN EXCELLENT ACTS of charity towards the neighbour, which cannot but draw on those who exercise them abundance of graces and the full pardon of their sins, provide a third series of means by which Purgatory may be avoided. "Charity," says Holy Writ, "covers a multitude of sins." If that is true of acts of charity in general, how much more so of certain practices of charity, particularly meritorious and excellent in their object, as those of which we shall now speak.

I.—THE APOSTOLATE OF PURGATORY

The Christian, we have said, does not live in isolation. He is part of a great family, the members of which people Heaven, earth and Purgatory. With all of these, he should be on terms of brotherly relations. He associates himself with the saints in Heaven by having recourse to their intercession, and by uniting himself to their perpetual praise of the Most Holy Trinity. His duty towards his fellow-men on earth is to aid them towards their eternal salvation. Every Christian ought to be an *apostle*, and he cannot be saved by a life of unmixed egoism. Those who are excluded eternally from the Kingdom of Heaven are those who have had no concern for their brethren. This is easily understood. To be saved, one must imitate Christ and become like to him. Now, the whole life of Christ was directed to one end: to procure the glory of His Father by the salvation of men, His brothers by adoption.

. . .

But the exercise of mercy and of active charity does not end this side of the grave. We have a group of brethren, who, while not among our earthly brethren, have not yet reached their end—eternal happiness. The souls in Purgatory are, in a certain sense, travellers and pilgrims. Properly speaking, of course, they do not advance ; they can no longer merit or demerit, and they are sure of their eternal salvation. But they have reached only the antichamber, and they are unable to reach Paradise. The wise virgins are here, who had oil in their lamps when the Bridegroom came : but their lamp itself was not sufficiently prepared, and therefore the door of the marriage-feast is closed against them for a time. Sad situation of these souls, all the more sorrowful because they have to pay the last farthing to divine justice. They nourish a hope, however : charity unites them to their brethren in Heaven and on earth. The first will succour them by their intercession, but the second can do still more for them, for to the simple force of prayer they can add that of sacrifice, and thus make direct satisfaction to the justice of God for the debt of sin. The souls on earth have at their disposal the inexhaustible treasures of the Church, that profusion of indulgences, fruit of the Saviour's Blood and of the superabundant satisfactions of the saints. Moreover, it is lawful for them to offer for their suffering brethren the satisfactory fruit of their own good works. It is by these means, as we have said above, that the living can aid the dead—that they can exercise what is called the Apostolate of Purgatory.

. . .

This Apostolate of Purgatory has the double advantage of being neither sterile nor dangerous. Purgatory is the good soil which returns a hundredfold. Nothing of the worker's labour is lost ; the enemy cannot sow his cockle ; all is germinated and brought to fruition for eternity.

It must be noticed, too, that this fecundity is not limited to the Church Suffering. It reaches in a marvellous manner to the Church Militant itself, for recourse can be had to the dead on behalf of the living. Helpless for themselves, the souls in Purgatory have still the prerogative of charity : they can sympathize with the miseries of others and speak to God on their behalf. The intentions of those who pray for their relief, will be always dear to the suffering souls.

We have, in the " Annals " of St. Dominic, a curious discussion between Fra Bendetto, who offered all his prayers and sacrifices for the relief of the souls in Purgatory, and Fra Bertrando, who did the same for the conversion of sinners. Fra Bertrando dwelt on the misery of these souls, exposed at every and any moment to eternal damnation, and he recalled the many instances of Christ's solicitude for the sinner. But the souls in Purgatory, he said, are sure of salvation. Surely, the plight of the sinner is more pressing. Fra Benedetto replied by pointing out that the chains of sin were self-forged chains, and that they could be struck off in a moment by a sincere 'Miserere.' Of two beggars, he asked, which was to be counted more worthy of pity: the one who, though strong and healthy, refuses to earn his living; or the other, who is paralysed and incapable of helping himself? Moreover, that Christ loved the sinner, is itself a strong proof of how much more He must love the souls in Purgatory who are united to him by the purest and most selfless charity, and whose torment is their desire to see His Face.

But Fra Bertrando was not convinced. Though a Dominican, he was not in agreement with St. Thomas, who wrote: "Prayer for the deceased is more agreeable to God than prayer for the living. The dead have a much greater need of help, by the very fact that they cannot help themselves, as the living can." The two disputants slept on their disaagreement, and the legend goes on to tell how the truth of Fra Benedetto's opinion was confirmed in a vision accorded to Fra Bertrando. The vision doubtless showed him that the two aims were not mutually exclusive: that in helping the souls in Purgatory, one could at the same time attend to the needs of sinners—but with a ten-fold efficacy.

. . .

The advantages which the practice of the Apostolate of Purgatory brings with it are well calculated to attract us to it.

Firstly, there could be nothing so sanctifying for us as to occupy ourselves with thoughts of our dead, and to live in their company by constant prayer. We have considered the power for good which the habitual thought of death can be, in helping us to avoid sin. The special remembrance of Purgatory teaches us, not only to avoid sin, but to practise all virtues, by placing before our eyes the example of saintly souls, who give themselves to expiation with a perfect conformity to the will of God, happy in rendering homage by their sufferings to His justice and His holiness, and aflame with His love.

To do good to the inhabitants of Purgatory is a sure means of winning their gratitude ; it is to make for ourselves friends, who will receive us, after our death, at the threshold of the eternal habitations. As we have already shown, the souls in Purgatory do not wait till they have entered Heaven, to repay our kindness to them. Baronius relates that a certain pious person, on his death-bed, was horribly tormented by devils. Suddenly, the dying man saw the Heavens opened and thousands of defenders coming to his aid and securing for him the victory. " We are," they said to him, " the souls your suffrages have delivered from Purgatory. We come by God's permission to thank you and to conduct you immediately to Heaven." The authenticity of this incident is not above suspicion, but one cannot doubt the truth it adorns : for gratitude, so rare a flower on earth, expands to full bloom in Heaven and in Purgatory. What a consolation will such a thought be to a person who can look back from his death-bed, or a life of remembrance of the Holy Souls ! " Blessed are the merciful," says Christ, " for they shall obtain mercy." And again : " Give, and it shall be given unto you ; good measure, pressed down, shaken together and flowing over, shall they give into thy bosom." The final judgment will be entirely in favour of those who have shown mercy : " Amen I say unto you, as often as you did it to one of my least brethren, you did it to me " (*Mat.*, xxv, 40).

The " least brethren " are certainly those who are the most unfortunate and the most worthy of compassion among men ; but one can also include the souls in Purgatory, whose distress, from a certain point of view, has nothing to equal it on earth. We know that they are helpless to aid themselves, and must look to earth and Heaven to aid them. Therefore, to show our charity to them is to accomplish in a splendid manner the works of mercy blessed by Our Saviour. This is the opinion of St. Francis de Sales, who writes :

" To obtain relief for the poor souls in Purgatory by our prayers—is not this, in some manner, to visit the sick ? Is it not to give to drink, to those whose thirst is for the vision of God? Is not prayerful aid to the Holy Souls, a feeding of the hungry? ..."

The blessing which Christ will declare publicly at the Last Judgment, He will already have declared privately to the soul who has faithfully practised the Apostolate of Purgatory. If material alms receives such splendid recompense, according to the Scripture, how great will be the reward for spiritual alms given to the souls of the dead.

. . .

We shall end with a word to the priest.

Many priests are made desolate by a sense of frustration and sterility in their ministry to the living; indifference is about them, and faith burns low with a smoky flame. It will be a source of splendid encouragement to such souls, if they remember that the dead are always accessible and wholly responsive to their zeal. Let them turn their eyes from the discouragements about their feet, and look on Purgatory as a huge field white for the harvest.

The same perspectives must be opened to those priests, members of Religious Orders and Congregations, who are zealous for mission work but are kept otherwise employed by holy Obedience. They seldom get an opportunity to preach or to administer the Sacraments, for the only congregation at their Mass is often the server who assists them. This distresses them, and desire for change, a common and very subtle temptation, obsesses them. Let such but get in touch with the Holy Souls, and they will find a sure way to satisfy their thirst for the ministry. They will soon acquire a taste for this apostolate, hidden from the eyes of men, but rich before God and full of profit to those who exercise it. They will even find in it the secret of an apostolate to the living, and will secure for themselves a blessed end.

II.—Prayer for the Most Deserted Souls in Purgatory

We must pray for all the souls in Purgatory in general, and in a special manner for the souls of our parents, our friends, and our benefactors, as well as for those who, or whatever title, have a right to our grateful remembrance. The Church teaches us to do so, for, at the Memento for the Dead in the Mass, express commemoration is made of souls who have been recommended to the priest, as well as of those whom he himself wishes to remember . . . But charity, which unites all the members of the Mystical Body, finishes the Memento with a remembrance of all the poor Souls: " and *to all those who rest in Christ*, grant a place of refreshment, light and peace." These common suffrages of the Church are specially for those for whom no one on earth prays in particular. Such souls must be in a majority in Purgatory. How many poor souls, even in Christian countries, have no Mass celebrated for them on the day of their burial, or are deprived by force of circumstances from religious burial. And if we look on the immense regions still sunk in paganism, who will count the huge number of souls who, at every instant, enter into the place of expiation ? When we think of the number of Christian souls who are forgotten in Purgatory, what must we think of those souls who lived their lives in the depths of paganism ? Thus, we should accord a very great part of our suffrages to these unknown, forgotten souls, and to the most desolate among them in a special manner.

In recent times, Catholic piety has come to take a special interest in these souls. On the occasion of Our Lady's second apparition to the three children in Fatima, among other things she said to them: " After each decade of the Rosary you will say: ' My Jesus, pardon me my offences, keep me from the fire of Hell and *console the souls in Purgatory, especially the most abandoned.*' " At the sixth and last apparition, Mary appeared, in fulfilment of her promise, in the company of St. Joseph and of the Christ Child, and confirmed by the nowfamous miracle of the sun, the supernatural origin of the apparitions. One of Our Lady's aims in these apparitions was to recommend the most abandoned souls in Purgatory to our prayers. It is with a thrill of pleasure that one again meets the sweet, maternal affection of Mary for the afflicted.

By responding to her invitation, we shall certainly merit her special protection. If we pray for the most abandoned souls, she will remember us, and will answer that " now and at *the hour of our death*," which we say so often in the " Ave." Is not this request from our Heavenly Mother a sufficient incentive to prayer for the great throng of the forgotten souls ?

. . .

Because they are the most abandoned, these souls are worthy of our compassion. If we find ourselves touched here below by the sight of extreme physical misery, we ought to be so too when we consider the awful abandonment of these souls who are to be our future companions in eternity.

Here below, perhaps, we have few friends, few occasions of doing good to our fellow men, and our contacts with our contemporaries may be slight. We envy the lot of those who are known to all, and whose name is on men's lips as the benefactors of mankind, while we live humbly, hidden and forgotten by all but a few. It seems to us that we shall find few intimate friends in eternity ; few of our brethren to whom we shall have done good on earth and who will thank us in eternity. Very well ! Here is an easy means of surrounding ourselves in eternity with many grateful friends, whose gratitude will augment our glory in Paradise : for we can make all the friends we wish in Purgatory. What we shall have done for them on earth shall establish between us and them, in eternity, a bond of unspeakable sweetness. God will reveal to them the good we have done them, and they will know us to eternity as their benefactors. We shall find them crowding around to intercede for us when we come before the judgment seat of God.

Add to all this that the act of charity by which we pray for these unknown souls is all the more agreeable to God, because it is completely disinterested and completely devoid of all human considerations, being wholly founded on the love of God. Everything in this prayer for the most abandoned souls in Purgatory, is of the supernatural order, and therefore its merit must be very great before God. Such merit is that of the good Samaritan, who stopped and stooped to the man who had been abandoned and poured oil and wine into wounds on which others would not even look.

While praying much and at all times, therefore, for our deceased parents, friends and benefactors, we ought also to have a care for the immense multitude of the forgotten. There are moments during life when we find ourselves in a state of depression, of frustration, of pain, of sickness, without consoler or friend. To remember prayerfully the Holy Souls at such moments is the best means of obtaining help and consolation from Him Who is the common Father of all human souls.

We may believe that it is also a means of preparing oneself for immediate entry into Heaven : for, if a constant devotion to the Holy Souls in general can merit this favour for us, how much more powerful must be the charity which inspires us to pray for the deserted and forgotten souls, with Him Who told the parable of the man who went down from Jerusalem to Jericho.

III.—The Heroic Act

There is one means of helping the Holy Souls which stands out from all the others as the " Heroic Act." It consists in offering to God, for the relief of the souls in Purgatory, all the satisfactory works done during one's life, and all the suffrages which shall be offered for one's soul after death. It is as thus understood, that the Church has recognised it and enriched it with indulgences.

It is called *heroic*, because it is indeed deserving of the title. If one were to offer the satisfactions which one offers to God on earth for the Holy Souls, that would indeed be heroic—but it would not be the extreme of heroism, for one would still keep the hope of being assisted after death by the prayers of the Church and the suffrages of relations and friends. But, in the heroic act, one renounces that hope. One despoils oneself of all, and there is involved a complete abandonment of oneself to divine justice for the complete debt of one's sins.

It is of the very essence of the Heroic Act that it be *perpetual and irrevocable in intention at the moment when it is made*. The renunciation of one's satisfactory works, for the benefit of the Holy Souls, during a part or even for the whole of one's life, while still keeping the suffrages which will be offered for one after death, is *not* the Heroic Act. This Act is not a vow, and therefore does not bind under pain of sin : it is only improperly that it is so called. To go back on one's offer is to show weakness and lack of grit : but there is no sin involved in doing so. For there is question of *heroism* here : and heroism is not obligatory, except when it is inseparably bound to the accomplishment of a duty or a precept.

By the Heroic Act, we do not renounce that element in our good works which we call *merit*—the inalienable and strictly personal increase of grace on earth and of glory in Heaven which these good works bring with them. The Heroic Act itself is a very meritorious work, and that merit is eternally ours, if we keep our engagement of honour to the Holy Souls. That Heroic Act has also a *satisfactory value*, and it may be asked whether the renunciation in question extends to *the satisfactory value of the act itself*. The answer is—no. The satisfactory value of the Heroic Act is *the last satisfaction which remains to him who makes the Act*. The despoiling of oneself for the benefit of the Holy Souls begins from the making of the Heroic Act, but does *not* include that Act. Thus the last act, reserved to oneself in every respect, is the Heroic Act itself. It is the last coin dropped into our personal purse. We may add that the Heroic Act does not include the abandonment of the privilege attached to the Scapular of Mount Carmel, because that privilege is not in itself a satisfactory act or an indulgence. But the Heroic Act does imply the renunciation of all the indulgences which a person could gain for himself. The *plenary indulgence at the hour of death*, being by very definition inapplicable to the dead, is the only exception to this.

The Heroic Act does not prevent one from praying for oneself or for others of the living. When a prayer, which involves some sacrifice, is said, three different virtualities are involved: *the meritorious fruit* which, as we have said, is necessarily personal; *the satisfactory value*, arising from the sacrifice involved in doing the act, is what one alienates in favour of the Holy Souls, when one makes the Heroic Act; *the impetratory force* of the prayer as prayer, which has a moral force in touching Him to Whom the prayer is addressed. God, the Immutable and the Impassible, wills to be touched by our prayer. The Heroic Act does not prevent us from using that moral force for ourselves or for others. He who has made the Heroic Offering can always implore mercy for himself. But he cannot play the rôle of a debtor paying his debts to divine justice, beacuse he has given away all and has nothing with which to pay. He has done in the order of satisfactory works, what the Religious does with regard to the goods of this world, when he takes his Religious Vow of Poverty. For just as all the fruits of a Religious' work belong to the community, so all the satisfactory works which follow on the making of the Heroic Act belong to Purgatory : with the difference, of course, that there is question of sin in the violation of the former, but not so in the latter, which, as we have said, is only improperly called a vow.

No set formula is necessary for the making of the Heroic Act, and an intention, purely interior, suffices. Some people have the habit of placing in the hands of Our Lady all that they have earned for the souls in Purgatory, in order that she may apply the suffrages to the souls of her choice. This practice is praiseworthy. P. Gaspar Oliden, a Theatine, recommends this practice at the end of the eighteenth century. But it is something which is not essential to the Heroic Act itself : but even after having made that abandonment to Mary, one can always express to her *the desire* which one has to succour some soul in particular.

Although it is not very ancient, the Heroic Act has quite a history. It was inspired by the Holy Spirit in certain saintly souls, before being officially sanctioned by the Church. St. Gertrude appears to have been the initiator of this pious practice, not that she herself made the Heroic Act as we know it to-day, but because she suggested the idea by her example, for she abandoned to the Holy Souls, all the satisfactory part of her good works. She does not appear to have thought of renouncing the suffrages which would be offered for her after death, but we may well believe that had she thought of it, her generous nature would not have hesitated to do so. She had full knowledge, however, that her act of renunciation was not a trifling matter, and that by it, she was exposing herself to the full weight of divine justice for her own faults. Overcome by this thought, she once said to Our Saviour : " I trust, Lord, that Thy Infinite Mercy looks more often on thy servant, entirely despoiled of merits and become as a beggar before Thee."—" What else could I do," answered the Saviour " for one whose charity deprives her of her treasures, but envelop her with the mantle of my tenderness, and work more diligently with her, that she may not be the loser by her loving charity "—" In vain do you work with me, my Saviour," she answered, "for I must always appear before Thee with empty hands, because I have given away not only what I have acquired, but all that I can possibly acquire." To this, the Saviour replied: "A mother who sees her children warmly clothed is content to place them near her, but she nurses the shivering child and covers it with her own clothes to warm it. Do you possess less than the other, if I place you now very close to the sea of graces? Will you envy those who rest on the bank of a stream?" Consoled by the divine words, the saint easily understood their hidden sense: the motionless people near the little trickle of water designated the souls whose jealous provision for the future caused them to cling to their good works. The sea symbolised the riches of God.

The first to make the Heroic Act, as we understand it, was P. de Monroy, in the 17th century. In 1728, Pope Benedict XIII approved this admirable practice, and accorded to it its first spiritual favours; Pius VI, in 1788, and especially Pius IX, in 1852, added new favours. They can be thus summarised:

1. A Plenary Indulgence at every Communion, on condition of a visit to a Church or public Oratory and prayer for the Pope's intentions.

2. A Plenary Indulgence every Monday, by assisting at Mass only, or every Sunday, if one is hindered from doing so on Mondays.

3. The Mass of a Priest who has made the Act, has at all times the benefits attaching to a privileged altar.

4. All indulgences are applicable to the souls in Purgatory, for those who have made the Heroic Act.

. . .

Having considered the nature and history of the Heroic Act, we pass on to review the spiritual advantages which it procures for him who makes it, and also the risks to which it exposes him, and to show the conditions necessary in order that it may be a means of avoiding Purgatory.

The indulgences which those gain who have made the Heroic Act are of no personal satisfactory value to them, since they have made all their indulgences over to the benefit of the Holy Souls. There is personal advantage however, based on the *merit* of the heroic act itself, for the Heroic Act leaves the treasure of merits, properly so-called, entirely intact. Merit is that which brings to us an increase of grace on earth and of glory in Heaven, and its greatness is relative to the value of the act. Inspired by charity, the queen of virtues, the Heroic Act is in the rank of perfect acts, for it is inspired, not by any kind of charity, but by *heroic* charity which causes us to forget our own interests that we may do good to our brethren and thereby increase the glory of God. We admire St. Martin, who gave to a poor shivering beggar, the half of his mantle. But they who make the Heroic Act are much more admirable, for they despoil themselves of all that could save them, not from the rigours of an earthly Winter, but from the expiatory flames of Purgatory. St. Martin kept the half of his mantle: they keep nothing. See, too, the nature of their alms. They give God to souls who are athirst for God. Still more : " Their charity is towards the whole Kingdom of Heaven. They cause an immense joy in that abyss of joy, for they add a new sun to that heavenly sky, a living melody to that concert of Life. Dante has watched a soul enter Paradise, and in a sublime line, has made the Elect to cry out : ' See, thus does our love grow and increase.' Whosoever causes a soul to be released from Purgatory, puts that cry on the lips of Heaven " . . . (*Mgr. Gay*).

The teaching of a wise theology is that he who makes the Heroic Act augments by that act itself his degree of grace on earth and of glory in Heaven. He will see God more clearly ; he will penetrate more into the knowledge of His divine perfections ; he will love God more strongly and more tenderly, and will unite Himself more intimately to Him ; his happiness will be greater, and for eternity.

All that is very beautiful and very alluring, you will say to me, and the advantage would be unmixed, if we were impeccable. Unhappily, this is not so. My weakness is such that I know I shall commit many faults, even after having pronounced the Heroic Act : venial sins and perhaps even mortal sins. You cannot, indeed, convince me that the Heroic Act will immunise me against sin and will *infallibly* secure for me the grace of final perseverance. I shall therefore still sin. And as I can no longer count on the suffrages which may be offered for the repose of my soul after death nor on the satisfactory works which I perform on earth, it is to Purgatory, and probably to a very long Purgatory, that you condemn me, in urging me to make this heroic gesture to the Holy Souls.

Of course, I say to you in reply, there are risks and serious risks in the Heroic Act. For how could it merit the name ' Heroic,' if it were merely an easy means of securing one's Heaven ? If it were so easy, everyone would do it and the world would blossom thickly overnight with heroes. That is why I warn you not to undertake it lightly, as one might lightly perform a passing popular devotion. Reflect on what you propose to do, with all the serious attention which the spirit of faith will suggest to you . Spiritual realities and realities of the next life are not nebulous affairs. The temporal punishment due to sin, even pardoned sin, is not a pious myth. Purgatory is a reality, and not a clerical fiction. God takes seriously the promises which one makes to Him. You would be greatly to blame, were you to indulge in a certain coquetry with this heroism, and be actuated, more or less consciously, by a vanity which permits you to confide to your intimates : " I have taken the heroic vow." This is secret pride, and far from the spirit of the Act. " Let one reflect and take advice," Mgr. Gay, " remembering what one abandons and the accumulation of debt that can undoubtedly be the consequence of one's action . . . Nothing could be less trifling than this act of renunciation, and the Church does not act stupidly in allowing the term " Heroic " to be applied to it. Let no one make this act, therefore, through inducement or through a mania for imitation . . . and, likewise, let him always respect the inviolable rights of others to choose their own devotional ways. Nothing is less according to God than that spirit of enthusiasm, exclusive and indiscreet, which would impose the preferences of its own piety and forms of devotion, on everyone else..."

This could hardly be better said. Let us add, however, that the risk run by these heroic friends of Purgatory, is greatly lessoned by the following considerations. 1° " Charity covers a multitude of sins " is a scriptural text which refers to the practice of charity to the neighbour. And what better exercise of charity than to despoil oneself generously of one's satisfactions for the benefit of the souls in Purgatory. 2° God does not allow Himself to be outdone in generosity ; for He takes as done to Himself whatsoever we do for our neighbour. "Martin, still a catechumen, has covered me with a mantle," said Christ in vision to St. Martin. How then could He forget the heroic benefactors of Purgatory. 3° Finally, what shall we say of the gratitude of those souls who benefit by this heroism? How they will intercede for their generous benefactors!

These considerations are consoling for those who are engaged in this heroic warfare: and it already begins to be clear how the Heroic Act can be a means of avoiding Purgatory, at the same time as it obtains for the hero a high place in Heaven.

Suppose that after mature reflection and consultation with your confessor, you decide to make the Heroic Act, what tactics are you then to use? Firstly, you must make every effort to regulate your account with divine justice, and to present yourself before God as on the day of your Baptism. There is but one means of doing this: to gain a plenary indulgence for yourself, and the Church offers these indulgences in such profusion that the only difficulty is one of choice among so many. To gain a plenary indulgence is not an impossible thing. It is even *easy*, one can say, to gain, when there is question of a person whose pious dispositions lead him to wish to make the Heroic Act. To detest all one's sins, even the least; to be resolved to avoid all voluntary sin, at any cost; then to fulfil the conditions necessary for the gaining of the plenary indulgence which one has chosen—what is there very difficult in all that? Good will—with the grace of God, which is never wanting to him who asks for it—will suffice.

To gain a plenary indulgence for oneself is therefore the first essential. This done, the Heroic Act is made by word of mouth or by intention. All the satisfactory works which you shall henceforth perform, and all the suffrages which shall be offered for you after death, will be for the souls in Purgatory and not for your own benefit. It is true that you have no need of them for the moment, since the plenary indulgence you have gained has delivered you from all your debts, but that will not be the case if you fall into new sins. In your own best interests, therefore, you must double your vigilance against the least faults from the moment you make the Heroic Act. You will certainly commit some sins, for your frailty is very great, but they will be small ones and not fully deliberate. An act of contrition or of love will suffice to remove them, and they will leave little or nothing of temporal punishment chalked up against them. This will certainly be the case, if care is taken, firstly to gain as many indulgences as possible for the Holy Souls, and secondly to perform as many works of satisfaction for them as we can—acts that are sore on our nature, whether of corporal or spiritual mortification ; material alms, pious exercises, services to the neighbour. You will understand the reason for this plan of action, if you consider that you are engaged in good works that are completely for the service of others. You are the servant of Purgatory. If you are a dilatory servant, to what purpose do you bear the label ' heroic ' ? Indeed, you must work as four men, precisely because you are not working for yourself.

If you do this ; if your zeal grows rather than diminishes, and perseveres to the end, so that you are all flame and fire to extinguish the flame and fire of Purgatory ; then, in the name of all reasonable theology, I assure you that you will have no need to fear Purgatory at the moment of your death, for Christ will return to you, ten-fold, the treasures you have relinquished on earth. The measure of your merits will be beyond belief—full, well pressed down, shaken together and flowing over. You will be surrounded by a multitude of the Elect who are your eternal debtors ; they will thank you effusively and will be your companions for eternity.

If, on the contrary, after having made the Heroic Act, you continue to multiply sins, even venial sins ; if you put little or nothing of satisfactory value into the treasury of Purgatory, it is in vain that you are branded with the sign ' Heroic.' and I tell you plainly that I foretell nothing of good for you. You will be cast into prison, and you shall not go forth from thence until you have paid the last farthing.

IV.—To Offer Oneself as a Victim

The Heroic Act is not the only extraordinary means of coming to the aid of the souls in Purgatory. There is another, more heroic still, which consists in offering oneself to divine justice as a victim for their release.

There are two ways of making this offering. The first is to place oneself under the hand of divine justice to suffer for the intentions of these souls, whatsoever it may please God to load upon us. The second is to ask God to transfer to us the suffering which some particular soul will have to endure in Purgatory, in order that this soul may be completely delivered and enter into Heaven. Such a transfer is possible because of the dogma of the Communion of Saints. Christ is the Head, says St. Paul, and we are the members. What is there astonishing in this, therefore, when one member of the great family, which is the Communion of Saints, substitutes for his brother in order to pay that brother's debts and even to receive the stripes destined for the brother's shoulders? Christ Himself has done so for us. With the consent of His Father, He offered Himself to pay the debt of our sins. He who offers himself as a victim for the souls in Purgatory in general, or for some soul in particular, imitates in this the action of Christ Himself. It is to interpret very literally that command of Christ that we should love one another as He has loved us (*John*, xv, 12).

In a family, when a brother offers to endure the chastisement of his brother, the father, touched by this voluntary devotion, softens the blows. It does not appear that the Heavenly Father did so in regard to His Only-Begotten Son, because Christ, in His immense love and His zeal for the justice of His Father, would suffer the maximum of punishment. "The Father has not spared his own Son," says St. Paul. But we may believe that in the case of a generous soul who offers itself to suffer as victim for a soul in Purgatory, divine justice will make some remission in consideration of the magnificent devotion of the victim and the frailty of our humanity. Divine justice will preserve the same proportion as that which exists between the expiation which is demanded on earth and that which is demanded in Purgatory for the same sin. The latter is much more severe than the former, as we can conjecture from the difference of the states and from certain revelations on the subject.

A flesh-and-blood illustration, so much more compelling than any dry theorising, can be taken from the life of St. Catherine of Sienna. Kneeling at the death-bed of her father, she prayed that he, who had been an upright and just man, should escape the torments of Purgatory, and go straight to Heaven. " And if it is otherwise, O my God," she cried, " send me the sufferings which he must endure, and I shall bear them for him ! " At the very instant of his death, she experienced a deep, searching, and strangely sweet suffering which gave her no rest. She knew her prayer had been answered, and while the others lamented around the remains, she bent down and gazed into her father's face, while she repeated in an ecstasy of joy : " Would that I were where you are now ! "

Gemma Galgani, that seraphic virgin who died in 1903 and was canonized in 1940, used offer herself as a victim for the conversion of sinners, but she did not forget the souls in Purgatory. She offered herself as a victim for them, too. " My Guardian Angel told me," she writes one day, " that Jesus would send me some special suffering, which would last for two hours beginning at nine o'clock." She gives an account of these two hours. " I had a frightful headache, and every movement caused me intense suffering." Heaven accepted these generous expiations of this heroic soul, and the souls in Purgatory found their sufferings lightened and the time of their captivity shortened.

Before imitating St. Catherine, St. Gemma and many other fervent souls, it is prudent to gauge one's spiritual forces and stamina, as well as to take advice from one's confessor. Experience goes to show that God generally takes such an offer seriously, and therefore one should not make it lightly and without mature consideration. But if the Holy Spirit inspires us, and if our confessor *ratifies the inspiration, and in the measure in which he approves of it*, let us go forward without fear. To take on ourselves the Purgatory of others must be an excellent means of doing one's own, in virtue of the principle that " charity covers a multitude of sins." We repeat here what we said when treating of the Heroic Act : If this means frightens our weakness, let us at least admire the heroes who have practised it, and let us strengthen our faith by considering the dogma of the Communion of Saints and the mysterious law which rules the divine family of which we are part.

V.—The Apostolate of Prayer

What is called the Apostolate of Prayer looks first and foremost to the living, and is thus distinguished from the Apostolate of Purgatory of which we have just spoken. Though the latter is also exercised by means of prayer, the Apostolate of Prayer, properly so-called, consists in collaborating by prayer in the salvation of souls who are still in danger of perishing.

An excellent means of securing one's own salvation is to work for that of others. St. Peter urges the faithful to make their salvation certain by good works, and there could be no more excellent work than the work of Christ Himself—the salvation of souls. Why did the Son of God become man, suffer, die, rise again, and perpetuate His tabernacle amongst us by His presence in the Blessed Eucharist ? The glorification of God His Father, by the salvation of souls—such was the one aim and purpose of Christ's life. Whoever works for the salvation of souls is a collaborator with Christ.

Prayer is the great alms which is in the power of all Christians, and which has a spiritual character far superior to material alms, to which however the Scripture gives such praise. By means of it, one works efficaciously for the salvation of souls. To save a soul is to give God to a soul and to give a soul to God : so that prayer becomes a double gift—to God and to the neighbour.

With what a look will not Christ look on him who has aided in the salvation of souls—the cause for which Christ was born, lived and died. This is surely the greatest proof of love we can give Him. As He said to St. Peter on the occasion of his triple confession of love, so He says also to us— " If you love me, have a care for my lambs and for my sheep. Use all the means at your disposal to procure their salvation. There is no question of the office of Sovereign Pontiff for you, as there was for St. Peter ; but whosoever you are, or wheresoever you may be, or whatsoever your condition in life, you can perform works of zeal ; you can be an apostle ; you can make your contribution to my work. For there is an Apostolate ready to your hand—the Apostolate of prayer. Prayer is one of the great laws of the supernatural world which I have established. Without prayer, nothing of any great efficacy is done in my Kingdom. Prayer is the first collaboration in my work which I ask of all that love me; and that collaboration is open to all, since the grace of prayer is offered to all. What can you do, feeble and poor creatures, but pray and stretch out the hand to Him who possesses all and who loves you as children? Have I not taught you the prayer of sonship: 'Father, hallowed be Thy Name! Thy Kingdom come! Thy Will be done on earth as it is in Heaven!'"

Truly, indeed, this is the apostolic prayer par excellence, which in its brevity embraces all the interests of the Kingdom of God, all works of zeal, all the forms of the apostolate—for the end of every apostolate is to establish the Kingdom of God among men. If we can do nothing else, we can pray for the success of every enterprise which has for its aim the advancement of the Kingdom of God, . . . For the Apostolate of Prayer is nothing less than the normal exercise of perfect charity, which has a care for all things that pertain to God as though they were each and all a deep personal concern. And as perfect charity covers a multitude of sins, you will find yourself on the straight way that leads directly to Heaven, if you persevere diligently in this Apostolate of Prayer.

VI.—Prayer for Those in Their Agony

The category of men who are in sovereign need of prayer, is surely that of the agonising, and above all of those in their last agony whose souls are burdened with mortal sin. The moment of agony is, indeed, the capital moment of existence, for it decides the eternal lot of each.

The precept that we are to love our neighbour as ourselves means that we are to assist him, in the measure of our strength and our means, when he is in grave need of our aid. Now, could these be a neighbour more necessitous than the agonizing; a neighbour more miserable, more worthy of compassion, than the agonizing in the state of mortal sin? Yet another few minutes—seconds, perhaps—and if he does not turn to God by an act of repentance, he will be lost for eternity. Every hour has its thousands of such souls, every minute its hundreds. Is there a means of aiding them? If there is such a means, how can we lay claim to true charity, if we neglect it?

The means exists. The means is prayer. God, who has commanded us to love our neighbour—meaning all men—has willed that we should constantly have at hand a means of aiding souls, which is both rapid and immediately efficacious. Listen to St. Paul recommending to his disciple, Timothy, " to make prayer, supplication, intercession, thanksgiving for all men ... This is good and pleasing in the eyes of God, who wills that all men should be saved and should come to the knowledge of the truth." (1 *Tim.*, ii, 1-4).

God wills that all men be saved, and He offers us an easy means of contributing to their salvation by prayer, supplication, intercession. Those who are in their agony and whose souls are stained by mortal sin should be the object of our constant prayer. We must use violence towards Heaven in their behalf: and know that, in doing so, we are pleasing Him, Who did not spare His Only-Begotten Son for the salvation of souls.

. . .

We have underlined the great truth, again and again, that God rewards in the next life, and sometimes in the present, acts of charity to the neighbour, which he takes as done to Himself. Now, it often happens that prayer is the only means many people have of aiding the neighbour. Apart from a few persons, prayer is the only means we have of assisting the dying. Under the general title of prayer, works of sacrifice for the dying are also to be included.

To pray for the dying, especially for dying sinners, is a common obligation, imposed on each of us in virtue of the precept of charity which commands us to come to the aid of those who are in extreme spiritual danger. We should have the habitual intention of coming to their aid by our prayers. But certain conditions are necessary before this common obligation becomes a means of avoiding Purgatory. This prayer made constantly and daily, so that it takes the form of a *veritable apostolate*, will place us in a state of perfect charity, in which all sin and the punishment due to sin will disappear.

Notice, too, that such prayer will compensate for our lack of charity towards the neighbour. Scandal is the first great way by which we fail in the charity we owe our neighbour. By prayer and sacrifice for those in their agony, we can turn aside the wrath of Him Who said : " Woe to the world because of scandals ! It must needs be that scandals come, but woe to him by whom the scandal cometh." In consideration of our present goodwill, our sins of scandal in the past will be blotted out.

.   .   .

Scandal is not the only way in which we can sin against the love of the neighbour : we can do so, too, by simply being indifferent, through that egoism which centres us on ourselves, and makes us insensible to our neighbour's needs. To love means to do good, and not merely to refrain from doing evil towards our neighbour. The evil rich man was condemned to Hell for having closed his eyes on the misery of Lazarus : and on the Last Day, Christ's words to all such will be : " I was hungry "—that is, I Myself, in the person of My poor— " and you gave me not to eat." This amounts to saying, that without acts of charity it is impossible to be saved. The act of charity which we can all perform, is to pray for our neighbours, especially for those who are in greatest need of our prayers. No need can be greater than that of the dying sinner. By praying for him, we are exercising a supreme act of charity, and it is such acts that will prevent us from appearing empty-handed before our Judge. For our works will follow us. Our charity towards the dying will give joy to the Eternal Father and to Christ: it will rejoice the angels, " because there is more joy in heaven upon one sinner doing penance, than upon ninety nine who need not penance " (*Luke*, xv, 7).

.   .   .

Every prayer approved by the Church can be offered for the dying. We have, above all, that great liturgical prayer —the Holy Mass, than which there is no more powerful means of aiding those in their agony. The " Stations of the Cross " and the Rosary can also be recommended as powerful in aiding them. Moreover, there are indulgenced ejaculations specially intended to aid the dying, of which the following is a well-known example :

" Divine Heart of Jesus, convert sinners, save the dying, deliver the souls in Purgatory." (300 *days, each time it is said*).

In 1914, Pius X founded " The Pious Union of St. Joseph's

Death," the members of which undertake to have a special care for the dead by prayer and in particular by the Holy Sacrifice of the Mass. Under Benedict XV, it was extended and richly endowed with indulgences for all, and with special privileges for priests. To avail of these privileges, one has simply to have one's name inscribed on the register of the Archconfraternity.

All this comes to saying, that this means of avoiding Purgatory is altogether in the spirit of the Church and has received her solemn approbation. It is for us to profit by it, and thus secure our immediate entry into Heaven after our death.

VII.—CATHOLIC ACTION

What is called " Catholic Action " in the strict sense of the word—that is to say, the apostolate of the laity to the laity to draw them to a truly Christian life, such apostolate being directed by the Ecclesiastical Hierarchy—can be an excellent means of securing one's own salvation, and of preparing oneself for immediate entry to Heaven, after one's death. It must be exercised, however, with the desired perfection, both of intention and of execution. Thus understood, Catholic Action is nothing else than the exercise of fraternal charity in its highest object—that object being the sanctification and salvation of our neighbour's soul. By example, by word, by devotion in all its forms, the apostle of Catholic Action seeks to gain for God and for His Church, the souls of those who surround him. What mission could be more beautiful and more conformable to the spirit of Christ! It is a participation in the work of the Apostles and their successors, who are charged to continue the work of salvation begun by Jesus Himself.

It is easy to see how Catholic Action, thus understood, can become a means of avoiding Purgatory. In the first place, it is certain that he who exercises this apostolate to his brethren, will find in it a powerful stimulus to work for his own moral and religious perfection. A Catholic actionist much necessarily give good example, if he wishes to have an influence for good on those around him. In devoting himself to Catholic Action, he *condemns himself*—pardon the expression—to become a model Christian. He must fly from sin by fervour of life—and such flight and such fervour are two excellent preservatives against Purgatory.

Add to this, that the practice of fraternal charity in its highest form wins for us the choicest graces, and a love of predilection on the part of Our Saviour. Christ will certainly heap His favours on those who cooperate directly in His work of salvation, according to the means at their disposal. He will certainly show His mercy at the end of their lives, to those who have laboured to win their neighbours for the Kingdom of Heaven.

VIII.—The Apostolate after Death

There is a story of a Neapolitan painter who found himself condemned to a long Purgatory on account of an immodest picture he had painted, and on account of harm that this picture had caused to many souls. In deciding our eternal lot, Jesus Christ takes account of the evils which we leave living behind us as the effects of our evil deeds—so that, for example, Voltaire must suffer a very heavy judgment for the great evil which his works will produce to the end of time. But the consoling reverse of this is that Christ will reward to the full, at the moment of judgment, all the good which He sees as flowing from our good works to the end of time. This conclusion, based on the consideration of the infinitely perfect judgment of Him whom St. Paul calls " the just judge," ought to encourage us to perform, during our lifetime, those works of charity the effects of which reach out across our grave, living after us. If I give an alms to the poor, or send a generous subscription to a good cause, I certainly perform an excellent work which God will reward. But it must be recognised that this is a transitory work, which *usually* receives its full spiritual reward in the very moment in which I perform it. This is not true, however, of certain particularly excellent works which, by their very nature, are capable of producing immense fruit during our whole life, and—indeed, especially—after our death. These works, though relatively numerous, are not generally possible to all. They usually demand the goods of fortune, or the talents of the spirit, or a particular vocation from God. St. Francis of Assisi founded an Order, and the mighty work accomplished and being accomplished by his sons was taken into account, when he came for judgment and reward before his Creator.

It is to these works, which live in their effects after death, that we give the name of " the Apostolate after Death." As the Scripture says: " Blessed are those that die in the Lord: their works follow them " (*Apoc.*, xiv, 13). That God will take account, in judgment, of all the effects of our good works that live after us, is a consoling thought for those who work the works of life while it is day: and a terrible thought for those whose legacy is compact merely of scandal and the fruits of scandal.

Of those works which live in their fruits after the death of their author, we shall consider these four which are particularly fruitful: 1°—the work of priestly vocations; 2°—foundation Masses for the Dead; 3°—the foundation of parochial missions; 4°—the good book.

I.—The Work of Priestly Vocations

The giving of priests to the Church is certainly one of those works of which we speak here. This work takes many forms, and has for its object the recruiting of good priests for the secular clergy, and for the many Orders, Congregations and Missionary Societies in the Church. By prayer, by alms, by devotion in all its forms, the faithful are called to collaborate in this holy work—which indeed can be called the work of works. The customary collections for seminaries, and the appeals for help from religious Congregations, afford us a splendid opportunity of performing a work, the fruits of which will live after us in the work of those priests whom we have helped towards the holy altar. God will certainly accredit to those who have helped in the preparation of priests, a share in the good done by these priests, and a share after death in the Masses they celebrate.

The most immediate collaboration possible in this work, is that of Christian families who give one or more of their sons to the Priesthood. Happy families, indeed, from which God selects one or more for His special service! Blessed families who can count on the special protection of the Saviour.

Those who are zealous for the work of priestly vocations have, next to the families of priests, a special right to the gratitude of the Church. Their devotion will be magnificently rewarded by God, and will constitute a special title to His mercy at the hour of death.

2°—Foundation Masses for the Dead

To set aside a part of one's fortune for the celebration of Masses for the souls in Purgatory, either in perpetuity or for a considerable time, is to exercise the Apostolate of Purgatory even after death. This generosity to the dead cannot remain without its recompense. It is an excellent means of securing the grace of a happy death, and after death, a merciful judgment before the throne of God. Happy those who, being rich in this world's goods, are rich also in the wisdom which prompts them to use these goods for the disarming of divine justice and the paying of their debts of temporal punishment for sin.

3°—Foundation of Parochial Missions

Another means of doing good after one's death is the foundation of missions to be given periodically in parishes. Those priests who have experienced their efficacy in their own parishes know how fruitful for the conversion of sinners and the sanctification of souls these missions can be. It is a work which is particularly necessary to-day in certain regions, where indifference grows apace and religious practices are almost totally abandoned. Nothing could be more salutary for converting these regions, for transforming lukewarm parishes into fervent ones and maintaining the fervent in their fervour, than periodical missions given by specialists in this kind of work. What a good use the rich can make of their riches, by giving money towards this great work! They can thus collaborate, directly and efficaciously, in the salvation of souls. They will find in it the secret of avoiding that peril of riches, which Our Saviour pointed out to His Apostles in such strong words.

It is related of the Curé d'Ars that he once debated with

himself whether he ought to throw all his resources into the building of a new church at Ars, and sacrifice to that end the work of the parochial missions. While he prayed, his favourite saint, St. Philomena, appeared to him, radiant and beautiful, and said twice : " There is nothing more precious than the salvation of souls." By that she meant the work of the missions.

This work is one of great social charity, the effects of which, constantly renewed, will stretch over many years beyond the death of the donor. It does not give a sure exemption from Purgatory, but it does enrich for Heaven. Christ will foresee and reward, at our judgment, all the good of our deed. Again, you have made yourself a perpetual collaborator in His work of saving souls, and it is hard to see how Our Saviour could condemn you to a long Purgatory. Yes, indeed ; the foundation of a mission ought to cover a multitude of sins.

4.—The Good Book

The good periodical is an excellent thing, but it seldom reaches beyond contemporaries, and is seldom re-read. It is the flower of a day which withers in the evening, and therefore it exercises an apostolate of a day. There is little chance of its influence being felt on future generations.

It is not so with the good book. No doubt, the majority of good books grow old and have their life span. But that life span can be one of centuries, though few indeed are the writings which can be labelled perennial. It would be a presumptuous pretence for the majority of writers to expect to rank with immortals like the authors of " The Imitation of Christ " and " The Introduction to the Devout Life." One can aspire, however, to a moderate life for one's work—a life beyond one's own life. The author of a good book has thus some chance of doing good after his death. It will be a sweet consolation to him when he comes before his Maker, for St. Paul has catalogued it among the works of light. Provided vainglory does not steal some of the merit, the good book will win for its author a recompense, proportionate in some manner to the future good of which his book will be the occasion and the instrument, just as the evil book is a blank cheque to be filled according to the evil which will be wrought by it throughout the ages. It can be said that this good, foreseen by God, is of great value in obtaining for the writer exemption from Purgatory. But it is certain that, on the day of the general resurrection, when Purgatory is no more, such a writer will be awarded the aureola of which the Scripture speaks: " They who instruct many unto justice shall shine like stars for all eternity " (*Daniel*, xii, 3).

IX—Material Alms

" There is more happiness," said Christ, " in giving than in receiving " (*Act.*, xx, 35). They know this by experience who, having fortune, use it to make others happy. " The happy heart is a continual festival "—and such a festival of intimate, true, constant, all-pure happiness, amounting to a foretaste of Heaven, is the lot of the generous giver. May we not believe that this secret of happiness, indicated by Christ Himself, is an assured means, not only of being happy on earth, but also of securing immediate entry into Heaven after death. Whoever gives alms as it should be given—that is to say, with the right intention of helping the neighbour—is sure to draw on himself the benevolence of Our Saviour, Who said : " Blessed are the merciful, for they shall obtain mercy."

There are different kinds of alms : material alms, which looks to our neighbour's bodily needs ; spiritual alms, which looks to the needs of his soul ; and what can be called a mixed alms, which contains elements of both, so that, in procuring material help for the neighbour, it also renders him spiritual aid. An example of this latter would be to give a sum of money to a poor church for the founding of Masses for the Dead. We have already said sufficient about the purely spiritual and the mixed alms. It remains to speak of material alms—the alms most often referred to in the Holy Scripture. Heaven is clearly promised, immediately after death, to those who practise this alms for the love of God and of the neighbour for God—not, of course, if it is merely the occasion of pride and vain-glory. We shall cite some passages from Holy Scripture in which God speaks of this matter.

The elder Tobias was inspired to speak these words to his

son, as his last counsel: " Do alms of thy substance, and turn not thy face from the poor, for it will then be that God will not turn his face away from thee . . . *For alms delivereth from all sin and from death, and it will not allow the soul to descend into darkness*" (Tob., iv, 8-12).

Notice very carefully the words we have italicized. To be delivered from all sin, in the Scriptural sense, means to be delivered both from the guilt of sin and from the punishment due to it. The rest of the text confirms this : " it will not allow the soul to descend into darkness." Hell is not the only place of darkness, for Purgatory, too, does not see the face of God. The Holy Souls detained there are deprived of the vision of God. They are truly in darkness. Alms, if you perform it, will prevent your soul from descending into darkness. As though to underline the words of the elder Tobias, the angel Raphael repeats his words before the throne of God: " Alms delivers from death, wipes out sin, and wins mercy and life everlasting." In the Prophet Daniel, the same doctrine is found, where Nabuchodonosor is recommended to buy back his sins by mercy towards the unfortunate (*Dan.*, iv, 24). *To buy back one's sins* is a happy expression, for it suggests the redeeming of our sins, both as to their guilt and their punishment, from the hands of divine justice, so that nothing remains to impede our immediate entry into Heaven. " As water extinguishes the hottest fire, so does alms expiate sin " (*Eccli.*, iii, 33). And listen to the Psalmist :

" Happy is he who hath a care for the poor !
In the evil day, the Lord will deliver him,
The Lord will deliver him and the Lord will give him life ;
He will be happy on the earth.
God will not deliver him to the will of his enemies ;
He will assist him on his bed of sorrow " (*Ps.*, xl).

Consider, then, the Psalmist's vision of God Himself assisting at the last moments of the merciful man. Will He, the next moment, consign this soul to the flames of Purgatory ? Assuredly not, for the word of God is firm. Consider another portrait of the merciful man, from the Psalmist :

" The light rises in darkness for the men of righteousness,

> For him who is merciful, compassionate and just.
> Happy is the man that giveth and is merciful :
> His cause shall prevail in justice,
> For it shall never be overthrown ...
> His heart is firm, confiding in the Lord.
> His heart is unshakeable ; he feareth not
> *Until he shall see his enemies overthrown.*
> He soweth alms ; he giveth to the poor ;
> His justice remaineth for ever " (*Ps.*, cxi).

The enemies of the just man, especially when the hour of death approaches, are the demons. He who has practised alms will not fear them, for, as the Wise Man says : " Better than a powerful shield, and better than a strong lance, his alms will fight for him against his enemies."

Turn now to the words of Christ, where He points the moral in the parable of the unjust steward : " I say unto you : Make unto yourself friends of the mammon of iniquity, *that when you shall fail, they may receive you into everlasting dwellings*" (Luke, xvi, 9). You know who these friends are. They are the poor whom you shall have aided with your fortune, more or less honestly acquired by you or by your ancestors, since it is so difficult to become rich without incurring some debt to justice. If you have friends of this sort, Christ assures you that their intercession will open Heaven for you, *when you shall fail*—that is, when you shall pass from this world. You will not, therefore, have to pass through Purgatory..

But Our Saviour has said something stronger and indeed startling, on the efficacy of alms. After having loosed on the Pharisees the storm of His just wrath, in those terrible anathemas we know so well, see how there comes a sudden calm and the sunshine of His mercy : " Give alms, and all shall be cleansed." Is it possible ? Will these Pharisees scale high Heaven without passing through Purgatory, because they shall have given alms ? It is Christ Himself Who says so ; the same who opened Heaven to the good thief, as the reward of a word said in recognition of His innocence and His Kingship.

One of the Fathers, St. Gregory of Nazianzen, says: " Nothing can win the love of God like alms, because goodness and compassion are the most distinctive characteristics of the

Divinity" (*Hom.*, xvii). This weakness of God—if the anthropomorphic expression may be pardoned—for those who give to the poor, may very well explain those unexpected conversions of certain great sinners, who, in the midst of their disorders, have been generous towards those in need and in misery. For, as we have remarked before, the Saviour considers as done to Himself whatsoever is done to the poor and afflicted. Whosoever aids God is sure of Paradise.

We shall conclude with this beautiful eulogy of St. John Chrysostom: "Alms is a heavenly work, and most many-sided of all good works. It protects those who practise it. It is the friend of God, and powerful in obtaining grace for those whom it loves ... It breaks the chains, dispels the darkness, extinguishes the fire ... It approaches, and the gates of the Kingdom open fully to it. When a queen comes, no guard would dare to question her right to enter, but all would hasten to open wide the gates. So is it with alms: for she is a queen and she knows how to make men like unto God ... She has wings and she flies easily: golden wings that glance in the light of heaven, rejoicing the angels ... She is always near to the throne of God, and when we appear before the tribunal of the sovereign Judge, she flies to meet us, and covers us with the protection of her wings." (*Hom.*, xxxii, *on the Epistle to the Hebrews*).